THE GOSPEL ACCORDING TO ST. LUKE

NEW TESTAMENT FOR SPIRITUAL READING

VOLUME 6

Edited by

John L. McKenzie, S.J.

THE GOSPEL
ACCORDING TO ST. LUKE

Volume 2

ALOIS STÖGER

CROSSROAD · NEW YORK

1981
The Crossroad Publishing Company
575 Lexington Avenue, New York, NY 10022

Originally published as *Das Evangelium nach Lukas 2*
© 1966 by Patmos-Verlag
from the series *Geistliche Schriftlesung*
edited by Wolfgang Trilling
with Karl Hermann Schelke and Heinz Schürmann

English translation © 1969 by Herder and Herder, Inc.
Translated by Benen Fahy

Library of Congress Catalog Card Number: 81-68166
ISBN: 0-8245-0115-2

OUTLINE

THE GOSPEL ACCORDING TO ST. LUKE

THE JOURNEY TO JERUSALEM (9:51—19:27)

Jesus' life of journeying was a life of renunciation, subjection to the divine imperative—it " had " to be so. His life set a pattern for those who follow him, and especially for his disciples. The first part of the story of his journey begins with a summons to follow Jesus on his way to Jerusalem (9:51-62). The second part emphasized his journey's goal, Jerusalem, the city where he died. Anyone who wishes to share his glory must be prepared to realize what a serious matter being his disciple is; he must be prepared to choose. The third part of the story brings us to the confines of Jerusalem. The kingdom of God had come; the Son of man was about to enter the city. What were the conditions which would ensure that his coming would mean salvation, and not judgment (17:11 —19:27)? The events which accompanied Jesus on his journey to Jerusalem are a lesson for the church. By means of its missionary activity, the church, too, must journey; it must journey through suffering and persecution to its glorification. The burning questions which affected the church in St. Luke's time are explained by appealing to Christ's example. They are not thrashed out systematically; they are resolved in the vivid scenes St. Luke knew how to describe so well.

On the Road (13:22—17:10)

Towards Jerusalem (13:22-35)

THE CITY WHERE HE WAS RAISED TO GLORY (13:22–30)

²²*And he traveled through the towns and villages, teaching and making his journey towards Jerusalem.*

3

This was a missionary journey. Traveling was his work, and his work was teaching. He taught that the promises of salvation God made in scripture were now being fulfilled in him (4:21); he taught God's way (20:21), the way of life God demanded of a man, the ways of salvation (Acts 16:17). All that was necessary to attain salvation formed the object of his teaching (see 13:23).

His teaching was given in the towns and villages to all. Everyone was asked to take a stand for or against God's will in the time of salvation which was now dawning. Behind the journeys stands the " must " imposed by the commission God gave his apostles (13:33), his saving will. Jesus appears as the model for his apostles in their travels; his paths set the stage for the testimony his apostles would bear him. We are told of the apostles that: " They bore witness and spoke the Lord's word . . . and they proclaimed the gospel in many Samaritan villages " (Acts 8:25; see also Acts 8:40). St. Paul in particular is portrayed in the Acts of the Apostles as an unwearying traveler. Jesus' mission in Israel looked forward to the future mission of the church; historically it was a necessary prelude to it. The goal of Jesus' journey was Jerusalem (9:51). There his " taking up " awaited him, his death and ascension, his passion and his glorification (see Acts 1:9). All that Jesus experienced on his journey, together with the teaching he gave, showed his disciples the way to their own personal resurrection and salvation. The apostles were " servants of the most high God and they proclaimed the way of salvation " (Acts 16:17). They " encouraged the disciples and exhorted them to persevere in the faith " (see Acts 14:22).

²³*Then a man asked him: " Lord, is it only a few that will be saved? "*

Who can enter God's kingdom? This is the burning question which occupies people as they go through life. Is there anyone who is not affected in the depths of his soul by the question of redemption and salvation? The man addressed Jesus as " Lord." He obviously

4

regarded him as the supreme authority in any question concerning the salvation promised for the end of time. Others had asked him similar questions (see 17:20; 18:18; 22:28 and Acts 1:6).

The Pharisees' teaching, which was the accepted teaching in Jesus' time, was that: "All Israel will have a share in the world to come" (Sanh. 10:1). Other teachers were less optimistic (see Ezra 5:47). Jesus did not decide the question; he had no wish to do so. Mentioning a number would hinder the purpose of Jesus' preaching. He summoned people to come to a decision concerning the offer God made them here and now. This was what mattered; knowing the number of the saved was unimportant.

[24]*But he told them: " Strive hard in the contest, that you may enter by the narrow door, for many I tell you will try to make their way in and not be able."*

An athlete summons up all his strength for the last few moments which decide the outcome of the contest. To be saved, a person must make every possible effort; he must draw on all his strength. This is what Jesus encourages us to do: "Strive hard in the contest." The " apocalyptic " writers in Jesus' time had a lot to say about the last stage of time and the glory which accompanied it. Among the greatest joys of those who practiced the most exalted virtue, they numbered the fact that " they struggled in a hard battle to subdue their innate wickedness and prevent it dragging them from life to death " (4 Ezra 7:92). Jesus himself had to fight such a battle in Gethsemane. He had to use all his strength to accept his cup of suffering and the death which awaited him (22:44). The way which led to his being taken up into heaven passed through this tense struggle. The way to salvation lies in following Christ on the path which leads by the Mount of Olives and Golgotha, by readiness to die and death itself (9:57–62; for St. Paul's comment on the effort see 1 Tim. 6:12 and 2 Tim. 4:7f.).

5

The narrow door remains open only for a predetermined length of time. Open ever since Jesus announced the time of salvation (4:21), this space of time will come to an end when the Lord comes for judgment. No one knows when this will be. Jesus' call summons us to make a decision which cannot be postponed. These are the last days.

" Many . . . will not be able " (see also Mt. 7:14). The disciples to whom it pleased God to give his kingdom are only a little flock (12:32). Jesus has no intention here of indicating a number. He wants to warn us, urging us and encouraging us to summon up all our strength. He calls on us to make a choice.

[25]" *Once the Lord has risen and closed the door, you will begin to bang on the door, as you stand outside, saying: ' Lord, open to us!' But he will answer you with the words: ' I do not know where you come from '.*"

Here we have a different situation. The master of the house has risen; the meal has begun and the door is closed. Those who have not yet made their way in must remain outside. It is Jesus that is the master of the house. All their knocking and pleading is in vain (11:9f.). They had not availed of the opportunity; the unique here and now, when they might have entered, has been lost forever. When the time of salvation has run its course, only the judgment remains (see 12:9).

[26]" *Then you will begin to say: ' We ate and drank in your presence. You taught in our streets.' [27]But he will tell you: ' I do not know where you come from. Go away from me, you evildoers '.*"

Those who were excluded remind the master of the house of the fellowship they once enjoyed with him, in a communion of give and take. But now all appeals to their former fellowship were in vain.

They had not taken Jesus' word seriously. He made known God's will, but they did not carry it out. They were evildoers.

God's will is that the call Jesus made should be heard and obeyed; we must follow his teaching and accept the offer God makes us in him. Being his fellow countryman or even his disciple will be no use if a person does not put his preaching into practice (see 7:21).

Neither baptism nor the fact of having shared a meal with Jesus, or listened to his word as his disciple, will bring a person to salvation, unless they are associated with effective obedience to his word and a personal decision for him (see 1 Cor. 10:1–11).

[28]" *You will cry out for distress and gnash your teeth when you see Abraham and Isaac and all the prophets in God's kingdom, while you yourselves are excluded.* [29]*People will come from the rising and the setting [of the sun], from the north and the south, and recline at table in God's kingdom.* [30]*And see, those are last who will be first; those are first who will be last.*"

Those who have been shut out realize with anguish that they have thoughtlessly rejected God's grace. Now it is lost irretrievably. They cry out. They torture themselves because they did not avail of the right moment and summon up all their strength to grasp the salvation which was offered them.

Their regret and remorse are all the greater because they can see in the patriarchs and prophets the glory of the salvation which had also been prepared for them, especially because Abraham, Isaac, and Jacob were their ancestors, and had interceded. They had the prophets' teaching to lead them to salvation. " Sinners cry out when they see how resplendent they [the virtuous] are " (Enoch 108:15). That they can see the reward reserved for those who believed the testimony of the Most High is a special penalty (4 Ezra 7:83). Jesus speaks of man's final destiny in the language of the apocalyptic

7

writings of the day. The new element in the message he preached was the fact that salvation or condemnation depended on carrying out his word, on following Jesus, and on a man's personal decision for him.

No one can blame God if he does not attain salvation. Even the pagans find their way into God's kingdom. The prophecy concerning the pilgrimage to the mountain of God which would take place in the last stage of time was now being fulfilled (see Is. 25:6–8). Then those who are saved will sing the song of thanksgiving (see Psalm 106:1–3).

The last stage of time produces a reversal of our entire scale of values: " The last will be first and the first will be last." The gentiles are taken into God's kingdom while the Jews are excluded. The Jews enjoyed a privileged position in salvation history. Yet the privileges they enjoyed were not sufficient in themselves to bring them to salvation. The gentiles had been forced to go without these privileges, yet they were admitted to a share in the festive meal which represents the kingdom of God. It is the man who welcomes Jesus' message that will be saved, if he takes his stand by it and follows Jesus.

In the time of salvation which dawned with Jesus, God offered salvation to Jews and gentiles alike. This salvation depends on the attitude a person adopts towards Jesus, and the person's willingness to follow Jesus to Jerusalem. No one can pride himself on having a right to salvation, but God has made salvation available to everyone in Jesus.

THE CITY OF DEATH (13:31–35)

[31]*At that very time, some Pharisees came and told him: " Go away and leave this place. Herod wants to kill you."*

Jesus was journeying through the territory of Herod Antipas

(4 B.C.–39 A.D.) which included Galilee and Perea which was east of the Jordan. The Pharisees who approached Jesus seem to have been acting on Herod's orders. Jesus' ministry disturbed him (9:7ff.). He was afraid of him, afraid that he might rouse his subjects. Consequently, he wanted to get him out of his area. It is doubtful if he really planned to kill him; he had had to be tricked into executing John the Baptist (Mk. 6:24–26), and after he had committed this crime, he could not forget it for a long time (9:9). When he had the opportunity to put Jesus to death lawfully, he did not avail of it (23:15). The message he sent to Jesus seems to have been a false alarm, a shot fired into the air to drive this mysterious and unwelcome person from the district. The suggestion that Jesus might be killed illustrates the situation in which he found himself. He was on the way to Jerusalem where death awaited him.

[32]*But he told them: " Go back and tell that fox: See, I will cast out devils and heal the sick today and tomorrow, but on the third day I will come to my end.* [33]*However, today and tomorrow and the following day I must journey on; it is not possible that a prophet should die elsewhere than in Jerusalem."*

Jesus' journeying was not to be governed by the powers-that-be in this world. Herod regarded his ministry as a political risk and a threat to the peace. He wanted to drive him out of his territory without resorting to force. He was a fox, with all a fox's cunning and cowardice. Foxes go out to steal only at night, in secret; while it is light, and consequently dangerous, they hide in their lairs (Ezek. 43:4f.). Herod wanted to rid himself of Jesus slyly, without taking any stand for or against him, and a number of the Pharisees agreed with him in this. Jesus confronted the people with an ineluctable choice.

Herod acted as if Jesus' life was at his disposal. However, it was God, not man, who decided what Jesus was to do. It was with God's power that Jesus cast out devils and healed the sick (see Acts 10:38).

9

He was Lord over the evil spirits and he had power to heal those who were sick; he could not be subject to the malice of a fox, of a small man such as Herod. Jesus' whole life, all his journeying and activity, was subject to the divine " must."

Today and tomorrow Jesus would continue to heal the sick; it was on the third day that he would reach his goal. His activity would continue for only a short time now. His words were a warning to those who warned him; the Pharisees, too, would share the responsibility for his death (6:11; 11:53). Jesus knew that death awaited him, but he did not flee from it; it was God's will which must be accomplished. Moreover, death would not mean the end of his work; Jesus' death was his crowning achievement; it brought his mission to completion (12:50; Jn. 19:30). The church continues to grow despite all opposition; St. Paul reached Rome, his missionary goal, despite the combined efforts of all the powers arrayed against him (2 Cor. 11:23–33).

Jesus speaks mysteriously of today and tomorrow and the third day, today and tomorrow and the following day. In the prophet Hosea, we find the words: " After two days, he [the Lord] inspires life in us; on the third day, he will make us rise again, to have life in his presence " (Hos. 6:2). The words come from a penitential hymn which the prophet puts on the lips of the two kindred peoples, Ephraim and Judah. In the national catastrophe which came upon them, the prophet saw God's avenging hand. However, he was firmly convinced that God would give both of them new life. Jesus' mysterious words seem to be an allusion to these words of the prophet. In that case, they announce his resurrection from the dead. The death he would meet in Jerusalem was not the end. It would be followed by his return to life and his glorification. All that the prophets had said, the whole history of the people of God, looked forward to this " third day " as the day of redemption. Jesus' journey to Jerusalem where death and resurrection awaited him fulfilled all the promises made by God in the course of salvation history.

Jesus knew that he was a prophet and he also knew that he would meet a prophet's fate. A prophet could not die elsewhere than in Jerusalem. The Jews were not merely " sons of the prophets " (Acts 3:25); they were also " sons of those who murdered the prophets " (6:23; 11:47f., see also Acts 7:52; Jer. 2:30; Neh. 9:16). It was at Jerusalem that the grace of close proximity to God and stubborn opposition to his will came into contact. The course of salvation history reached its climax when Jesus journeyed to Jerusalem. This was the greatest grace of God's closeness, and he was rejected to the extent of being executed.

[34]*" Jerusalem! Jerusalem! You who kill the prophets and stone those who are sent to you. How often I tried to gather your children as a hen gathers her chickens under her wings—and you did not want it. [35]See, your house will be left to you deserted. I tell you, you will not see me any more until the time comes when you will say: 'All praise to him who comes in the Lord's name'."*

Jesus himself, the great prophet, now pronounces a final lament for Jerusalem. The history of its rejection of God was now reaching its climax. The message Jesus preached was God's final word, a call to make the decision demanded by the last stage of time.

All the love God showed in his saving activity in the course of history is summed up in Jesus' mission and his preaching. The image of the protective and solicitous mother bird occurs again and again in the Old Testament (see Deut. 32:10f.; Is. 31:5; Ps. 36:8), but it was never evoked so tenderly as in Jesus' words

Jesus wanted to gather Jerusalem's children, the whole of Israel, and place them under God's protection; he wanted to shelter them in his love and bring them to salvation. But arrogantly presuming on what Jerusalem was and the privileges they enjoyed, the Jews rejected Jesus when he tried to bring them a new word from God. They felt safe. God had nothing more to demand from them. The story of God's love and the story of sin in which man rebels against

God reach their *dénouement* in Jesus' journey to Jerusalem (Mt. 21:33–39).

Jerusalem will be destroyed because it refused to answer the call of God's messengers or accept their guidance. Its greatness and glory were the result of God's choice of it as his dwelling. Jesus brought this to its full accomplishment. In him, God's glory appeared in the temple (2:21–37). But when he was put to death in the city, disaster came upon it. God's protective care was withdrawn and it was abandoned to its own inhabitants. Destruction was its final end. The words of the prophet Jeremiah (Jer. 12:7) were fulfilled. Jesus takes up the threats of condemnation made by the prophets (1 Kings 9:7f.) and completes them. The end Jesus met in Jerusalem also meant the end of Jerusalem.

The death Jesus went to meet in Jerusalem was not the end. The time would come when he would be greeted with the blessing with which those who made the pilgrimage to the temple were greeted at the end of their journey: " All praise to him who comes in the Lord's name " (Ps. 118 [117]:26). Jesus is the one who is to come; he is the Messiah who comes in the name of the God who gives salvation. Jerusalem, the city of his death, was also the city of his glorification. The death which was being prepared for him there ends with his being raised to glory, with his coming as the Son of man in power and glory (see 22:69).

Jerusalem's secret is that God lives in it. The city was given up to destruction, but not without a ray of hope. Its inhabitants will say: All praise to him who comes in the Lord's name. Israel will be converted before Jesus comes in his glory, and when he comes they will pay homage to him (see Rom. 11:25f.). The persecuted church is not an embittered church. It does not withdraw to a ghetto and abandon the world to itself and to the power of the devil. The church is still active even where it appears to be dying, because it believes in the promise of victory and glory God has given it. It believes in his saving will.

Table Talk (14:1–24)

By means of the key word " meal " (having a meal, a wedding feast, an early meal, a supper, a great supper) four scenes are now linked together to form a composite unity; a miracle of healing performed on the sabbath (vv. 1–6), two exchanges which took place during a meal (vv. 7–11; 12–14), and the parable of the great supper (vv. 15–24). St Luke interweaves this traditional material artistically, according to a literary plan. The first and last parts are held together by being situated in the context of a meal; both mention eating bread, putting a part for the whole, to indicate a meal (vv. 1, 15). The two center sections are similarly constructed. There is an introduction, followed by a negative and positive formulation of the rules concerning a meal. These are then given an eschatological orientation (an antithetical saying with an eschatological final verse). The final section is connected with the rule for meals which precedes it by the mention of the same guests (vv. 13, 21). Only one of the guests is portrayed as saying anything and Jesus dominates the rest of the conversation. Yet we get the impression that everyone was drawn into the conversation and that there was a lively exchange. In the parables, the master of the house, the servants, and the guests all have something to say. All those who assisted at the meal are addressed, the guests, their host, and a particular guest.

Plato and the other philosophers in antiquity aired their most profound thoughts in the form of table talk at after-dinner conversations (" *symposia* "). In the same way, St. Luke collects a number of the Lord's sayings in a *"symposion."* He cast the traditional material of the gospel in a mold taken from the Greek world. By adapting it in this way without falsifying it, he did it a great service. Jesus gave the sabbath meal a particular impress and added a touch of splendor to it; he performed a miracle of healing for the man who was sick and he gave them all the gift of his word. The meal is a symbol of the eschatological meal in which God's kingdom is represented. When Christians assemble for the " Lord's Supper " on Sundays, they recall the meals the Lord shared with his disciples; they should remember his presence which brings salvation and the time of salvation which is to come.

A MEAL ON THE SABBATH (14:1–6)

¹*It happened that he went into the house of one of the leading*

Pharisees on the sabbath to have a meal, and they were watching him. ²And there a man suffering from dropsy appeared before him.

Jesus even accepted invitations which came from those who opposed him; he came to bring salvation to everyone. His host at this meal was a " leading Pharisee," the president of a synagogue who was also a Pharisee (8:41), or perhaps even a member of the supreme council in Jerusalem (23: 13, 35; Jn. 3:1). The house he entered was a focal point of piety based on the law and traditional customs which were rigidly observed.

It was the sabbath. The Jews were accustomed to hold a festive meal on this day. On weekdays they ate twice, but on the sabbath they had three meals. The principal meal was taken at midday, after the religious service in the synagogue. " On a feast day, people must either eat or drink, or sit down to study." Guests were invited as part of the celebration and they were entertained royally. Kindness had to be shown to the poor, to orphans, and strangers. Their hunger must be satisfied.

The sabbath was consecrated to the memory of God's great benefits, creation (Ex. 20:8–11), and the liberation of the Jews from the slavery of Egypt (Deut. 5:12–15). It was shrouded in the festive atmosphere evoked by the Israelites' faith that God had made choice of Israel: " The Lord blessed the sabbath, but he appointed no other people or nation to celebrate the sabbath except Israel. Israel alone was permitted to eat and drink and keep a sabbath on earth. The Most High blessed this day which he created before any other day, to be blessed and to be consecrated, for his glory " (*Jubilees* 2:31f.). The sabbath was a symbol of God's fidelity to his covenant. It was meant to show the Israelites that God was their Lord, that it was he who sanctified them (Ex. 31:13). Eternal life was thought of as a sabbath which would never end (Heb. 4:9). The sabbath meal to which Jesus was invited in the Pharisee's house recalled God's great benefits; it was enveloped in the hope

14

of a future world where men would share in God's sabbath of rest. Jesus would bring all God's saving activity to completion.

Jesus was the guest of honor at the meal to which he had been invited as a doctor of the law. It was customary to get famous teachers of the law to speak at the religious functions in the synagogue and to invite them to lunch afterwards. The news about Jesus had spread all over the country (7:17). The people looked on him as a great prophet (7:16) and the Pharisees, too, discussed his identity among themselves (7:39). They watched him. Every time he was a guest in a Pharisee's house, they watched him, measuring him by their own Pharisaical standard of virtue. Simon the Pharisee (7:36–50) judged him by his attitude to the sinful woman, while another unnamed Pharisee (11:37–53) based his estimate of him on his neglect of the prescriptions concerning ritual cleanliness. On this occasion, he would be judged on the way he interpreted the obligation to keep the sabbath holy. The conclusion drawn was: He cannot be a prophet sent by God. He does not speak God's word. The Pharisees set up their own teaching, their own interpretation of the law as the measure of God's will and of his word. They did not believe that Jesus had a commission from God to speak and act as he did; he did not measure up to their expectations, to what they taught.

Among the guests were scribes and Pharisees, people who shared their host's views. Jesus did not ignore them; he had not broken with them. St. Matthew portrays the woes Jesus pronounced against them (Mt. 23) as a sentence of condemnation; St. Luke (11:42–52) presents them as an invitation to repentance and conversion. The Pharisees excluded sinners from the fellowship of the chosen people; they were scrupulous in observing the laws of ritual purity, and they tried to promote the sanctification of the sabbath. In all this, their aim was to keep the people holy for God. They looked on their own way of life, on their own interpretation of the law, and on their traditions, as the way appointed by God. They were so convinced of it that they never gave a thought to the possibility that God might have prepared a different way to bring his people to holiness. So they made it impossible for themselves to adhere to Jesus, when he proclaimed and inaugurated the new order of salvation.

There was one more guest present who had not been invited. He was an intruder; he had come only to see the guest of honor (see 7:37; 19:3). It was surprising that he should be there. See, a man suffering from dropsy appeared before him! Another firm belief of the scribes and Pharisees was that illness was a punishment for an immoral life. They even claimed to be able to decide which crimes were responsible for a particular illness. Dropsy, they believed, was the result of sins against purity. All eyes were on Jesus and the sufferer.

3Jesus addressed them, speaking to the scribes and Pharisees and saying: " Is it permitted to cure someone on the sabbath or not?" But they remained silent. 4And he grasped the man and cured him. Then he let him go.

Jesus acted like a man who had authority; he addressed them. The question he asked was a common one in the rabbinical schools, and it had been answered long ago. If a person was ill and in danger of death, he could be assisted, even if it meant violating the sabbath. But if there was no immediate danger of death, nothing could be done for the sick person until the sabbath was over. There was no immediate danger in the case of the man who had dropsy. Jesus' question was intended as a challenge. He forced his audience to reconsider the law; they could not be content only with the " traditions of the ancients " (Mk. 7:5). Jesus claimed to interpret the law and renew it as a prophet who spoke in God's name (Mt. 5:17-48). The Pharisees were silent. They were reluctant to dispute with Jesus; their doctrine was inalterable. How could he convince them?

Jesus grasped the man who had dropsy. He took him into his fellowship, healed him, and let him go. This miraculous cure was a sign; it showed that God was with him, that he acted with God's power and authority (Acts 10:38). It showed that it was with God's authority that he interpreted the law concerning the sabbath; the time of salvation, the last stage of time, had dawned. God's sabbath of rest was beginning to produce its effect. This miracle was an anticipation of the restored world which is to come, the final " restoration of all things " (Acts 3:21).

Jesus restored its true meaning to the sabbath rest, the meaning God attached to it. The scribes concentrated on the discussion concerning the obligation to rest on the sabbath; they forgot God's saving will, his love, which gave this day its character: Jesus filled the sabbath once again with God's mercy and love. He took the sick man to himself, healed him, and let him go. He acted with authority; he was in control of the situation. The sabbath centered around him and he gave it its impress. It became the " Lord's Day " (Rev. 1:10). In him, God appears as the God of mercy and compassion for all those who are poor, while the sabbath becomes a day to help others and save them, a day when everything will be brought to completion.

⁵And he asked them: " If one of you has a son or an ox which falls into a well, will you not pull it out immediately on the sabbath day?" ⁶And they were not able to find a suitable reply.

The Damascus document from Qumran says: " If an animal falls into a cistern or a pit, it must not be pulled out on the sabbath." According to the stricter of the two opinions found among the scribes, such an animal should merely be given food on the sabbath, to prevent it dying before the following day. The more lenient view was that, although the animal could not be pulled out, it could be enabled to make its own way out, by placing cloths and padding under it. Jesus did not condemn this lenient interpretation of the law. He let it stand and even went further. The law sets no limit to love, just as God's love is without limit. God's kingdom which Jesus proclaimed is a kingdom of his divine compassion.

Jesus put the sabbath rest at man's service (13:15f.). The miracles he worked on the sabbath were so many signs that the time of salvation had come; God manifested his glory by showing mercy. For Jesus, the sabbath rest was a symbol of God's good will towards his creation, a symbol of peace and salvation. Now that the last stage of time had come, God manifested his glory through Jesus; in everything he said and did Jesus proclaimed God as the God of grace and love, who gives and forgives. The joy which is characteristic of the sabbath in the last stage of time is really an outburst of joy at the great things God has accomplished in his mercy. The cure of the man suffering from dropsy filled the sabbath meal in the Pharisee's house with the joyful atmosphere which belongs to the time of salvation.

The sabbath rest, as it was prescribed by the law, was based on humanitarian and social grounds, on consideration for the family, the household, and even the animals owned by the master of the house (Ex. 23:12f.; Deut. 5:14f.). The simple rules of life Jesus gave became the basic rules for admission into God's kingdom (14:7–14). Jesus' explanation of his conduct was in perfect harmony with human wisdom and prudence; the scribes were at a loss for an answer. The wisdom he taught was far superior to theirs. He was sent by God to teach men (Mt. 7:29).

Christ's work of redemption which is represented in word and action by this cure forms the center of a Christian Sunday, and it is constantly reproduced by Jesus in the eucharistic meal. This is intended to transform us, so that we may become true symbols of God's love among men. The sabbath meal in the house of this leading Pharisee looked forward to the eschatological meal which will be celebrated in " God's sabbath of rest " (Heb. 4:9ff.). The meal

18

Christians celebrate on the Lord's Day is midway between the Jewish sabbath meal and this eschatological meal in God's kingdom. In each case, the Lord is present to share his saving gifts.

A Word for the Guests (14:7–11)

[7]He told a parable to those who had been invited, because he noticed how they chose the first places for themselves. He said to them: [8]" When you are invited by someone to a wedding feast, you must not sit down in the place of honor, for fear your host may have invited someone more important than you. [9]The man who invited both you and him might come to you and say: ' Give this man your place'—and you would have to take the last place, to your embarrassment. [10]On the contrary, when you are invited, go and sit in the last place, so that when the man who invited you comes, he will say to you: ' Friend, move higher up.' Then you will be honored before all those who are at table with you. [11]Everyone who exalts himself will be brought low, while the man who lowers his own dignity will be exalted."

The Pharisees were well versed in the law and festive meals in their homes were spiced with conversation concerning the correct knowledge of God. Jesus spoke as one of the company, not as a prophet issuing a warning. His words were graphic, but they were also loaded; they were a parable. His purpose shone through them, the message he preached, God's kingdom. The incident he observed became an image of his saving teaching.

It was customary in antiquity to seat guests, not according to age, but according to their dignity and rank. Each one chose a place in keeping with the rank he claimed for himself. Jesus saw how all the guests tried to take the first place. The Pharisees were very particular about their dignity; they loved the first seats in the synagogues, and they saw to it that special greetings were reserved for them in public places. They claimed precedence over others; they were convinced they had the right to the first places. They claimed to have the same certainty concerning their place at God's table as they had concerning their right to the first place at a meal. They were sure of entering God's kingdom. Were they right?

Jesus was prompted to remark on what he saw and he began with a " rule for the table." An ancient proverb formed the background to his words: " Do not give yourself airs in the presence of a king. Do not take the place reserved for important persons. It is better to have someone say to you: ' Come up here,' than to be moved to a lower place in the presence of a nobleman " (Prov. 25:6). The scribes, too, had a similar rule of prudence: " Stay two or three seats away from the place [which belongs to you] and wait until someone tells you: ' Move up! Move up!' This is better than having someone say: ' Move down! Move down!' " For the scribes these words were no longer merely a rule of thumb, to avoid being embarrassed. They used them to illustrate an attitude which was the result of a moral judgment.

Jesus' " rule for the table " expresses a truth concerning God's kingdom. Anyone who wishes to enter God's kingdom must be small; he must make himself small and avoid all false, self-righteous claims. It is the last verse which gives us the true meaning of the parable. Lowliness is the first condition for admission into God's kingdom (6:20). The story of the Pharisee and the tax collector in the temple ends with the same sentence.

The guests' conduct at the meal made it clear who could assist at the banquet in God's kingdom. For a Christian, there are no such things as rules which are merely a matter of courtesy or courtly politeness. For him, even his conduct at an ordinary meal is full of significance; it is overshadowed by the mystery of God's kingdom. God's kingdom embraces everything; it encompasses a man, his meals, and the customs he observes at his meals, every sphere of his life and activity. God is all in all. Nothing can be withdrawn from him; the good news of the kingdom demands that a person should be converted.

A dispute broke out among the disciples concerning precedence at the Last Supper (22:24). Jesus demanded that his followers should humble themselves, even as he humbles himself (22:26–27). The Eucharist is celebrated in a context of service and self-abasement. Once more a bridge stretches from the meal where Jesus was a guest to the eschatological banquet; between the two stands the holy meal celebrated by the church. The bridge which connects the three of them is the attitude of self-abasement.

A WORD FOR THE HOST (14:12–14)

12He also told the man who had invited him: " When you arrange an early meal or a supper, do not invite your friends; do not invite your brothers, your relatives, or your wealthy neighbors, so that they in turn may not invite you, in which case you would have been repaid. 13Rather, when you are holding a reception, invite the poor, the cripples, the lame, and the blind. 14It will be well for you, because they have nothing to repay you. Then you will receive your reward when the just rise again."

Jesus' host who invited him to the meal is also drawn into the conversation. The word which was addressed to him is no longer referred to as a parable. By means of a command given for a particular case, Jesus pronounces a truth which is valid for all time. The words he spoke to his host are intended to have binding force. Jesus wants the directions he gives to be followed, but not only in the way he gives them.

Jesus is not content with behavior which is inspired by self-love, politeness or hope of something in return. Those who were to be invited were the poorest of the poor, the cripples, the lame, and the blind. Nothing could be expected of them. They could not return the invitation; they could add nothing to a person's honor or his influence. Moreover, eating in the company of such persons is not very enjoyable. No one likes to see them about. No one who was lame or had a bad hand could enter the Qumran community; those who had a limp were excluded, together with those who were deaf or dumb. Deaf-mutes, the blind, and those who were mentally retarded were forbidden to lay their hands on the heads of the sacrificial animal in certain sacrifices in the temple. They were excluded from the official temple worship. And these are the very people who must be invited, to exclude all hope of a reward. In the Sermon on the Mount, Jesus demanded even more of his disciples; they must love their enemies. Such love could not hope for anything in return (6:35).

The man who practices such selflessness will receive a share in God's kingdom. The man who seeks God alone in everything he does will experience his favor; God will reward him and show him gratitude (6:1). A Christian is meant to be an image of God (5:16); he gives without expecting anything in return; his intention is directed towards God and God reveals himself to him (see Mt. 5:16).

The rules governing the celebration of a meal become the " rules " of the heavenly banquet in God's kingdom. The early church went to great lengths to ensure that these rules were also observed in the celebration of the Lord's Supper. We may ask, did it succeed? St. Paul complains about the church at Corinth that, when they came together for the Lord's Supper, each one ate his own meal first, so that some were drunk, while others went hungry: " Are you not showing disrespect for God's church and embarrassing those who have nothing?" (1 Cor. 11:20–22). In the Epistle of St. James, we read: " Suppose a man wearing a gold ring and splendid clothes comes to your meeting, and at the same time a poor man comes in whose clothes are dirty. If you turn to look at the well-dressed man and say to him: ' Please sit down here,'

22

while you tell the poor man: 'You there, stay standing here, or else sit at my footrest,' have you not introduced distinctions among yourselves? You have set yourselves up as judges and your attitude is wrong " (Jas. 2:2–4). God's grace and generosity are never more apparent than in the celebration of the Eucharist. Man is never more a beggar than he is at this meal, when he receives a divine food and drink " for the remission of his sins " (Mt. 26:28).

As the parable which preceded it, Jesus' instructions in this passage also end with a reference to the last things. At the end of the parable, Jesus promised that God would exalt certain persons; here he promises that the just will rise again. The way pointed out in the parable was the way of self-abasement; here it is the way of selflessness. Serving others in unselfish love, giving everything and expecting nothing, these are the characteristics of a true disciple who follows Jesus on his journey to Jerusalem, where he was " taken up."

Jesus speaks of repayment, of a reward. The thought of a reward is inspired, not by the disciple's behavior, but by the Father in heaven. The man who behaves in this way will receive the gracious gift of fellowship with God in God's kingdom. He will be repaid when the just rise again. All men, both just and unjust, must rise again (Acts 24:15; Jn. 5:29). Tyre and Sidon will find it easier to endure the judgment than the towns of Galilee which refused to believe in Jesus (10:14; 11:31). They will rise to meet their sentence. The mention of the resurrection is intended to be a joyful promise; it is the reason why Jesus says: " It is well for you."

THE GREAT SUPPER (14:15–24)

¹⁵*When one of those who were reclining at table with him heard this, he said to him: " It will be well for anyone who eats bread in God's kingdom."*

One of the guests expressed in explicit terms the unspoken reality which formed the background to this conversation—the feast to be held in God's kingdom. The earthly meal was a symbol of the feast to come which represents the final consummation, God's kingdom (13:28). The guest proclaimed anyone blessed who could partake of this meal. All Israel's hope and longing centered on this feast. This was the "feast of the redemption" which would never end. The apocalyptic writings described it in glowing colors: "At his last coming, he [God] will lead out Adam and our fore-fathers and bring them here [into the garden of Eden], where they will rejoice. God will be like a man who has brought home his beloved to take a meal with him. When they have come, they will converse in front of his palace, eagerly looking forward to his feast, the enjoyment of all that is good, of his infinite wealth. Joy and happiness will be there, in light and life eternal" (*Slav. Book of Enoch* 42:5). The early church reiterated the blessing pro-nounced by this guest when it recalled the life to come (Rev. 19:9). The two symbols, the eschatological meal and the eschatological marriage feast, tended to be confused. They give us some idea of the joy the last stage of time will bring. When the early church at Jerusalem met to "break bread," it was filled with joy at the thought of what was to come, with the jubilation which accom-panies salvation (Acts 2:46). The meal they celebrated reminded them of the fullness of salvation which was to come; "breaking bread" in the eucharistic meal assured them that the eschatological meal would come one day. At the Last Supper, Jesus himself re-called the feast which is to come in God's kingdom (22:16, 18, 29). "It is well for anyone who eats bread in God's kingdom." Our gaze is led from the sabbath meal to the eucharistic meal, and from this to the meal in God's kingdom.

The Pharisee who pronounced the blessing never doubted that he would share in this meal and its happiness. To be sure of sharing in that eternal life which would free him from all distress, he endured the burden of the law gladly. He was scrupulously careful to observe every letter of it, and he constructed an artificial rampart about it, to prevent it from being violated in any way. Such obedience was not easy; it could be realized only with great self-denial, so that a pious Jew drew courage from the thought of the happiness with which God would reward his service. Surely it would be well for those who are invited to the feast God has prepared for the just, when he reveals his kingdom! The Pharisee was convinced that he would be there; he knew he was a " son of the kingdom " (Mt. 8 : 12).

16But he said to him: " A man arranged a great supper and sent out numerous invitations. 17At the hour fixed for the supper, he sent his servant out to tell those who had been invited: ' Come, [everything] is already prepared '."

Jesus did not elaborate on the blessing pronounced by the guest; instead, he spoke about the behavior of those who were invited. He was always careful to avoid describing the glory of the eschatological feast; God's kingdom surpasses anything a man can imagine. He passed from the blessing to the personal decision which is necessary, if a person is to be able to partake in this feast (see 13 : 23f.). The false sense of security must be dispelled; Jesus' call for repentance must be welcomed.

The evening was the time appointed for the great feast; it was great, because numerous invitations had been sent out. First of all, the guests received a preparatory invitation which announced the meal. This did not indicate the exact time. Shortly before the banquet was due to begin, the host sent a servant to remind those who had been invited to come, as they had already promised they would. In issuing the invitations in this way, the host followed a rule of courtesy which had won acceptance in leading circles in Jerusalem. " In Jerusalem, no one attends a banquet without being invited twice." When the second invitation arrived, courtesy demanded that it should be accepted.

[18]*"And at once they all began to excuse themselves. The first said to him: 'I have bought a field and I must go out and have a look at it. I beg you, hold me excused.'* [19]*And another said: 'I have bought five teams of oxen and I am on my way to try them out. I beg you, hold me excused.'* [20]*And another said: 'I have married a wife, and so I cannot come.'* [21a]*And when the servant came back, he told his master this."*

To be invited to a feast is an honor and a cause for joy. But, with one accord, all the guests began to make excuses, although they had already promised to come. They did so at once; things were becoming serious! To refuse an invitation, especially at the last minute, was regarded as an offense. The way in which it was refused in this case must have been offensive in the extreme to the man who had given the dinner. The guests rejected the call sent to them; their interest in the invitation was destroyed.

[21b]*"Then the master of the house became angry. He said to his servant: 'Go out quickly into the streets and lanes of the town and bring the poor, the cripples, the blind, and the lame in here.'* [22]*And the servant told him: 'Lord, your command has been carried out, but there is still room.'* [23]*And the Lord said to him: 'Go out to the roads and the hedgerows and force them to come in, so that my house may be full'."*

The meal was ready and the master of the house had no intention of abandoning it. He was determined to share the joy of this meal with someone. Consequently, someone must be found to take the place of those who were invited first. The new invitation failed to muster sufficient guests to fill the banquet hall, so that the servant was sent out once more with an invitation. The host is a generous and big-hearted person. His high-mindedness is in sharp contrast to the short-sightedness of those who were invited first. God's true nature becomes ever more clear. God is generous, condescending love.

First of all, the poor who were found in the streets and lanes of the town must be invited. They had no home of their own, but at least they spent their lives within the sheltering walls of the town. These new guests were not merely to be called or invited; they were to be brought in. They could not conceive that they should come to the feast; they would not even dare to go, when they received the invitation. They would have to be brought.

The servant's second mission was directed to those who lived by the roadside outside the town. Country roads in those days were bordered by hedges. The people who lived out there were foreigners; they had no rights in the town and they would have to be compelled to enter. Oriental courtesy demanded that even the poorest guests should try to refuse an invitation until they were taken by the hand and brought into the house by " gentle force " (24 : 29). These people who could only find a place to live outside the town were now to be compelled to come to a " great supper " in the town. For them, this was unthinkable; they felt unworthy.

²⁴" For I tell you: ' None of those men who were invited will taste my feast '."

The concluding words of the parable are spoken, not by the master of the house, but by Jesus himself. We could say that he himself now speaks to the world at large. The parable gradually focused on him. It is Jesus himself who speaks the threatening words about the exclusion of the guests who refused his invitation.

The Pharisee who pronounced the blessing at the meal was convinced that he would be present at the feast promised for the end of time. Was he really entitled to be so sure? It is certain that in saving history God invited the whole of Israel. Now the final, decisive, and definitive summons concerning the invitation was being issued by Jesus. The supreme hour of salvation history had dawned (see 2 Cor. 6:2; Is. 49:8; Lk. 4:21). Everyone must turn to Jesus now; his invitation must be accepted (13:24, 25f.). And what happened? His invitation was refused. The conclusion is: "None of those who were invited will taste my feast." Where was the Pharisee's assurance now?

The reasons quoted in excuse by the guests are so detailed in the version given by St. Luke that we must stop to consider them. Property (a field), business interests (teams of oxen), and a wife (marriage) were the obstacles which prevented them from accepting the invitation. The three influences which prevented God's word from growing and bearing fruit were similar (see 8:14). "The seed which fell among thorns stands for those who hear the word, but are then choked by the cares and riches and pleasures of life, so that the fruit they bear does not come to maturity" (8:14). In St. Matthew's gospel, Jesus issues an appeal for poverty and renunciation (Mt. 19:21); this appeal is not addressed to everyone.

The parable is an appeal for self-examination and conversion. A person's share in the feast of God's kingdom is endangered if he does not listen to Jesus' word and keep it. The three guests refused the invitation because their worldly possessions, their own affairs, and the satisfaction of their desires meant more to them than the appeal Jesus made and the church's preaching which brings Jesus' invitation to mankind. People may rouse themselves for a moment, perhaps, as when the three guests received the first invitation, but they make no definite or determined decision which is translated into action. They are anxious for their own well-being and they want to make the most of it.

Two groups of men were brought into the feast, to take the place of those who were invited first. This, too, needs to be examined.

They were the very people the Pharisees excluded from God's kingdom, the poor (the cripples, the lame, and the blind) and the gentiles. They were not members of the holy community of Israel. They had no right to hope for a place at God's table in his kingdom. But Jesus thought otherwise. It was precisely for the poor and the gentiles that he opened the way to the eschatological feast. In them, he found the attitude which is the essential condition for admission, according to his preaching. The poor and the gentiles who accepted the invitation did not dare believe that they had been invited; they had to be brought, to be " compelled " to enter. They knew they were poor and unworthy in God's eyes like the sinful woman in the Pharisee's house (7:36), the chief tax collector Zacchaeus (19:1), the tax collector in the temple (18:8), the prodigal son (15:11), and the thief who was crucified with Jesus (23:41).

The parable of the great supper brings St. Luke's *symposion* to a close, but not without throwing light on the meal the church celebrates on Sundays. Who are the people who come together for this meal? St. Paul gives us the example of the church at Corinth: " He [God] has chosen all that is low and worthless in the world for himself " (1 Cor. 1:26-28). Why is that so? At the meal in the house of a leading Pharisee, a festive sabbath meal, only one man found healing—the poor, despised sufferer from dropsy.

The symposium is enveloped in the splendor of God's generous, merciful love which delights in giving everything to those who have nothing, and who were excluded from the shelter of God's city. Those who thought they had something went away empty-handed (1:53). It is the belief that the greatest thing a man can hope for is a gift, a grace, that gives rise to the true fellowship which makes the Lord's Supper what it is. The realization that the important thing on the way to salvation is to adhere to the Lord discloses the purpose of the Eucharist, to make us share in the Lord's death, until he comes (22:20; 1 Cor. 11:23-25). The symposium was held on the way to Jerusalem.

29

The Serious Character of Discipleship (14:25–35)

A person must follow Jesus' call if he is to enter God's kingdom. The parable of the great supper has already made it clear that there are obstacles to this. In a new literary composition in which various traditional sayings of Jesus are incorporated the conditions for the most radical form of following Jesus are laid down; the renunciation of all domestic security and readiness to give one's life (vv. 25–27), the need for careful consideration and trial, to see whether a decision to undertake such a radical form of life should be taken (vv. 28–32), and the renunciation of all possessions (v. 33). It is only in this way that a person will succeed in living up to the real meaning of discipleship and complete surrender to Jesus, and the responsibility this involves (v. 34). In the church, there are Christians who are voluntarily poor and who renounce marriage by choice (1 Cor. 7:8; Acts 4:37). What are we to think of them?

RENUNCIATION AND DISCIPLESHIP (14:25–27)

²⁵*Great crowds journeyed with him and he turned and spoke to them.*

The great crowds wanted to be his disciples; they followed after him. But did they realize what this meant, what it involved? Jesus was on his way to Jerusalem where glory awaited him, but it was there, too, that he would meet his passion and death. We have already heard some of the demands Jesus makes of his disciples; some of the conditions for being raised to glory have already been mentioned: " Strive hard in the contest " (13:24). Anyone who wishes to share in the great supper must accept the invitation immediately (14:18–20). What does journeying with him mean?

The crowds followed behind Jesus. He turned when he spoke to them. They had taken the first step towards discipleship. They became acquainted with Jesus and attached themselves to him, despite the opposition of so many others. They went about after him and listened to his word. It is only by adhering to Jesus that we can be saved. What does following Jesus mean?

²⁶" *If a man comes to me and does not hate his father, his mother, his children, his brothers, his sisters and his own life as well, he cannot be my disciple."*

The man who comes to Jesus to be his disciple must put him before everything; everything else must take second place to him. Jesus preached love, not hate. He had no intention of abrogating the fourth commandment (18:19f.). To hate here is a Semitic expression which means to put something deliberately in the second place, to neglect. St. Matthew paraphrases St. Luke's meaning with the words: " The man who loves his father or mother more than me " (Mt. 10:37). To " hate " oneself is to deny oneself (9:23). Adhering to Jesus (in some form or other) is an essential condition for admission to God's kingdom, the highest value of all. At least if a conflict arises, Jesus must be put before everything else; every other tie must be broken.

Levi, the ancestor of the Levites who served in the temple, said about his father and mother: " I do not know them." He had never seen his brothers and he did not know his own children (Deut. 33: 9). Levi felt himself bound to the temple, the law, and the covenant in a way which allowed of no compromise. Because of this commitment, he reduced all his obligations to his family to a very secondary place. Levi was consecrated to God; God's law and the covenant were his sole concern; they took precedence over everything else. Similarly, Jesus himself must be the sole and unique concern of his disciples. He is the law, the new order of salvation; he is God's revelation, the truth (Jn. 14:6), the reality compared to which everything else is only a shadow. Salvation can be found only in him (Acts 4:12).

31

²⁷" Anyone who does not carry his cross and come after me cannot be my disciple."

This saying was pronounced on the journey to Jerusalem, where Jesus was to meet his death on the cross. If a man wishes to follow him, he must be determined to carry the cross, like him. Jesus' words were metaphorical. Death on the cross was the penalty for disreputable persons, such as slaves and deserters. Anyone who carried the cross forfeited his life and honor; he was given up to total annihilation (see Gal. 3 : 13). Anyone who undertakes to follow Jesus must be prepared to endure all this. Jesus, the master and Lord, bore his cross; this was his way to " being taken up."

What does going after Jesus mean? Were the crowds who accompanied Jesus to Jerusalem prepared to give him precedence over everything? Were they ready to endure his fate, to accept the cross, to risk their lives if God so decreed, in imitation of Jesus? That there are such persons is implied in Jesus' words and the appeal he made.

A DELIBERATE DECISION (14:28–32)

²⁸" Who among you, wanting to build a tower, would not first sit down and count the cost, to see if he has enough to finish it, ²⁹to avoid being unable to complete the building when he has laid the foundations so that those who see it begin to mock him, ³⁰saying: ' This man began to build and was not able to finish the building '."

The parable begins in the style of a Semitic discourse. Those who hear it can and must judge for themselves. The case is put that a man wanted to build a tower. In a vineyard, a structure such as this served a dual purpose. When there was plenty of work to be done, it served as a dwelling place, while it was used as a watchtower the whole year round. A clear view could be had from its flat roof, and

32

a man could see whether thieves or robbers were breaking in. Every vinegrower must have dreamed of having a proper tower in his vineyard, instead of a small shelter made of branches. It is with this supposition that Jesus' parable begins. If one of you owns a vineyard and wants to build a watchtower in it, he will not engage bricklayers immediately and gather the necessary material. First he will consider whether the means at his disposal will permit him to finish his project. Only when he is sure that he has enough money will he begin with the work. Anyone who dispenses with such reflection and allows the workmen to begin some day when the idea comes to him runs a serious risk.

[31]" *Or what king who is on his way to make war on another king will not first sit down and take counsel with himself, to see if he is strong enough with his ten thousand men to advance against the other who is coming with twenty thousand?* [32]*If he decides he is not, he sends ambassadors, while the other is still far off, to ask for conditions of peace.*"

This second metaphor is not taken from the lives of ordinary people any more; it comes from the world of politics. Unlike the first metaphor, it begins, not with: " Who among you," but with: " What king." It is supposed that a king is about to make war on another king who is already on the march. What will the king who is attacked do? The king sat down and took counsel with himself. He will do battle only if the result of his investigation gives hope of a favorable outcome. If not, he asks what he must do to make peace and surrenders unconditionally.

By means of the contradictory pair of " great and small circumstances—a small farmer and a great king," the double parable expresses the same idea. The man who undertakes anything big must first check carefully, to see whether the strength and the means he has are sufficient. The message of the double parable is: think first, then act. It is better not to start something at all than to attempt it with insufficient means and suffer a fiasco. Jesus did not intend these ideas to be a rule of thumb for everyday life; St. Luke incorporates the two parables in Jesus' teaching about the need to take his discipleship seriously. Anyone who feels an inclination to follow Jesus and become his disciple must consider well whether he has the serious and determined will and the strength which will enable him, not merely to become Jesus' disciple, but to be and to remain one. If a person does not feel up to this, it is better for him to abandon any such venture; failure in this case would endanger his salvation.

When they are interpreted in this way, the two parables give rise to a difficult problem. In the matter of which he was speaking, did Jesus really leave us free? Surely following Jesus is necessary for everyone's salvation? Does Jesus want those who come to him to ask themselves whether they want to follow him, or whether they would prefer to abandon the idea? His appeal to them to follow him has already excluded this " whether." If this is so, what is the meaning of the parables?

Following Jesus can take different forms. A person who listens to his appeal for repentance and faith in the message he preached, and obeys him, follows Jesus. But the gospels also recognize another way of following him; this consists in attaching oneself permanently to Jesus. Consequently, it means renunciation. This was the way the apostles followed Jesus. Jesus did not demand that all his disciples should renounce marriage, but only those whom God " had enabled to grasp this word " (Mt. 19:12). In the same way, he did not demand that everyone should renounce their money or possessions. After his conversion Zacchaeus, the tax collector, did not give up all his belongings (19:1–10). The women from Galilee who followed Jesus did not abandon all their possessions (8:3). According to the present passage of St. Luke, when Jesus spoke of the need to take his discipleship seriously, he was referring to this strict imitation of himself. Mere eagerness or momentary enthusiasm is not enough for this.

It involves a radical renunciation which must extend even to what seems indispensable for life. It is important to consider this before a person undertakes to follow Jesus in this way (see 9:57f.). Jesus wanted to prevent enthusiasts from attaching themselves to him; they might be full of ardor at the beginning, but they would soon tire of such a difficult life, and might eventually lose the faith (Jn. 6:60–71).

The choice of images in the parables probably alludes to the form which the following of Jesus took in the case of the apostles, building a tower and waging a war. They were charged with building an edifice and with conducting a war (Rom. 15:20; Phil. 2:25). Both tasks demand determination, careful consideration, and total self-surrender. Honor and peace were to be the crowning glory of these works; shame and cruel servitude had to be overcome. The salvation the Messiah brings confers honor and peace.

THE QUALIFICATIONS OF A DISCIPLE (14:33–35)

³³" So, then, none of you can be my disciples unless he renounces everything he possesses."

A disciple must decide unreservedly for Jesus; those who are dearest to him, his own life and honor, must take second place to Jesus. All a disciple's thoughts and desires must concentrate on the interests of God's kingdom (see 5:11; 18:28). Many Christians in the early church at Jerusalem dispossessed themselves (Acts 4:36–5:11), but it was possible to be a member of the church without giving up everything one possessed (Acts 5:4).

³⁴"Salt, too, is good; but if salt becomes tasteless, what can it be seasoned with? ³⁵It is no use either in the fields or on the dung-heap. It will be thrown out. Let him hear this who has ears to hear with."

35

Salt is good as long as it keeps its seasoning power. Jesus' disciple is good as long as he preserves the spirit of genuine discipleship, as long as Jesus is everything to him so that he thrusts everything which would come between them into the background; as long as he is radically detached from everything, so that he can live solely to follow Jesus " wherever he goes " (9:57). If a disciple who has decided to follow Jesus in the strictest way possible is not sufficiently radical in doing this, he is like salt which has gone stale. He is not qualified to serve the world and he incurs guilt (Mt. 5:13). Jesus' words about what happens to salt which is useless are meant to be reflected upon, as is evident from their length. They are a warning and a threat.

The word about the salt contains a hidden meaning. A man's ears must be open if he is to understand it; it calls for reflection and a readiness to accept it. The man who really hears and obeys it receives God's power to bring him to salvation (see Mt. 19:12). Not everyone is capable of following Jesus in this radical way. In the church, there will always be a need for those who renounce everything radically in this way, to remind all of Christ's disciples that God's kingdom and its blessings are superior to all earthly possessions. Every Christian must be inwardly detached from his possessions and from everything else so that he can renounce them outwardly when the time of decision calls for it. He must be prepared even to give his life if he is compelled to lose his life as a martyr confessing Jesus. In these disciples, we can see what following Jesus means in its deepest sense. Jesus' words about the need to take his discipleship seriously were addressed to the crowds; they were to be in no doubt about what following him means ultimately. The demands his words make are not intended for everyone indiscriminately. " Not everyone can find room for this word " (Mt. 19:11). However, Jesus' words remind us all what a serious matter being his disciple is.

Conversion, faith in Jesus' word (Mk. 1:15), and attaching oneself to him are the basic requirements for anyone who wishes to become his disciple. If a man wants to follow Jesus, his former life will be no obstacle to salvation provided that he has been truly converted. This is illustrated by the double parable of the lost sheep and the lost drachma (vv. 3–10), and the parable of the prodigal son (vv. 11–32). God's love for sinners which is proclaimed in this passage was vitally important for the mission among the gentiles. The tradition on which St. Luke drew showed that, when he proclaimed God's merciful love for sinners, Jesus was forced to defend himself against the Pharisees' objections. Ideas similar to those entertained by the Pharisees may have been prompted in the early Christian churches by the sight of sinners receiving baptism and sharing the common meal with the " saints."

The Pharisees take Offense (15:1–2)

¹All the tax collectors and sinners drew near him, to hear him.
²And the Pharisees and scribes complained, saying: " This fellow here welcomes sinners and eats with them."

Jesus was a prophet, powerful in word and work (24:19). The tax collectors and sinners had seen him and what he did. They came to hear him. What they saw was explained by what he said. Jesus offered salvation and called for a moral conversion. Hearing is the beginning of faith, and faith is the beginning of conversion and forgiveness. Hearing is crowned by the obedience which consists in faith and the faith which consists in obeying. The sinners drew near to Jesus, and through him they drew near to God whose prophet he was. A prophet is one who speaks on God's behalf. They drew near to hear God (see Jer. 29:14f.).

The scribes and Pharisees referred to Jesus in terms of contempt: " This fellow here." They watched him in every way, because they felt that they were responsible for the holiness of the chosen people.

37

They were annoyed and they complained: " He lets sinners come near him; he takes their part and eats at the same table with them " (5:29). By behaving in this way, he frustrated their efforts to preserve the sanctity of the chosen people. The Pharisees' basic principle was: " A man must have nothing to do with sinners." Sinners and those who violated the law must be isolated; they must be excluded from all fellowship with God's holy people. So sin would be punished and vice prohibited; sinners would be outlawed and order restored. The people's sanctity would be preserved. Jesus' behavior must have seemed scandalous. To make matters worse, he acted like a prophet and claimed to speak and act in God's name.

Jesus gives the Pharisees their answer in a trilogy of parables. The first two are in reply to the complaint: he welcomes sinners. The third reaches its climax in a festive meal and is in reply to the reproach: he eats with them. Jesus was quite conscious that it was God's message he preached and that he had nothing to take back. The gospel was being preached to the poor and this included sinners who were prepared to be converted.

THE JOY OF FINDING WHAT WAS LOST (15:3–10)

3But he told them the following parable, saying: 4" What man among you who has a hundred sheep and has lost one of them will not leave the ninety-nine in the wilderness and search for the one that is lost until he finds it. 5And when he has found it, he lays it across his shoulders for joy; 6once he comes home, he calls his friends and neighbors together, saying to them: ' Rejoice with me, for I have found my sheep which was lost.' 7I tell you: there will be joy in heaven in the same way over a single sinner who repents —more than over ninety-nine just men who had no need to be converted."

Palestine is a land of sheep and goat pastures. Everyone was familiar with shepherds and the life they lived. What Jesus sees in them and emphasizes is their care for their flock, their love for their animals.

The parable begins with a question (14:21, 31). Those who heard it were to judge by their own experience. A shepherd would behave just as Jesus said. He takes as much care and trouble over each lost sheep of his flock as if it were his only one and he had not got ninety-nine others besides. He is not indifferent to any of them; he refuses to lose even one. The ninety-nine others will not make up for the loss of one.

The shepherd takes the sheep which has been found on his shoulders. This is a fact of experience. When a sheep has strayed from the flock, it wanders about aimlessly. Finally, it lies down dejectedly and has to be carried. The shepherd treats it more gently than he treats the others, even though searching about the rocky highlands is strenuous and exhausting work. Everything is forgotten because now he has the lost sheep back once more.

His joy is so great that he cannot contain himself. He announces it to his friends and neighbors, saying again and again: " I have found my sheep which was lost."

The shepherd rejoices over a single sheep that was lost and has been found again; in the same way, God rejoices over a single human being who was a sinner and has been converted. That is what God is like. He can never be indifferent to even a single sinner; he refuses to be comforted with the thought of the many who are good. He searches for the sinner; he, too, belongs to him; he will never give him up. He has a care for him and he mourns over him even though he has entered on the wrong path.

If the sinner who is lost is converted, and allows himself to be found, he will not be greeted with reproaches, distrust, or severe precepts. God is a saviour; he will forgive him and bring him home, joyfully and with every indication of affection (Jn. 3:16).

There will be more joy over a single sinner who repents than over ninety-nine just who do not need to repent. The scribes, too, made a distinction between " penitents " (who did penance and were converted) and those who were " perfectly just." Both could say: " It is well for the man who has never sinned, and for him whose sins have been forgiven." Jesus went further. Even the Old Testament recognized that God felt no pleasure in a sinner's death; it was God's will that he should be converted and have life (Ezek. 18:23). God's great joy celebrates the creative omnipotence of the love which makes everything new.

Jesus defends his love for sinners by vindicating God's love for them. A paradoxical situation in which the all-holy God must be defended against the reproaches of human beings. Only the man who believes that God's kingdom has dawned, and that God reigns by means of his mercy, is capable of believing that it is love for sinners which makes the people holy. The Pharisees did not realize that history's great turning-point had come; they refused to accept the message Jesus preached.

[8]" *Or if a woman has ten drachmas and she has lost one, does she not light a lamp and sweep out the house and search carefully until she has found it?* [9]*And when she has found it, she calls her friends and neighbors together and says: ' Rejoice with me, I have found the drachma which I lost.'* [10]*I tell you: there is joy among God's angels, in the same way, over a single sinner who repents."*

Jesus confirms what he had already said. When a person recites the same poem twice, it is impressed more firmly on people's minds; it makes them think. The theme of a song is repeated in its many verses. It is absolutely certain that God is as Jesus describes him. He is not as the pious, the scribes and the learned men of Israel believed and said they knew him to be.

A drachma was worth a silver denarius, and a denarius was a day's wages for a laborer (Mt. 20:2). Ten drachmas was not a fortune, but it was a lot for the poor woman. The woman searched for the lost drachma with the greatest care. This was a difficult task in a Palestinian house. Everything was stored in the same room and the light was bad. She lit a lamp and shone it on everything; she swept out the house, scouring every corner and searching until she found the coin. She was so happy that she had to share her happiness with others. Those who had shared her sorrow must also be told of her joy. Over and over again, she explained the reason for her excitement: " I have found the drachma which I had lost."

This is the way God rejoices over a repentant sinner. His joy is manifested in the angels' joy, in the joy of the heavenly court; their joy is a reflection of the divine joy. In both parables, Jesus says: " God finds joy in a sinner who repents." The distinction between sinners and the just is not abolished; it is not passed over in silence or treated ironically. Jesus never spoke as if sin were not sin. Like the prophets, he called for conversion and repentance; his demand was more radical than that of any prophet before him. He regarded the appeal for repentance as the basis of his mission : " God's kingdom is approaching. Repent!" (Mk. 1:15). Everyone must repent, because everyone is guilty in God's eyes. Jesus' appeal for conversion was accompanied by the threat of judgment and condemnation. Even his proclamation of God's love for sinners was an appeal for conversion; it was a way of preaching salvation and repentance.

The scribes were determined to believe that God did not love a sinner before his conversion. It was only when he abandoned his evil practices and atoned for them that God bestowed his love on him. The words were put on God's lips: " Be converted and then I will welcome you . . . When a man is truly converted, God forgives him." Jesus has a different message; it is God who takes the initiative. The shepherd goes after his lost sheep; the woman looks for the coin. They express their joy with the words: " I have found what I had lost." " Love consists in this; it is not that we loved

41

God, it was he who loved us and sent his Son to atone for our sins. . . . He loved us first " (1 Jn. 4:10.19). Of himself, a sinner could never find his way back to God; God must bring him back (Jer. 24:7).

THE PRODIGAL SON (15:11–32)

11Then he said: "A man had two sons, 12and the younger of these said to his father: ' Father, give me that part of the property which is coming to me.' And so he divided his fortune between them. 13Not many days later, the younger son put all he had together and went off to a distant country, where he squandered his wealth living a dissolute life."

The two parables concerning the search for what was lost revealed God's way of dealing with sinners; the parable of the prodigal son goes further and tells us what takes place in the sinner who is lost. The other parables mention repentance, but without saying what it means; here the meaning of the word is made clear. In this parable, as in the first two, Jesus' purpose is to defend God's merciful treatment of sinners through him. The father in the parable treated his son as a mature person. This was the risk he took.

Life in his father's house, with its regularity and the limitations it imposed, had become burdensome to the younger son who was eager to be independent and wanted to live as he pleased. He left his own country and went to the region east of the Jordan. Palestine was not capable of supporting the population there. Anyone who wanted to get ahead had to go abroad. The diaspora counted four million Jews, while only half a million stayed in the home country. His home country did not allow this young man enough scope. Other countries enticed him with a promise of freedom and independence. But it was not long before he had spent all his money: " The man who loves wisdom gives joy to his father; he who associates with prostitutes sacrifices his wealth " (Prov. 29:3).

14" When he had spent everything, a great famine came upon that country, and he began to suffer want. 15He went and attached himself to a citizen of the country, who sent him to his farm to look after his pigs. 16He longed to fill his stomach with the husks on which the pigs were fed, and no one gave them to him."

In times of famine, even a wealthy person finds it hard to make ends meet. But what about a person who has no means whatever? A Jewish scribe would say he must run footsore until he reached the nearest Jewish settlement, where he should ask for assistance and for work. What did the " prodigal son " do? He did something which was unthinkable for a pious Jew. He made an urgent approach to a citizen of that heathen country and attached himself to him, like an importunate beggar. He wanted work so that he could live; he was willing to undertake anything to avoid starvation. There was nothing he would not give up simply to prolong his life, destitute as it was. He was in a pagan country where there was no sabbath rest, no ritual meals, where the laws of ritual cleanliness were not obeyed. He lived in the company of sinners and those who knew no law. The work he accepted was unthinkable for a pious Jew: " May a curse come upon the man who cares for swine." He was occupied constantly with animals which were unclean (Lev. 11:7), thereby denying his religion. The prodigal son had become a sinner, and a rebel; he had abandoned God. What had he left?

The truth of the proverb: " Drunkards and gluttons will be reduced to penury " (Prov. 23:21) was strikingly demonstrated in the prodigal son. He was forced to go without everything a human being has need of to live a genuinely human life (Jn. 12:6).

17" He came to himself and said: ' How many hired laborers of my

43

father's have more than enough bread, while I am dying of hunger here! ¹⁸I will set out and go to my father and say to him: Father, I have sinned against heaven and before your face. ¹⁹I am no longer worthy to be called your son. Regard me as one of your hired laborers'."

The Jews had a proverb: "When the Israelites are reduced to eating carob-beans, they turn [to God]." This was certainly true of the prodigal son. He came to himself; he gave himself up to reflection. He refused to give up the struggle; he was determined to live. Neither God nor his father formed the center of his reflections; his immediate desire was to save himself from dying of starvation in a foreign land. The Jewish scribes quoted God as saying: "If a godless person returns to his senses, I plait a crown for him at his death [the crown of eternal life] . . . If a godless person returns to his senses, he can make constant progress [in coming closer to the saints]." The path of self-analysis ends in God's presence.

The prodigal son entered into himself; he turned to his father, and ended by turning to God. The words expressing his repentance are taken from scripture (see Ex. 10:16; Ps. 51:6). The memory of his father's house with its abundance and its religious observances—and the memory of his father who was behind all this—reminded the prodigal son of God. It aroused in him a consciousness of his guilt and prompted him to turn to God.

The picture of his devoted father convinced him that he would be forgiven. How could he set out to go to his father otherwise? In the picture of his father, he saw an image of God (see Jer. 3:12f.). The prodigal son recognized his guilt and acknowledged that he had forfeited his rights as a son by the life he lived. He only asked to be one of his father's hired laborers.

²⁰*" And he rose to his feet and went to his father. He was still far off when his father saw him and was moved with pity for him. And*

44

*he ran and fell upon his neck and kissed him. *²¹*But the son said
to him: ' Father, I have sinned against heaven and before your face.
I am no longer worthy to be called your son '."*

The prodigal's reflection was translated into action. An inner
conversion must bear the " fruits of repentance." It demands that
a man should break with his old life and return to God, rising to
meet his Father. The father did not wait until everything demanded
by a true conversion had been accomplished before forgiving him.
In the picture of this father, we see an image of the Father in
heaven who always takes the initiative with his love.

*²²" But the father told his servants: ' Quick, bring out the best
festive robe and clothe him with it. Put a ring on his finger and
shoes on his feet. *²³*And bring out the fatted calf and slaughter it.
We are going to celebrate and have a feast. *²⁴*For this son of mine
was dead and has come to life again. He was lost and now he has
been found.' And they began to celebrate a joyful feast."*

The father did not call his son to account; he imposed no conditions, and he prescribed no trial period. He did not express his
forgiveness in words, but his behavior showed his forgiveness more
than any words. He gave his son the right to be a free man again.

This father's joy is the joy of the time of salvation. The gospel of
mercy is a gospel of joy. Jesus saves those who are lost from death.
He came " to give light to those who sit in darkness and the shadow
of death " (1 : 79). The words spoken by the prodigal's father are
like a refrain; they close the first and second part of the parable,
and the story of the father's love and big-heartedness, and the story
of the pitiless severity and intolerance of the elder son. That is what
God is like—and that is what the Pharisees are like. But Jesus tells
us: " Be merciful as your Father is merciful " (6 : 36).

²⁵" But his elder son was out on the farm. And as he came and

45

drew near the house, he heard music and dancing, 26and he called over one of the servants and inquired what this might mean. 27He told him: 'Your brother has come and your father has killed the fatted calf, because he has recovered him safe and sound.' 28aBut he was angry and he refused to go in."

The elder son had given faithful service, day in and day out. He came in from his work on the farm. The meal was over and the men had begun a dance of joy. Music and the beat of dancing feet could be heard from the house. The son who had been so conscientious about fulfilling his duties was surrounded by a festival atmosphere of happiness and rejoicing. The servant who explained the reason for the festivities saw only what was obvious, the prodigal's return, the killing of the fatted calf, and the fact that he had come back safely. Indeed, how could he have seen what went on in the father's heart and in the heart of the prodigal son. He saw nothing of the drama of his repentance, the change which had taken place and his resurrection from the dead, all of which were involved in this. Repentance is an anticipation of what will happen at the end of time. What passes between God and a sinner who repents is an image of the world-wide event which is still to come, but is already taking place. The time of salvation is a time of joy.

The elder son's reaction is an image of the Pharisee's attitude. In him we have a picture of a pious Jew. He rejected his father's behavior angrily; he protested against the way the moral order was being endangered; he complained about such incomprehensible mercy. Surely, the day of the Lord, when God's kingdom will be established, is a " day of anger " on which those who have violated the law will receive a sentence of condemnation. Go in to the feast? That would mean associating with a sinner; it would mean sitting at the same table with a man who had sullied himself with prostitutes, gentiles, and pigs. The elder son acted like a "just " man, a pious person, or a Pharisee. " This fellow here welcomes sinners and eats with them " (15:2).

²⁸ᵇ" *Then his father went out and spoke to him.* ²⁹*However, he answered his father: ' See, I have served you for so many years. I have never disobeyed your commands, yet you never gave me a kid to have a feast with my friends.* ³⁰*But when your son, this fellow here who squandered your fortune with prostitutes, came back, you killed the fatted calf for him.' "*

The father went out to his elder son; he was by no means indifferent to him. He spoke to him pleadingly and tried to placate him, but it was as if a raging torrent had burst its banks, and the elder son poured out his heartfelt indignation. What his father had done provoked him; the just man was ignored while they celebrated the return of a sinner. His " so many years " of faithful service are contrasted with the prodigal son who " squandered your fortune "; I " never disobeyed your commands," with " spent everything in the company of prostitutes "; you " never gave me a kid with which to celebrate," with " you killed the fatted calf." The mystery of God's love and mercy is something which cannot be gauged by human standards. By revealing God as a loving Father, Jesus proclaimed that God's kingdom was close at hand, the kingdom which brings forgiveness and salvation.

³¹" *But he replied: ' My child, you were always with me, and everything I have is yours.* ³²*But it was necessary to hold a feast and celebrate, because your brother was dead and has come to life; he was lost and has been found '."*

The father defended himself. Did the elder son not remember all that he had received from his father, everything he had? He was his dear child; this is the way his father addresses him; he enjoyed his father's love and fellowship with him at all times. He lost nothing of his share of the inheritance. The father confirmed that everything he had was his. Did his father do him an injustice by being so good to his other son (Mt. 20 : 15)? Did he lose as a result of his goodness?

The three blessings the father mentioned form a picture of God's covenant with his people; my child—my people; I am with you—you are with me; and the community of property which exists between the father and the son. Jesus inaugurated a new order of salvation which restores the old order and gives it new depth and perfection. The new covenant which remits sins is founded in his blood (22:20; see also Jer. 31 : 34).

It was God's will that they should hold a feast. The prodigal, after all, was a brother of the elder son. The elder son thought only about the law; he had no love for his brother. According to Jesus' message, however, this was the essence of the law; this was God's will. Here we find once more the attitude revealed by the dispute about the sabbath (14:5). The Pharisees guarded the sabbath rest jealously, but they did not trouble themselves about fraternal charity. It is by his miracles of love and mercy that God manifests his glory.

Would sin not gain the upper hand and break over everything like a flood if it was forgiven too easily? Would the revelation that God rejoiced at a sinner's conversion not be catastrophic for morality? Surely Jesus' preaching about the mercy God showed sinners was a threat to the entire moral order? Jesus' words mention two regulatory forces—repentance and brotherly love. The prodigal son repented and came back to his father; the elder son received a lesson in fraternal charity. Such repentance and charity were a sign that God's kingdom had dawned; the time of salvation had come. Under the guidance of the Spirit, the apostles' preaching led those who heard it to conversion; it incorporated them into the fellowship of those who are assembled in Jesus' name and constitute a

" single heart and a single soul " (Acts 2:37–47). Repentance and fraternal charity are the foundations of the moral order.

The early church, too, was forced to reflect on the question: How are sinners to be dealt with among the people of God who are holy? St. Matthew's gospel describes a process which is really " juridical " in nature; first a fraternal correction should be given privately, after which it could be repeated in the presence of witnesses. If this failed, the matter could be brought before the whole church and the guilty person expelled (Mt. 18:15–17). St. Luke, on the other hand, shows us the way of mercy and goodness in love. Both approaches go back to Jesus; both are rooted in the proclamation of the imminent coming of God's kingdom. God's kingdom is at once a kingdom of mercy and judgment.

The feast is mentioned three times in the parable of the prodigal son. When Christians gather for the eucharistic meal, they recall the salvation and forgiveness God accomplished in Jesus (22:20; 1 Cor. 11:26) in a spirit of joy (Acts 2:46). Once they were not a people at all; now they are God's people; once they were without grace, but now they have received God's grace (1 Pet. 2:10). At the Lord's Supper, the Lord's blood is proffered " for the remission of sins " (Mt. 26:28). The new order of salvation and our adoption as God's sons are celebrated with joyful gratitude.

The parable ends without telling us what the father did about his elder son. Jesus was not passing judgment; he was making an offer of salvation. He was anxious to bring the Pharisees to salvation too. Everyone needs to repent, both sinners and those who imagine they are just (18:9–14). " We are all subject to sin " (Rom. 3:9).

The Children of this World (16:1—17:10)

Sin is no obstacle to salvation if only a person will repent. But what are the obstacles to salvation? This new section seems to answer this question. It can be divided into two similarly constructed parts: 16:1–18 and 16:19—17:10. Each of these begins with a story which then receives var-

49

ious "applications." The first part ends with a number of sayings addressed to the Pharisees in which Jesus demands that they should fulfill the law in a much more radical way (16:14–18). The second part ends with a number of verses concerning the need for the self-surrender demanded by faith (17:5–10). These are intended for the apostles. Of the two stories, the first shows how a man can use his wealth to attain salvation, while the second shows how it may bring him to damnation. In each, three characters appear. In the first story we have the rich man, his steward, and the debtors; in the second, the rich man, the beggar, and Abraham. The steward ensures his future by giving; the rich man incurs damnation because he would not give anything.

Wealth and marriage prevented the guests in the parable from turning up at the hour appointed for the great supper. The man who is determined to follow Jesus in the most radical way possible will renounce his wealth and his family (14:25–34). However, such extremism is not demanded of everyone. On the other hand, it is impossible to be Christ's disciple without some form of renunciation. This new passage can be entitled " The Children of the World " (16:8) because it deals with the question: How can Jesus' disciple, whose thoughts must be fixed on heaven where Christ now reigns in glory (Col. 3:1), defend himself against the world's attacks? The world is determined to bring him under its influence. "Everything that is in the world, the lust of the flesh, the lust of the eyes, and the arrogance of life [the folly of thinking that all our wellbeing depends on ourselves alone] comes from the world; it does not come from the Father " (1 Jn. 2:16). The proper attitude towards wealth (the two stories with their " applications "), the new interpretation of the law of marriage (16:18), and humility (17:10) are so many bulwarks against these three dangers. A similar literary composition is found in St. Matthew (19:2–20). There the problem, its solution, and the conclusion are all the same. Salvation is a gift from God; man has no claim to it, even when he has done his best. The traditional material St. Matthew uses for his purpose is different.

THE DISHONEST STEWARD (16:1–13)

1aBut he also told his disciples:

What Jesus said about the joy God feels when a sinner repents was meant for the scribes and Pharisees (15:1). The tax collectors and sinners heard this good news. But the crowds who accompanied Jesus on his journey were also present. Jesus now turns to his disciples, to those who had decided to listen to his word and obey it They, too, needed his teaching to show them what was necessary if they were to attain the glory which awaited him at the end of his journey.

[1b]*" There was a rich man who had a steward, and a complaint was brought to him that he was squandering his estate; [2]he summoned him and asked him: ' What is this I hear about you? Give me an account of your administration. You cannot be my steward any more '."*

The rich man was a landowner and very likely a foreigner. He employed a local man to run the estate as his steward. The steward was independent to a great extent, but he was bound to give the owner an account of his administration. Rightly or wrongly, he had now been denounced to his employer for squandering the property entrusted to him. This was enough to make the owner call him to account for his actions. This meant that he would have to hand over all the deeds and promissory notes, as well as the accounts; bookkeeping in the ordinary sense was unknown. At the same time, the steward was given notice. The reproachful question he asked made it clear that the owner was highly displeased. He was determined to dismiss his steward, who consequently found himself in a difficult position.

[3]*" The steward then said to himself: ' What am I to do? My master is depriving me of my office as steward. I have not got the strength to dig and I would be ashamed to beg. [4]I know what I will do, so that people will welcome me into their houses, when I have been dismissed from my post '."*

The difficulty of the steward's position is clear from his monologue He had lost a good position, and all hope of a " sinecure " had disappeared. He was not strong enough for manual work, and his self-respect made it impossible for him to go begging. Like the warring king and the farmer who built a tower, the steward took time to consider. He will " forgive " others their debts; then they will give him what he needs in return. What must be done to ensure the future? This is the great question we all face as we go through life.

The steward was not troubled by scruple of conscience. He was still in a position to win himself friends, putting them under obligation to him, so that they would later give him shelter. He was still steward. He could still make use of what had been entrusted to him. All he was interested in was ensuring his future survival. He did not hesitate; time was short, and precipitous action was the order of the day. The whole parable bears the mark of the last stage of time which was now being announced.

[5]" He summoned each of his master's debtors singly, and said to the first: ' How much do you owe my master? ' 'A hundred measures of oil,' he replied. [6]Then he told him: ' Take your account and sit down quickly and write fifty.' [7]Then he said to another: 'And you, how much do you owe?' 'A hundred bushels of wheat,' he replied. He said to him: ' Take your account and write eighty '."

The debtors were wholesalers who were behind in their payments. Only two are mentioned: wine and oil were the most important agricultural products in Palestine. A hundred measures of oil was the yield of from one hundred and forty to one hundred and sixty olive-trees. This would be about ninety gallons. A hundred " bushels " of wheat could be harvested from about one hundred and five acres of land. This would be about one thousand bushels. The steward took fifty percent and twenty percent respectively off the two bills. In monetary terms, both would come to about the same amount, five hundred denarii. A silver denarius was the usual wage paid to a hired laborer for a day's work (Mt. 20:2-13). Oriental storytellers were fond of large numbers; the steward wanted to ensure a lengthy future for himself and so he was forced to take a great risk.

"And the Lord praised the dishonest steward, because he had acted prudently. The children of this world are wiser than the children of light in dealing with their own age."

Who was the Lord who praised the steward? Was it the land-owner? Would he have been able to take such a detached view of things? Would he have had such a sense of humor that he could praise the dishonest steward for his " prudence "? The Lord is Jesus (7:6; 11:39). But how could Jesus praise this sly and cunning embezzler for his " prudence "? The story is not a factual account; it is a parable. Where is its real point?

Jesus' praise was not intended for the thief's underhanded cunning or his shameless audacity; it was for the bold stroke by means of which he availed of his present position to provide for the future. What he praised was not his dishonesty as such but the fact that he provided for the future with such foresight, while there was still time. The steward is referred to as the " dishonest steward "; he was a fraudulent, unjust, and wicked administrator. Parables are intended to make people listen attentively and think about the lessons they contain.

A disciple is prudent if he remembers that his Lord may come and demand an account (12:42–46), if he refuses to live only for the day and is familiar with the demands of the hour. He must act boldly and decisively, so that he will be able to stand fast in the end. He must forgive others, and so earn the right to his heavenly home. The parable is an eschatological appeal : Be prudent. In this last hour provide for your future in the final age.

The conclusion Jesus draws sounds almost like a complaint : " The children of this world are more prudent than the children of light in dealing with their own age." " This world " is subject

53

to Satan's influence and power; he is the prince of this world (Jn. 12:31), its god (2 Cor. 4:4). The "children of this world" are guided solely by the principles, the self-interest, of godless men. They do not trouble themselves about God or his will, about his promises or his threats for the future. For them, life begins and ends in this world. They allow themselves to fall under Satan's influence; they are his disciples, his kingdom. The "children of light," on the other hand, are guided by the light in all their thoughts and actions (see Jn. 8:12; 12:36; 1 Jn. 1:5 and 1 Thess. 5:5).

The dishonest steward is a child of this world. He was guided solely by anxiety for his earthly life. He acted vigorously and decisively in putting everything which represented an advantage for his life on earth to the best possible use. The children of light have eyes only for what life, man, and the world itself are in God's sight. Through their faith in God's word, they have knowledge of the world to come, that world which proclaims its presence in the background of this present world; they know about God's kingdom and its promises, including eternal life. Yet compared to the children of this world, the children of light are indecisive and feeble in their efforts when they should be preparing for the glorious future which will be theirs. Jesus had good reason to complain.

However, the children of this world are not more prudent than the children of light in every respect. They are "more prudent . . . in dealing with their own age." They are more prudent especially where their aim is to make life more worth living. In one thing, however, they are not prudent. Their gaze does not go beyond the realities of this world; they are totally ignorant of the world to come.

9"And I tell you: use your unjust mammon to win yourselves friends, so that when it is no more they may welcome you into eternal tents."

With the property he administered, the dishonest steward won himself friends who would look after him when he was no longer steward. Like the steward, Christ's disciple, too, must win himself friends with his wealth; they will intercede for him at the hour of death, when his earthly possessions will lose their value (12:20). Alms and works of charity intercede for a man before God (12:33); they make him worthy to see God face to face; they give him a share in the world to come. This attitude is characteristic of the new people of God Jesus founded.

Jesus refers to temporal riches as mammon; this is something on which a man builds, in which he trusts (see 12:15f.; 16:11; Sir. 27: 2; Mt. 6:24).

God welcomes those who have done good into the eternal tents. " There are many dwellings in the heavenly Father's house " (Jn. 14:2). Whenever Jesus speaks about the life to come, he likes to use the language of the world in which he lived. We have an example of this in the words: " I saw another vision, the dwellings of the just, and the places where the saints repose. With my own eyes I saw their dwellings with his holy angels and their resting places among the saints, and they prayed, interceding for the children of men and pleading for them " (Enoch 39:4f.).

[10]" *The man who is faithful in the smallest matter is also faithful in much; he who is dishonest in the smallest matter is also dishonest in much.* [11]*If, therefore, you are unfaithful with your unjust mammon, who will entrust you with genuine wealth?* [12]*And if you are not faithful with what is alien, who will give you what is ours?* "

Worldly wealth is not God's greatest gift. In fact, it is the least; it is not much. On the other hand, genuine wealth on which a man can build confidently is much. This is the world to come, the right to share in God's kingdom, the new eternal life. Temporal possessions are the least of all; they are incapable of making our lives really secure. They cannot ward off death (12:22–31); they cannot even add the slightest thing to the length of our life or to our height (12:25). What is greater will be entrusted only to the man who knows how to administer what is less properly. " If you are not faithful in small things, who will give you what is greater? " (Mt. 25:21). God gives the heavenly blessings which are to come only to the man who knows how to administer his earthly possessions faithfully, in accordance with God's will. The steward was expected to be faithful (see 12:42; 1 Cor. 4:2).

It is the mammon that is alien. What is ours is the new life, God's kingdom. In our present state, we human beings would never entrust what is ours—something to which we are deeply attached, which is near and dear to us—to a man who is incapable even of looking after what belongs to a stranger who bears no relation to us. When God gives us his kingdom and a share in his own life, he gives us something which is his very own, something in which—to speak in human terms—he himself is personally involved. Mammon is alien to him; it is not related to him personally in any way. If we do not administer what is alien faithfully, how can God entrust us with what is ours, as he calls it? Fidelity in the administration of earthly goods is a test for a disciple to see whether he is fitted to possess the good of the world to come.

[13]*" No servant can serve two masters. Either he will hate the one and love the other, or he will attach himself to the one and despise the other. You cannot serve God and mammon."*

Jesus' discourse concerning wealth and property closes with a word of warning. The service of God and the service of mammon are incompatible. Both God and mammon claim man entirely for themselves. God wishes to be loved with a person's " whole heart, and his whole soul; with all his strength and his whole mind " (10:27). As experience shows, mammon, too, makes an exclusive claim on a man. How could the service of two masters such as these, both of whom demand total self-surrender, be reconciled? Could a slave serve two masters as a slave? Each of his masters could demand his service at any given moment. No one could serve two masters like this. Jesus' words make it clear that no compromise aimed at serving God and mammon is possible. They impose a choice, God or mammon (see also 1 Tim. 6:17f.).

Which must we choose? God is great beyond all comparison. The man who is faced with a choice between God and mammon must choose between two things; to hate God or to love him, to despise him or to attach himself to him. But who would relegate God to the second place? Who wants to hate or despise him? Jesus' words are a summons to reflection; they are disturbing.

THE AVARICIOUS PHARISEES (16:14–18)

14But the Pharisees who were fond of money heard all this, and they sneered at him. 15And he told them: " You are the very people who pretend to be virtuous in the sight of men, but God knows your hearts. What is exalted among men is an outrage in God's eyes."

The Pharisees were regarded as being avaricious. Jesus charged them with devouring the property of widows (20:47). The Qumran community referred to them as " liars who are interested only in feasting and having more than they need." The rabbi Jochanan (d. 287) is quoted as saying: " The members of the body are suspended from the heart, and a person's heart is suspended from his purse." The Pharisees regarded poverty as a curse. Wealth was the reward of virtue; poverty was a punishment for sin. " Wealth, honor, and [a long] life are the reward of humility and the fear of God " (Prov. 22:4). Anyone who attacked the Pharisees' wealth cast doubt on their fidelity to the law and on their piety. Jesus dared to do this; he overthrew their teaching completely. He went about the country as a mendicant (8:1); he preached renunciation of one's wealth and proclaimed a blessing for the poor, while pronouncing a series of " woes " on those who were rich (6:20, 24). The Pharisees had a long tradition on their side. They sneered at him, arrogantly despising him.

The Pharisees were avaricious; they tried to secure their earthly lives by means of their wealth, and their existence in God's sight by performing the "works justice demanded." They did good deeds and never transgressed the law. They declared that they were just, and they were convinced that God concurred in this judgment. Their wealth was a sign that God agreed with their opinion of themselves. But Jesus quashed this judgment; he destroyed their security and demolished the pious construction behind which they had taken refuge. God looks at a man's heart (see Mt. 5:3), at the attitude from which his actions spring. The Pharisees did not seek God; they sought only their own honor, their own selves (Mt. 6:1-18). It is the man whom God makes just that is really just (see Is. 5:5).

In Jesus, God reversed the Pharisees' judgment: " The brother who has no claim to fame [who is poor] can boast of his exalted dignity. The rich man must boast of his lowliness. He will disappear like the flower of the grass " (Jas. 1:9f.).

[16]" *The law and the prophets lasted until John; from then on, God's kingdom is proclaimed and everyone forces their way in by violence.* [17]*It would be easier for heaven and earth to disappear than for [even] one little flourish of the law to fall away."*

The Pharisees scorned what was new in Jesus' preaching. They failed to recognize the significance of the period of salvation history which had dawned in him. The first period of salvation history, the age of the law and the prophets, the time of the promise, ended with John the Baptist. Now the good news of God's kingdom, the message of victory, was being proclaimed. The time of fulfillment had come. In Jesus, the salvation which had been promised was present at last. He inaugurated the new era (4:16ff.).

Everyone was forcing their way into God's kingdom; they used all their strength to attain salvation. The idea of a struggle crops up here once more (13:24). It was in keeping with St. Luke's historical work to picture a great multitude of people welcoming the good news of salvation and pressing their way into God's kingdom, despite persecution and difficulties of every kind. His gospel shows how the people, the tax collectors and sinners, entered by this door which had now been thrown open to everyone, despite the opposition of the leaders among the people. The Acts of the Apostles particularly is penetrated with the idea that everyone, including the gentiles, realized that this was the hour of salvation and availed of it. The joyful pathos involved in the word " everyone " shows that there was nothing to obstruct the way of salvation. However, the fact must not be overlooked that everyone must force their way in if they wish to enter. The radical character of Jesus' words was appropriate; the time of decision had come. No one had anything to lose by deciding in favor of Jesus' teaching. Everyone was forced to make a determined effort. Even the Pharisees who thought that they were holy could not refuse to yield to the demand made by Jesus' forceful words.

The Pharisees regarded themselves as being just; they were convinced that they knew the law and observed it perfectly. Was this opinion of themselves justified? Surely their zeal for the law entitled them to scorn Jesus' extremism? What reproach could be made against them? The preaching of the kingdom and its presence in Jesus did not abrogate the law. It would be easier for heaven and earth, all that was most permanent in man's experience, to disappear than for the law to come to an end. The law expressed God's will; this could never lose its force. The law is for all time. This had to be reaffirmed in the face of those who were full of enthusiasm for the salvation which had come in Jesus and wanted to cast off all restraint.

God now asserted his sovereign rule; consequently, his will, which is contained and expressed in the law, was being fully accomplished. It was accomplished so radically that not even the law's least provision was overlooked. The little flourish Jesus mentioned is a tiny decoration with which many Hebrew letters are adorned. God's will attains its perfect accomplishment in God's kingdom; at the same time, every effort must be made to see that it is obeyed perfectly. The decisive turning point which marked the transit from the time of the promise to the time of salvation was also a decisive turning point in the history of man's surrender to God's will. A man may no longer reserve anything for himself. Everything he has, including the very depths of his personal existence (his heart), must be put at God's disposal.

Properly understood, the law remains valid. It was more than fulfilled by Jesus who placed it under the sign of the all-powerful grace of God's kingdom. That was why he could say: " If your justice is not greater than that of the scribes and Pharisees, you will not enter into the kingdom of heaven " (Mt. 5 : 20).

[18]" *Everyone who sends his wife away and marries another commits adultery, and anyone who marries a woman who has been abandoned by her husband also commits adultery.*"

The advent of the time of salvation does not do away with the Old Testament law; on the contrary, it makes it more stringent. God's will which it expresses is enforced without any concessions to human weakness.

The Old Testament admitted the possibility of divorce (see Deut. 24 : 1 and Mt. 19 : 3). Jesus, on the other hand, proclaimed the indissolubility of marriage. A man might give his wife a writ of separation, but it had lost its juridical force. The marriage still existed. Consequently, remarriage on the part of those who had been divorced was equivalent to adultery. Both men were at fault: the man who took a second wife, and the man who married a woman who had been divorced. Both offended against the sanctity of marriage.

The Pharisees regarded themselves as being just, because they observed God's law. But God demands a more exalted justice than that practiced by the scribes and Pharisees (Mt. 5:20). Jesus reproached them with ignoring God's law to observe human traditions (Mk. 7:8). Moreover, the Old Testament law was not a complete expression of God's will. It was Jesus who revealed the law's real intent by proclaiming God's sovereign rule. He went straight to the heart of the matter and reasserted God's will as it had been from the beginning.

The message Jesus preached imposed the demands of the law in a far more radical form. He did away with all concessions to human weakness and restored the full force of the commandments; this was true of oaths (Mt. 5:33–37) and of divorce (Mt. 5:31f.), where the result was bound to be more drastic. The change was particularly marked in the case of revenge (Mt. 5:38–42) and love of one's enemies (Mt. 5:43–48). Of all the extreme demands Jesus made, St. Luke mentions only the indissolubility of marriage. Why was this? The guests who were invited to the great supper did not come; two were prevented by their possessions and the third by his " wife " (14:20). It was because of the Jews' hard-heartedness. Attachment to wealth and attachment to a wife endanger the readiness of a man's heart to answer God's call. This readiness can be attained in a radical fashion by poverty and the renunciation of marriage (Mt. 19:12, 21). Practical charity and the indissolubility of marriage are characteristic marks of Jesus' disciples and are the first steps towards perfect detachment from wealth and marriage for the sake of God's kingdom. By means of them, they force their way with violence into God's kingdom. They must prove themselves anew each day by means of them, and decide in favor of God's call. They can never say they have already done everything.

THE RICH MAN (16:19—17:4)

[19]" *But there was a man who was rich, who was clothed in purple and linen and held a sumptuous feast every day.* [20]*There was also a pauper whose name was Lazarus who lay at his gate, covered with sores.* [21]*He would have been glad to fill himself with what fell from the rich man's table [but no one gave it to him]. The dogs came and licked his sores.* [22]*However, it happened that the poor man died and was carried by angels to Abraham's embrace. The rich man died, too, and was buried.* [23]*And there in the lower world, he raised his eyes as he was in an agony of torment and he saw Abraham a great distance away and Lazarus in his embrace.* [24]*He cried out and said: 'Father Abraham, have pity on me and send Lazarus to dip the tip of his finger in water and moisten my tongue. I am suffering agony in these flames.'* [25]*But Abraham replied: 'My child, remember that you received good fortune in your life, while Lazarus suffered ill fortune. Now he is comforted here and you are in agony.* [26]*Moreover, there is a great abyss between us and you, so that those who might want to go from here to you cannot do so, and no one can cross from there to us'.*"

St. Luke's account of Jesus' words reaches its first climax in this passage. In vivid, dramatic language, Jesus explains the real meaning of the woes he pronounced on the rich who laugh and have plenty to eat, and of the beatitude of the poor who mourn and are hungry (6:20ff.). The picture of the poor man is in sharp contrast. He was a cripple and he lay at the gate leading to the rich man's palace, where his friends brought him every day. He was tormented with hunger. In antiquity, people ate with their hands, and in well-to-do homes it was customary to use the bread crumbs to clean them. These were then thrown under the table. The beggar would have been glad to have them, but no one gave them to him. The half wild dogs which roamed in the alley-ways licked his sores and he could not prevent them, he was so helpless. The beggar's name was Lazarus, *El-azar,* " God helps." He was one of those poor who bore their misery with patience and put their trust in God. Their life was bearable only because of their trust in God. They found comfort in God's promises in the Psalms and in the prophets. The beatitudes of the Sermon on the Mount were intended for them.

The rich man lived his life without any reference to God. He had everything. What did he need from God? He had no time for God or for a starving beggar. He was well off and he was totally absorbed in the fine life he led. He was not against God; he did nothing to make the beggar's lot worse. It was " only " that he was blind to God, the poor man, and " Moses and the prophets."

The point of the story is in what happens after death. Now that they were dead, the two men found themselves in different places, according to whether they had obeyed God's will or not during their earthly lives. Man's existence is not limited to his life on earth; it continues even after death. The whole story shows the continuity between the present life and the life to come; it shows the significance of this world for the world to come. Being well-off in this life is not the only thing that matters.

" After the judgment, the pit of torment will be visible and likewise the place of life; hell's furnace will be visible, and on the other hand the joy of Eden [paradise]." This is the conception found in the Fourth Book of Ezra (7 : 36). The inhabitants of the two places could see one another and converse together. In the lower world, the rich man raised his eyes and saw Abraham far away. According to the source just quoted, the souls of the reprobate are tortured by the fact that they can see how the angels keep watch over the dwellings of other souls in deep silence (4 Ezra 7:85). What Jesus tells us about the life to come in this story was in keeping with the ideas current at the time. He does not mean that the world to come is like that. The story of the wealthy spendthrift is not a " tourist guide " to the next world. Jesus makes use of traditional images to drive home his teaching more effectively.

The beggar had a place at the banqueting table; the rich man suffered torments outside. The beggar enjoyed the happiness of the place of honor; the rich man endured burning thirst. The rich man's situation in eternity was hopeless. The Jews were convinced that their father, Abraham, could free them even from hell by his intercession. " Those who walk in the valley of tears are those who at this hour are sent to Gehenna [hell]. Then Abraham, our father, comes and makes them rise up and takes them with him." In his torment, the glutton appealed to Abraham, but it was in vain. Between the place of torment and the place of happiness, there is an insurmountable gulf. There is no road leading from one to the other. No form of intercession can save anyone; there can be no change in a person's circumstances. All hope is destroyed. What should the rich man have done?

[27]" ' In that case, father, I implore you to send him to my father's house. [28]I have five brothers; he can give them a warning, so that they, too, may not come to this place of torture.' [29]But Abraham said: ' They have Moses and the prophets; they should listen to them.' [30]But he said: ' No, father Abraham, but if one comes to them from the dead, they will repent.' [31]But he told him: ' If they do not listen to Moses and the prophets, they will not be convinced if someone comes back from the dead '."

Now it is clear why the rich man was tormented. He had given himself up to the enjoyment of his wealth; he was quite insensitive to the comfort and hope held out by scripture (Rom. 15:4). He was deaf to God's word and to his call. His wealth and the fine life he led had made him blind—blind to God, to the poor, to the " life to come." They had closed his heart to the " other " world. The beatitudes addressed to those who have placed their hope in God, whose hearts are open to him because of the distress they feel, are followed by those addressed to people who are open to their fellow men and their needs (see Mt. 5:3-6; 5:7-10). " Lazarus " was forced by his distress to put his hope in God and he was given a share in the banquet prepared in God's kingdom.

In scripture, in Moses and the prophets, God has given us his word to warn us and enlighten us; it guides us so that we may not come into the place of torment. " We are secure in our possession of the prophets' words, and you do well to pay attention to them; they are like a light shining in the darkness, until the day dawns and the morning star rises in your hearts " (1 Pet. 1:19). It is this prophetic word which leads a man to mold his thoughts according to God; it marks the beginning of conversion and repentance. The whole of scripture is devoted to Jesus Christ, his death and resurrection (24: 27, 46). The man who listens to the word about Jesus and puts it into practice will be spared the rich man's fate; when the message of Jesus' death and resurrection is preached, it gives rise to repentance (Acts 2:37f.).

Anyone who refuses to listen to scripture will also refuse to be convinced if a messenger comes from the other world. Even the greatest miracle, the resurrection of the dead, would be in vain.

A rich man who is in danger of relying completely on his wealth must inquire what is God's will. The result of such a conversion is active love for one's neighbor (3:10f.). " This is the kind of fasting which appeals to me: loose the unjust chains and undo the thongs of the yoke; let the oppressed go free and break every yoke. And you must share your bread with the hungry. Bring the poor who have no home to your house. When you see a person naked, clothe

him, and do not hide from your own flesh [your fellow men] "
(Is. 58:6–9). Christians needed to be reminded of this, and it was of
them St. Luke was thinking particularly when he wrote his gospel
(see also Jas. 2:5, 12f.).

17:1*But he said to his disciples: " It is impossible that there should
never be scandals. But it is too bad for the man through whom they
come! *It would have been to his benefit if a millstone had been
hung round his neck and he had been thrown into the sea, rather
than that he should have given scandal to one of these little ones.
aWatch over yourselves."

" Scandal " (" *skandalon* ") or " offense " is regarded almost as a
personal force. It is an obstacle to faith and it leads to apostasy.
Those who give scandal are the devil's children (Mt. 13:38, 41). A
man can hold fast to Christ by faith and obey God's will which he
proclaimed only by struggling against such " scandals " (Mt. 7:23).
It is impossible that they should never arise; they are part of God's
plan and consequently they are necessary (Mt. 18:7). The preaching
of the gospel was bound to give rise to scandals; they will be rooted
out only when the time of fulfillment has come (Mt. 13:41).

Scandal makes use of human beings to attain its end. It is through
men that it comes, when men allow themselves to be used as instruments. It is to such men Jesus addresses his prophetic woe with its
threat of damnation. Their end is eternal damnation. The crime
committed by those who allow themselves to become instruments of
scandal is unspeakable. Its gravity is indicated by the penalty appointed for those who lead others astray: they will be drowned in
the sea with a great millstone hung about their necks. The limitless,
brooding sea, with its unfathomable depths, is an image of hell.
Scandal must be prevented from making its way among men by
force; the way must be blocked before it.

It is to everyone's benefit that the person who gives scandal should be disposed of rather than that one of these little ones should be scandalized. It is their salvation which is in danger. The expression: "these little ones" does not mean children; it means the poor, those who are deprived of their rights and are despised. These are the people Lazarus the beggar represents, and it is they whom God has chosen for himself, making ready his kingdom for them (6:20ff.). Each single one of these little ones is of great worth in God's eyes. His will is that not a single one of these little ones should be lost (Mt. 18:14).

[3b]" *If your brother is guilty of a fault, confront him with it, and if he repents, forgive him.* [4]*And if he wrongs you seven times in the day and turns to you seven times saying: ' I am repentant,' you must forgive him."*

As a community of brothers, the disciples are not a society of saints who never commit any fault. If a brother is guilty of a fault, if he has wronged a brother, the other cannot be indifferent. His brother's salvation is at stake. The first course of action to be taken is described in the words: " Confront him with it." The man who lets his brother get away with his wrong-doing, and refuses to worry about the sin he commits, is guilty: " Do not hate your brother in your heart. Approach your neighbor frankly, so that you will incur no guilt on his account " (Lev. 19:17). The rebuke a brother gives is intended to bring his brother to repentance. If he realizes his guilt and repents, brother must forgive brother.

The disciples as a community receive an increase of holiness when one of them forgives his brother, when he forgives him again and again despite frequent relapses, " seven times in the day," an unlimited number of times. If a disciple forgives his brother, God will forgive him his guilt (11:4). When Christians are anxious for their brothers' salvation and forgive the personal injuries or affronts they have received, the people of God become a holy people. Here, too, the effective motive is repentance, as it is when God forgives.

BLESSED ARE THE POOR (17:5-10)

⁵And the apostles said to the Lord: " Give us greater faith." ⁶But the Lord replied: " If your faith was even as great as a mustard seed, you could say to this mulberry tree: ' Uproot yourself and plant yourself in the sea,' and it would obey you."

The apostles realized that the faith they possessed already would have to be strengthened if they were to live up to the demands Jesus made. They looked to Jesus for the strength to accomplish what he asked. He made known the conditions necessary for salvation and he gave his followers the strength to fulfill them. He is powerful in word and action.

Faith is the saving gift which is the basis of all other gifts. The greatest difficulties can be overcome by means of faith; it bears the promise of salvation. A mustard seed is the smallest of all seeds used for sowing (Mk. 4:31); it is scarcely as big as the head of a pin. Even the least degree of faith and surrender to God can work wonders. The roots of the black mulberry (sycamore) tree are so strong that it can stand for six centuries, despite the storms to which it may be exposed. Yet a mere word spoken with the slightest trust in God and surrender to him could transplant this tree from the land into the sea. God will give the believer a divine power to enable him to live up to the demands Jesus makes. The message Jesus proclaimed was God's merciful sovereignty.

The man who acknowledges his poverty and his helplessness by placing unlimited trust in God's saving activity in Jesus will be raised to a suprahuman level; he will receive new life. God will make known his glory in him.

⁷" Who among you, who has a servant at the plough or keeping watch, will say to him, when he comes in from the fields: ' Hurry, come here and recline at the table?' ⁸On the contrary, will he not say: ' Prepare something for me to eat and gird up your clothes to serve me, while I eat and drink? You can eat and drink yourself afterwards.' ⁹Does he feel grateful to the servant merely because he did what he was told? "

The people to whom Jesus was speaking would certainly have acted like the farmer described here. The servant was a farm hand who was hired by the farmer for a year; this gave the farmer a right to all his labor. The servant had to do the ploughing and watch over the animals, besides looking after the house; he had to do the cooking and wait at table. The farmer himself was only an ordinary person; he had only one servant to do all the work, but the demands he made were exorbitant. The servant had been working in the field, while the farmer was at home. He came back worn out, but the farmer reclined at the table and made him serve him. The servant was hungry after his day's work, but he had to wait until his master had eaten. The farmer gave him no thanks; he was acting within his rights. A servant is a servant and must do what he is told. Jesus did not comment on this social situation which would seem so unacceptable to us. He merely made use of it in his parable.

¹⁰" It is the same with you. When you have done everything you were told to do, you must say: ' We are only miserable servants. We did what we were obliged to do '."

This parable is not meant to be a description of God; it merely describes man's relationship to him. The service a man offers God is a slave's service. Jesus' prophetic words are really an " inconsiderate " expression of the demand God makes; those to whom it is addressed are reduced to the brink of annihilation. But it is precisely this which makes a man free; he is empty and open, so that God can bestow the blessings of his kingdom on him. "Blessed are the poor; the kingdom of God is theirs."

The scribes and Pharisees believed that the relationship between God and man was a form of contract: I give something that you may give something in return, *quid pro quo*. They thought that when a man had observed the law and done what God had enjoined on him, God owed him a reward. Jesus' parable rejects any such idea. God owes no one anything, not even thanks. Man is purely and simply a servant. In St. Luke's gospel, the parable is addressed to the apostles. They had left everything and followed Jesus (5:11); they had complied with his radical demands. Had they any right to presume on the act of renunciation they had made? Had they a claim on God? According to St. Matthew, Peter asked Jesus: "See, we have left everything and followed you. What reward shall we have?" (Mt. 19:27). He expected a reward, an idea which was rectified by the parable of the workers in the vineyard (Mt. 20:1–16). The reward God bestows on a man is not a return for anything the man may have done. What we call a reward is really a gift which God gives us in his goodness.

St. Luke closes the section which he devotes to the radical demands Jesus makes with the parable of the man who is only a miserable servant. The apostles had left everything; yet all they could say was: We have only done what we were under obligation to do. They are God's servants; through them, God establishes his kingdom; he shows his mercy and proclaims it, and manifests his glory. In this ministry, they are purely and simply servants; what they do is only what they are obliged to do. St. Paul writes: "If I preach the gospel, that is no credit to me. I am under obligation to preach it. It would be too bad for me if I did not preach the good news" (1 Cor. 9:16). A Christian who thinks he has done "everything" has no right to make demands on God. The attitude which Jesus describes helps to maintain peace among Christians—despite the variety of temperaments (Rom. 15:1–2).

The Last Stage of the Journey (17:11—19:27)

A Glimpse of the Glory to Come (17:11—18:8)

The Grateful Samaritan (17:11–19)

¹¹It happened that as he was journeying towards Jerusalem, he passed right through Samaria and Galilee.

Jesus' journeying and all his activity were dominated by Jerusalem; it is only from Jerusalem, where he was raised to glory, that the way Jesus followed, his journeying and his ministry, can be understood.

St. Luke's account of the journey begins with an incident which occurred in Samaria, and the last stage of the journey is also introduced by an event which brings Samaria to mind. Samaria was the bridge by means of which God's word came from Galilee to Jerusalem and from Jerusalem to the gentiles. The commission the risen Christ gave his disciples ran: " You must bear me witness in Jerusalem and in the whole of Judea and Samaria and to the ends of the earth " (Acts 1:8). The road the church must travel is indicated by the road Jesus traveled; the church's way is the result of Jesus' way.

¹²And as he was going into a village, ten men who were lepers came to meet him. They stopped some distance away, ¹³and raised their voices, crying out: " Jesus, Master, have pity on us! " ¹⁴And he looked at them and said to them: " Go and show yourselves to the priests." And it happened that, as they went, they became clean.

Jesus' journey still led from town to town, and from village to village (13:22). Their sickness and misery formed a common bond among the ten lepers and prompted them to forget the national animosities which existed between the Jews and the Samaritans (9:53; Jn. 4:4–9). Lepers were allowed to enter villages, but not walled towns. They were especially forbidden to enter Jerusalem, the holy city. They were not permitted to come near their fellow men (see Lev. 13:45).

They addressed Jesus as " Master." Previously, only the apostles had addressed him in this way, when they were overcome by his power (5:5; 9:49), astonished at his glory (9:33), or in need of help in their distress (8:24). The lepers accompanied this address with an appeal to him to have pity on them. Jesus was a scribe who was full of power and mercy. God's kingdom which is revealed to all men in power and mercy had dawned in him.

Before they were cleansed, Jesus told the men to obey the law concerning lepers who were made clean (see Lev. 14:2; 16:29).

15When he saw that he had been cured, one of them returned and glorified God in a loud voice. 16He fell on his face before Jesus' feet; and this was a Samaritan.

The miracle probably took place while they were still on their way to the priest. One of the ten returned immediately, giving glory to God with grateful praise. God worked through Jesus. The man who had been cured offered his praise to God in Jesus' presence, as he fell on his face at his feet. God accomplishes our salvation through Jesus. In him, God's grace has appeared. The leper acknowledged this by giving thanks.

Ordinary decent humanity leads a man to salvation if it is accompanied by faith in Jesus' words which are borne out by the law and the prophets. The word bears fruit when it finds acceptance in a " beautiful and good heart " (8:15). The way by which the gospel would reach the gentiles was indicated in the Samaritan.

17Jesus answered and said: " Were not ten made clean? The other nine, where are they? [18]*Could they not find their way to come back and give God the praise, with the exception of this stranger?"* [19]*And he said to him: "Stand up and go. Your faith has saved you."*

Only the stranger came back. As a stranger who was not one of the children of Israel, the Samaritan did not dare to imagine that he had any claim on God. He welcomed what was given to him as a gracious gift from God, and he gave thanks. The Jews offered no thanks, because they were Jews; they regarded God's gifts as their due. In their eyes, what they received from God's spokesman was only what was owing to them. They lacked the basic attitude necessary for the reception of salvation. Only the stranger possessed the dispositions which make a person receptive: gratitude, praise, and a consciousness of one's poverty in God's eyes. The way to salvation is open to all, including " strangers," sinners, and gentiles. It is faith that brings a man to salvation, that faith which involves a conscious choice in favor of Jesus' word and an attitude of self-surrender to the saving activity God accomplishes in him.

THE COMING OF GOD'S KINGDOM AND THE SON OF MAN (17:20–37)

The second part of St. Luke's account of Jesus' story was introduced by a number of questions regarding the last stage of time (13:22ff.). Similar questions are found at the beginning of the third part. As Jesus was on the way to his goal, questions concerning the end of all things weighed on people's hearts. He spoke to the Pharisees about the coming of God's kingdom (17:20–21), and to his disciples about the Son of man's coming (17:22–37). God's kingdom is already present, but the Son of man has still to come. This discourse connects a series of sayings which are peculiar to the third gospel with similar sayings in Matthew ch. 24f. The construction of the passage is clear: Introduction (v. 22); the coming of the Son of man as an event which cannot be ignored (vv. 23f.); the inevitability of the Son of man's passion (v. 25); the Son of man's second coming which surprises an age totally given to earthly pursuits (vv. 26–30); an exhortation to be fully prepared (vv. 31–33); the separation of the good from the bad at the second coming (vv. 34ff.); and a conclusion (v. 37).

[20]*When he was asked by the Pharisees when the kingdom of God would come, he answered them with the words: " The kingdom of God is not subject to observation as it comes.* [21]*No one will be able to say: ' See, it is here or there.' You must realize that the kingdom of God is among you."*

The expression " the kingdom of God " summed up all Israel's hopes for the future. When God asserted his supreme dominion everything would be well. The question as to when this great hope and expectation would be realized was one which agitated all classes of society, the Pharisees, the apocalyptic visionaries, and Jesus' disciples (19:11; 21:7; Acts 1:6). God's kingdom was the object of Jesus' preaching. Surely he would answer the question as to when it would come. But his answer was disconcerting. God's kingdom cannot be seen as it comes. All their calculations were in vain. " The kingdom of God is among you "; it is already present.

Jesus' ministry made it clear that God's kingdom had already " appeared." He cast out demons by God's finger (11:20); Satan was reduced to powerlessness (10:18) because God's kingdom had come. The law and the prophets lasted until John; from that time on, the kingdom of God was proclaimed as a gospel of victory (16:16; 4:21). Jesus was the fulfillment of the hopes Israel held out for God's kingdom. In him, the promised time of salvation had come. For those who have faith the presence of God's kingdom is " visible " in the effects produced by the Holy Spirit (24:49) whom the glorified Christ sent to his church (Acts 1:4).

What Jesus said referred only to the presence of God's kingdom among his contemporaries; he did not say that it was he who brought it, that it was present in him. He acted as the prophet of the salvation promised for the end of time; he was its herald and he knew the mystery of God's kingdom. Yet he was more than this. It was through him that God asserted his rule. Jesus' word must have given the Pharisees to think.

²²But he told his disciples: " The days will come when you will long to see even a single one of the days of the Son of man—and you will not see it."

The days will come—this was the phrase used by the prophets who foretold disasters to come. Jesus here announces that a period of terror would come. These disasters would be so great that his disciples would look forward ardently to the days of the Son of man and long for the Messiah's coming. To enjoy even a single one of those days would give them strength and courage; but they must wait and endure patiently. This period of distress occurs between Jesus' ascension and his second coming. Christ's disciples will be afflicted and go with bowed heads (21 : 28); they will be persecuted and put to a severe test. It is the hope of the Son of man's coming that gives the church courage in this period.

Israel's salvation history continues uninterruptedly into the last stage of time. It began with Jesus, in whom the past was brought to completion and the final state has already been inaugurated. Yet the final restoration of all things has not come yet. God's kingdom has come, but the Son of man has still to come. Christ's disciples live in a state of tension between what is already a fact and what has not yet been manifested. The life of the church therefore is lived between fulfillment and expectation, between having and hoping, between joy and fear; the church is " joyful in hope " (Rom. 12:12).

²³" They will say to you: ' See, [he is] here; see, he is there.' But do not go there. Do not run after them. ²⁴As lightning, when it strikes, lightens from one place under heaven to another, so will the Son of man appear, when his day comes."

75

The affliction they suffer will make people receptive to every voice which proclaims the immediate coming of salvation. They must not let themselves be duped. When the Son of man comes, he will not go unnoticed; there will be no doubt about his coming. This over-powering event will be its own light, a light which cannot be ignored. When the Lord comes in his glory, no one will need to be told by anyone else. Everyone will see for himself and realize: he is there.

²⁵*" First he must suffer much and be rejected by his own people."*

The Son of man was to endure the fate of the suffering servant of Yahweh who was despised and abandoned by men. He was to be a man of sorrows, no stranger to weakness, a man before whom people would avert their gaze (Is. 53:3ff.). In the way Jesus walked, the way his disciples and his church must follow was indicated. They experience the divine " must " which imposes suffering and affliction on them before they can attain glory.

²⁶*" In the days of the Son of man, it will be as it was in Noah's days. *²⁷*They ate and drank; they married and were given in mar-riage, until the day when Noah entered the ark, and the flood came and destroyed them all. *²⁸*Everything will be as it was in the days of Lot. They ate and drank, they bought and sold, they planted and built. *²⁹*But on the day Lot went out of Sodom, fire and brimstone rained from heaven and destroyed them all. *³⁰*It will be the same on the day the Son of man is revealed."*

The days of the Son of man will begin when the Son of man leaves the concealment of heaven (Col. 3:3) and reveals himself openly. It is then that the final redemption and the judgment will come; the Son of man is a judge.

The coming of the Son is at once a promise of happiness (17:22) and a threat which inspires fear. As yet there is no sign of his coming; we must wait for it. Consequently, people do not " reckon " with it in their lives; they do not let the thought of his coming disturb or upset them. Life continues its normal course. The needs arising from hunger and thirst and the care of one's family are satisfied, and this makes a person's earthly life secure. People work, do business and build homes. The gravity of the situation escapes them. The Son of man will come without warning; they do not give a thought to the fact that he is coming to pass sentence and that on his sentence their life in the world to come will depend.

Two events in salvation history underline the gravity of the situation: the fate of the contemporaries of Noah and Lot (Gen. 6:11-13; 18:20ff.). These disasters were provoked by fire and water. These two elements underline the frailty of the foundations on which men build; they show how quickly everything they have can disappear; both are symbols of the divine judgment (see also 2 Peter 3:5-7).

[31]" *On that day, the man who is on the roof and whose belongings are in the house should not go down to get them. The man who is in the field must act similarly, not turning back to get what he left behind.* [32]*Remember Lot's wife.* [33]*If a man tries to save his life, he will lose it, and if a man loses his life, he will keep it safe."*

On that day, the day on which the Son of man will appear in the glory of his sovereign reign and pronounce judgment on men, what will be of lasting value? On that day, the only thing of any importance, the decisive thing, will be the Lord who is coming. Everything else loses its value once the only thing of any value has appeared. This is the right to stand in his presence (21:36). The whole life of Christ's disciple must be characterized by this eschatological attitude. It is only in this way that he will be able to earn true life, a life in God's kingdom, salvation.

True life and eternal salvation can be attained only by the man who is prepared to lose his earthly life and renounce its enjoyment if that is the only way to obey God's word. It is death which brings life to birth. The Son of man had to endure the passion and be rejected before he could enter his glory.

If the Son of man's coming is to bring salvation to a man, he must be animated by the same disposition as the disciple who is determined to follow Jesus. This attitude is described in the words: " If anyone wants to come after me, he must renounce himself and take up his cross day by day and follow after me. The man who is determined to save his life will lose it, but if a man is prepared to lose his life for my sake, he will save it " (9:23f.). And again: " No one who puts his hand to the plough and looks back is qualified for God's kingdom " (9:62). In the age of the church, " following " Jesus means being on the watch for the Son of man's coming. This watching is patterned on the way his disciples follow the " Jesus of history."

[34]" I tell you: on that night, two men will be reclining on the same couch; one will be taken and the other left. [35]Two women will be in the same place milling corn; one will be taken and the other left."

The Jews believed the Messiah would come on the night of the Passover. The night in which he comes brings the judgment. This begins with the separation of the good from the wicked (Mt. 25:32). The just will be presented to the Lord (1 Thess. 4:16f.), while the others are given up to eternal damnation (Mt. 13:48). What decides the sentence? The life of one of the men and one of the women is totally taken up with eating or working at the mill; the life of the other two looks forward to the Son of man's coming. The judgment, therefore, is decided by a person's attitude towards Jesus; it depends on obedience to his word (13:26ff.).

³⁶They answered and said to him: " Where, Lord? " ³⁷But he replied: " It is where a body lies that the vultures will gather."

The discourse dealing with the last stage of time began with the question " When "; it closes with the question " Where." Curious and superficial questions distract people from what is essential. God's kingdom has come; the Son of man will come. The promise has already been fulfilled, but it has not yet been fully accomplished. What follows from this?

Carrion attracts vultures (Rev. 19:17). That is common knowledge. As carrion attracts vultures, sinful men call down the judgment which condemns them on their own heads. It is not the question where the judgment will take place that is important; it is the question of freedom from sin and of repentance. When Jesus preached that the last stage of time had come, his preaching was intended as an appeal for repentance. He proclaimed God's merciful rule, so that the Son of man's coming might not result in condemnation.

UNWEARYING PRAYER (18:1–8)

¹He told them a parable, to show that it is necessary to pray always and never give up.

Christians must wait for the Son of man's coming. Their distress is great (17:22); they are tormented by persecution; the temptation to fall away is a constant threat. The burning question on their lips is: " How long more?" (Rev. 6:10). Only the Son of man's coming can bring salvation.

By unwearying and persevering prayer, Christians must win from God the fulfillment of this the greatest of his promises. The day of the Lord can be hastened if Christians lead a good life (2 Pet. 3:12), if they do penance (Acts 3:19) and pray perseveringly. Jesus taught his disciples to pray that God's kingdom might come (11:2). The salvation Christians long for will begin when the Son of man comes in glory (21:28). Christians must pray constantly that the Son of man may come, and never give up, even when their prayer seems to go unheard and weariness and disgust prompt them to stop.

²" There was a judge in a town who had no fear of God and was not overawed by men. ³There was also a widow in that town and she approached him repeatedly and said: ' Grant me justice against my adversary.' ⁴And for a long time he refused. ⁵Then he said to himself: ' Even though I have no fear of God and I am not overawed by men, I will give this widow justice nonetheless, because she is pestering me. Otherwise she will come to the end of her patience and fly at my face '."

The judge was a godless person whose wickedness is expressed in the proverbial words: " Having fear neither of the divine anger nor of human vengeance." He fulfilled his office as a judge in an arbitrary fashion, as if there were no God to whom he must render an account. His conduct was the exact opposite of what it should have been. The command God gave judges was: " Grant justice to those who are oppressed and to orphans; acquit those who are poor and in need. Rescue the oppressed and the poor, saving them from the power of evildoers " (Ps. 82:2-7). A widow was regarded as the most typical example of a person who was poor; without the support of her husband, she was oppressed and defenseless. Scripture repeatedly directed that God-fearing persons should take their part: " Grant justice to orphans, and appear on a widow's behalf " (Is. 1:17). " Pure and unstained holiness in the eyes of God the Father means visiting orphans and widows in their misery and keeping oneself undefiled by the world " (Jas. 1:27).

When a lawsuit involved a claim to a sum of money or an inheritance, an approved lawyer had to be called on to judge. The judge did not want to help the widow to vindicate her rights; he was indifferent, ill-humored, and spiteful. He was deaf to God and man. The widow was sure she would win the case if only it could be heard. But how was she to force the judge to do this? She was not in a position to bribe him; the only thing she could do was to approach him repeatedly and petition him, insistently and perseveringly. She did this, and the judge grew tired of her.

The judge's soliloquy reveals what he is thinking. He is, and he wants to be, exactly as Jesus described him. The motive which induced him to grant the woman her rights was the lowest possible one. He wanted peace. He was forced to realize that the woman would not give up and, on the other hand, he was tired of being annoyed. In the end, he says to himself ironically: " She is boxing my ears," " She is attacking me to my face." It is not fear that moves him to act; it is the desire to put an end to her annoying insistence.

⁶Then the Lord said: " Listen to what the unjust judge says! ⁷Will God not grant justice to his elect who cry out to him day and night, and not delay their case? ⁸ᵃI tell you: he will vindicate them—and quickly."

Jesus' explanation of the parable starts with the words of the unjust judge, not with the widow's persevering prayer. The point of the parable is not persevering prayer; it is the certainty of being heard. The judge was a godless and inconsiderate person; sheer selfishness, the desire for peace and quiet, alone moved him to come to the widow's aid when she prayed insistently. Surely God will be far more ready to listen to the cries of distress of his elect. God is certainly not like the godless judge.

The persecuted church has every reason to hope that its prayer will be heard, because the church is the fellowship of God's elect.

81

He has already given proof of his mercy towards them; he chose those who had the least claim on his mercy (14:16–24). In them, he loves the image of his Son, his chosen one (9:39), God's anointed (Christ), his elect (23:35). Even if their prayer is not heard immediately, so that the elect must persevere in suffering and persecution, the fate of God's Son, the Christ, his chosen one par excellence, should encourage them. Jesus did not receive the title "God's chosen" without first enduring the cross. He was revealed as the chosen one at the transfiguration when his path to glory via the cross was made known. The Jews used this title to mock him as he hung on the cross; to them it seemed impossible that a man who was crucified should be God's chosen one (23:35). Jesus is God's chosen because he attained his glory through the passion. God's elect must follow the same path as his chosen one.

The persevering prayer of the elect who are oppressed will not remain unheard. God will grant them justice quickly, without delay. For the sake of the elect, God will cut short the difficult times that are coming (Mk. 13:20–23). He will not delay in coming to the help of his elect. God's saving intervention will come, this intervention which consists in a new presence of Jesus. It is not without reason that the church prays countless times and without tiring: "Thy kingdom come"; that it celebrates advent each year, and keeps watch in the eucharistic assembly until he comes (1 Cor. 11:26).

[8b]" *Will the Son of man, when he comes, find faith on the earth?*"

The great temptation in the time of distress is the temptation to fall away from the faith; not even the elect are immune to this. God's choice of a man never gives him the right to feel secure and become lazy. On the contrary, it demands that he should constantly renew the decision he has once made in favor of the God who chose him. St. Paul could look forward with assurance to his death and judgment, because he had kept the faith (2 Tim. 4:7). This saying of

Jesus concludes his explanation of the parable and it is a serious question addressed to us. God will never fail, but how do things stand with you? Salvation is coming, but no one will attain it without a hard struggle (13:24), without making every effort to persevere steadfastly.

The Conditions of Admission (18:9–30)

On what conditions will the Son of man's coming bring salvation? Who will be able to stand his ground at the judgment? Who will enter God's kingdom in its final state? The answer to these questions is given in three stories: in the example of the Pharisee and the publican (18:9–14), in the story of Jesus' affectionate welcome for the children (18:15–17), and in the story of the rich man's refusal (18:18–30). Poverty as a condition of admission into God's kingdom forms the background to the three stories. The tax collector is poor in moral and religious matters; the rich man must become poor in material things; a child is poor in every way, he is completely dependent on adults. The beatitudes and the conditions of admission to the kingdom prescribed at the beginning of the Sermon on the Mount occur here once more. St. Matthew talks of the "poor in spirit"; he emphasizes a person's moral and religious attitude. St. Luke, on the other hand, speaks of material poverty. "Jesus must have addressed his saving appeal to definite groups among the people, not simply because of their straitened circumstances, but because of the religious openness and moral preparedness he encountered among them. For St. Matthew, these groups incarnated the religious and moral dispositions which are demanded of all, including those who were to believe in Christ in the future. For St. Luke, however, they remained a vivid reminder of the saving message Jesus preached to the poor, and of the threats he uttered against the rich who refused to be converted."

THE PHARISEE AND THE PUBLICAN (18:9–14)

⁹" He told the following parable to some who placed all their trust in themselves, believing that they were just, and despised others."

The marks used to describe the " some " who trusted in themselves are taken from the conventional picture of the Pharisees. The Pharisees belong to history; they are not mentioned by name. But even in the church there will always be a secret inclination to present one's fidelity to the law before God, and presume on one's own efforts by setting oneself up as God's free partner in the work of salvation.

Such Pharisaic assurance of his own holiness on a man's part, and of his ability to please God and gain entrance into his kingdom, is based on his own achievements, on the confidence he has in himself. The man who thinks like this despises those who cannot point to any such achievements on their part. The Pharisees looked down on the ordinary people because they did not observe the law. They knew nothing about the law and had no idea how to interpret it (Jn. 7:49). The Pharisee set up his own virtuousness as the norm by which others were measured, exhorted, praised, despised, or rejected. His condemnation of others led to his own condemnation (6:37).

¹⁰" *Two men went up to the temple to pray. One was a Pharisee, the other a tax collector.* ¹¹*The Pharisee stood up and prayed in his heart:' God, I thank you that I am not like the rest of men, thieves, deceivers, and adulterers, or like this tax collector here.* ¹²*I fast twice a week. I pay tithes on all I earn '."*

The two men who climbed the temple hill presented a study in contrasts. Both prayed. They were convinced of the truth of what they said in their prayers; a man who prays is addressing the omniscient God (Mt. 6:8). What the Pharisee said was an accurate reflection of his deepest disposition. Jewish prayer is primarily an expression of gratitude and praise. The Pharisee, therefore, prayed as their teaching prescribed. He was " just."

The thanks he offered God revealed his self-righteousness and the contempt he felt for others. He even went beyond the law and performed various good works of supererogation. He wanted to be certain that he was doing nothing which might even remotely resemble a violation of the law. The psalmists who were genuinely religious men had also enumerated their good deeds in their prayers (Ps. 17 [16] : 2–5), but God was completely overlooked in the Pharisee's prayer; the principal role was reserved to his own ego: " I am not like the rest of men, I fast, I pay tithes . . ." The rest of men are merely the dark background to the Pharisee's shining portrait of himself. His prayer is a perfect expression of the man who is just of and by himself and despises others.

¹³" *But the tax collector stood far away and refused even to raise his eyes to heaven. He struck his breast and said: ' God, be merciful to me a sinner '."*

By describing himself as a " Pharisee," a man proudly claimed to be " separated " from others: " I thank you, my Lord and God, for giving me a share with those who occupy the place of learning, and not with those who sit at the street corners . . . I run, as they too run; I run to do the work which concerns the world to come, while they run for the well springs in the pit." As a sinner, the tax collector, too, is " separated "; virtuous Jews avoided him and excluded him from their company. He remained standing at a distance; he did not deserve to stand among good people. He did not dare raise his eyes to God; an impious man could never endure the gaze of the God who is the All Holy. He struck his breast, the seat of his conscience; he regretted his guilt. His prayer was only a few words, the address " God," the petition " Be merciful to me " which is reminiscent of Psalm 51, the penitential psalm (Ps. 51 [50] : 3), and the confession of his sinfulness. The tax collector's situation was hopeless. According to the Pharisees' teaching, he would have to make restitution of all his ill-gotten gains plus an additional twenty per cent, before he could hope for forgiveness. The tax collector could only hope that God would accept the offering of his " contrite heart " (Ps. 51 : 19) and, in his mercy, forgive him his sins.

¹⁴" I tell you: this man went home justified, unlike the other."

Who is just in God's eyes? The Pharisee was scrupulously exact in fulfilling the many difficult precepts of the law. The tax collector was dishonest; he collaborated with the enemies of his own people. Jesus knew what his listeners thought, and the judgment he proclaimed was in direct contrast to theirs; this was something unheard of, something which left them surprised and dismayed : " *But I* tell you." He is God's spokesman. The judgment he pronounced is God's own judgment. God pronounced the tax collector just, and it was as a just man that he went home.

And the Pharisee? The tax collector went home as a just man, unlike the other. In these words, does Jesus compare the Pharisee's justice with that of the tax collector and rate the tax collector above the Pharisee? Or does he go deeper? Does he refuse to credit the Pharisee with the justice he attributes to the tax collector? The first interpretation would be shocking enough; it implies that God is better pleased with a sinner who repents than with a just man and all his merits and self-assurance. But if Jesus meant that the Pharisee has no claim whatever to be just, his sentence can only be described as terrifying. What is the use, then, of human achievements? This was what Christ meant by his words. " What is exalted in men's eyes is an outrage before God " (16:15). Man attains justification, not by his own efforts, but by God's gift. It is the gift of God's kingdom which satisfies a man's hunger and thirst for justice (Mt. 5:3). Human justice and holiness are frail qualities (Mt. 5:20), until God intervenes and bestows his justice as a gift. The man who realizes this will never despise anyone else.

An unattached saying which crops up here and there throughout the gospel is used to explain the example of the Pharisee and the publican in the temple (14:11; Mt. 23:12). The man who trusts in himself exalts himself; Christ's judgment, which is an anticipation of God's final judgment, humbles him. The man who humbles himself, and acknowledges his insufficiency by bowing before others, is exalted by Jesus' sentence. God himself justifies him when the judgment begins.

A Childlike Attitude (18:15–17)

¹⁵They also brought young children to him, for him to touch them. When his disciples saw this, they were inclined to rebuke those [who brought them].

Mothers or older sisters brought children, very small children, to Jesus. Little children such as these are utterly helpless; they are incapable of doing anything and are completely dependent on adults, for better or for worse. They wanted Jesus to touch them, not with a fleeting touch, but laying his hand on them and filling them with his power and blessing. Children ask for their parents' blessing, while pupils seek the blessing of their teachers. Before the evening meal on the sabbath, the father of the house blessed the children by laying his hands on them. Anyone who implores a blessing acknowledges his own insufficiency; he commits himself to the power of someone who is greater than he; he admits that he does not suffice for himself.

The scribes had no time for children: "Sleeping late, taking wine at midday, talking to children and delaying in meeting places frequented by the ordinary people bring a person to ruin." The disciples wanted to stop the children being brought to Jesus. They were inclined to rebuke them but they did not do it (as they did in Mk. 10:13). The " holy " apostles did not scold the children. After the first Easter, the church came to a true understanding of Jesus.

¹⁶Jesus called them [the children] to himself and said: " Let the children come to me. Do not stop them. The kingdom of heaven belongs to such as these. ¹⁷I tell you truly: the man who does not welcome the kingdom of God like a child will not enter it."

Jesus called the children to him without being annoyed with his disciples (Mk. 10:14). He respected children, without idealizing them or glorifying their " childish innocence "; he knew how perverse they could be (Mt. 11:16). His eyes were alert to everything which recalled God's kingdom, and he saw in a child two traits which are necessary for admission into it; these are lowliness and helplessness. A child cannot presume on his own achievements; he can only indicate his poverty imploringly. By nature, he has the attitude demanded of those who wish to enter God's kingdom. The man who does not welcome this like a helpless child will find no entrance. The self-satisfied person who relies presumptuously on his own efforts will be excluded. God's kingdom is a gift, a grace God wishes to confer on those who are poor, who look to him for everything and acknowledge their own insufficiency.

THE RICH RULER (18:18–30)

¹⁸"A man who was a ruler asked him a question saying: ' Good Master, what must I do to inherit eternal life?' ¹⁹But Jesus said to him: ' Why do you call me good? No one is good except only one, and this is God '."

The ruler was a councillor, a member of the Sanhedrin (synedriums), or the president of a synagogue. Whatever he was, he was a leading figure, a man who incarnated the Jewish outlook. The question he asked was typical of a pious Jew: What must I do? How is the law to be observed in practice? He was probably thinking of some particular action he could perform to ensure eternal life. He wanted to gain eternal life and ensure his salvation—even at the cost of considerable effort (13:24), even if it meant using violence (16:16). The ruler was hungry for salvation and he had the necessary readiness.

The question of eternal life is a burning question (10:25). The man who receives eternal life possesses the fullness of all God's promises. Eternal life is an inheritance. God promised the land of Canaan to the patriarchs of Israel as an inheritance; they were to possess it for all time, as a gift from God. The promise of the land of Palestine really looked forward to a more glorious gift: " The man who does evil will be destroyed, but the man who waits for the Lord will inherit the land . . . Those who have been brought low inherit the land and find joy in the fullness of salvation . . . The Lord takes care of just men's days. Their inheritance will last forever " (Ps. 36:9–18). The Promised Land is a symbol of salvation. The inheritance is God's kingdom (Mt. 5:5), eternal life (10:25).

Life in the full sense means indestructible life. Such life belongs to God alone. He is the living God (Mt. 16:16). Life which is subject to death does not deserve to be called " life." True life is a gift from God which he bestows in the last stage of time. This life is eternal, and anyone who enters God's kingdom will enjoy it. When God asserts his rule to the full, death will be overcome and eternal life will dawn.

Jesus raised no objection to being called " master," " rabbi," but he rejected the description " good." The Jewish scribes were jealous of their honor: " A man's respect for his teachers should almost equal his fear of God "; it should surpass that which he had for his parents; they only brought him into this world while his teachers bring him into heaven. Jesus did not look for honor for himself; he sought only God's honor (Jn. 8:50). By refusing to be called " good," he gave praise to God for his goodness. God alone is good. The Pharisees thought they were good, because they observed the law and performed works of supererogation. But a human being is good only when God makes him so. The new covenant which had been promised contained the assurance that God himself would bestow every blessing on his people (Jer. 32:34). Only the man who acknowledges that he is not good longs for salvation and becomes good.

[20]*"You know the commandments: You shall not commit adultery, you shall not kill, you shall not steal, you shall bear no false testimony, honor your father and your mother."* [21]*But he replied: " I have observed all this from my youth."*

Anyone who wishes to enter God's kingdom and enjoy eternal life must keep the law (16:17, 29). The " ten commandments " are the basic law of the Old Testament (Ex. 20:13–16; Deut. 5:17–20). According to the Old Testament, the ten commandments were divided into two equal groups of five each. The first five referred to God, the second to one's neighbor. Jesus cited four commandments from the second group in addition to the commandment to honor one's parents which is included in the first group. This commandment was included in the first group because the honor paid to one's parents really referred to God; it is God who is the source of life; a man's parents merely transmit it. A man's attitude towards his neighbor is given precedence over his attitude towards God, because love for his neighbor proves the sincerity of a man's love for God. Jesus appeals to the prophets and says, with reference to God: " It is mercy I want not sacrifice " (Hos. 6:6; Mt. 9:13).

The ruler stated that he had kept the law from his youth. He was conscious that it was possible to fulfill the law despite all the demands it imposed. This was confirmed by the scribes who said: " Lord of the world, I have gone through the two hundred and forty-eight articles you framed for me, and I have not found that I have angered you with any of them." A Jew knew from the law what he had to do. At the same time he was able to do what he realized was just. Consequently, he knew that he had fulfilled God's will and that he was just. The ruler spoke from conviction; that was why Jesus, too, took his words seriously.

It is clear that the ruler could have spoken with such assurance only because God's will was known to him exclusively from the letter of the law. A man who compares his conduct with the demand made by the letter of the law may perhaps be able to say: " I have done everything demanded of me." Can he still say this when he is faced with the demand the living God makes, the God who is good, who alone is good? Can he say it when he is faced with the God who now asserts his sovereign rule and is determined to be all in all? Who has obeyed the demand Jesus proclaimed as coming from God: " You are to be merciful as your Father is merciful " (6:36)?

²²*When Jesus heard this, he said to him: " One thing still remains [to be done]: sell everything you have and distribute [the proceeds] among the poor, and you will have a treasure in heaven. Then come and follow after me." ²³When he heard this he was very sad, because he was extremely rich.*

Jesus' words are not intended to add yet another prescription to the precepts of the law. They go much deeper than that. Jesus made known the will of the living God here and now to the ruler; this was God's will for him, the demand he addressed to him personally. He must renounce everything he possessed. The proceeds from the sale of his property must be used for alms and works of charity.

But the most important thing was that he must become Jesus' disciple and follow him. Jesus revealed what God's will was, the way which leads to life.

By giving alms and performing works of charity, a man amasses a treasure in heaven. He can enjoy the interest accruing from this here on earth, but the capital is kept safe for the world to come. Jesus did not ask only that the ruler should give alms; he asked that he should renounce all his possessions, thereby renouncing even the possibility of giving alms and amassing a treasure in heaven in the future. It is not merely to be able to give alms that the rich man must renounce his possessions; Jesus simply indicates a good way in which a person may rid himself of his belongings.

Jesus demanded that the ruler should renounce everything he had because he was to follow him wherever he went. The radical form of discipleship to which he was called could no longer be reconciled with the ownership of property, with mammon, which claims a man's service and makes it impossible for him to devote himself completely to God's service (16:13). By renouncing his wealth, the ruler would be free to follow Jesus. What God wanted from him above all was that he should attach himself to Jesus and follow him, so he would fulfill the law and the prophets, and do God's will. This incident gives us the final answer to the question of worldly wealth. The complete renunciation of ownership is not a general law imposed on everyone (10:38ff.). Every Christian is bound to practice interior and exterior renunciation to such an extent that he can put God before everything else (12:31). It is probable that the demand made on a particular person may be of a different kind; he may not be asked to renounce his possessions.

The councillor was overcome with sadness. He was deeply disillusioned because he was very rich. His wealth held him bound; mammon deprived him of his freedom. He felt incapable of giving up his material security and relying on God for everything by following Jesus. Jesus' call to renounce everything showed him where he stood. He was convinced that he had accomplished God's will to the full because he had observed the law from his youth. Now Jesus' call made it clear to him that he rejected God's will and refused to obey it. He came to Jesus in search of security for his life; now he realized that he could only secure it by giving himself completely to God. " If a man comes to me and does not hate . . . his life, he cannot be my disciple " (14:26). It is only in the encounter with Jesus that God's will is revealed.

²⁴When Jesus saw him like this, he said: " How difficult it will be for those who have wealth to journey into God's kingdom! ²⁵It is easier for a camel to pass through a needle's eye than for a rich man to enter God's kingdom."

Jesus is no longer speaking to the rich ruler; he is proclaiming his message for everyone. The man who is wealthy will find it hard to enter God's kingdom; he will journey in only with difficulty. This expression occurs only in St. Luke's version of the saying which he situates in the course of Jesus' journey to Jerusalem. Life is a journey whose goal is God's kingdom. On his journey to Jerusalem, Jesus appears as a master who teaches the way to life.

A drastic metaphor underlines the difficulty. A camel is a huge animal and with its high humps it certainly could not penetrate a needle's tiny eye. A rich man cannot enter God's kingdom. The metaphor is not meant to imply that what is difficult is impossible; it merely underlines the difficulty. It is intended to shake people up, to make them think, and to frighten them. Wealth as such is not something harmless; it is a force which constitutes a threat to salvation because it takes complete possession of a man and does not leave him free for God (16:13).

²⁶But those who heard this said: " Then, who can be saved?" ²⁷But he replied: " What is impossible for a man is possible for God."

93

Salvation, entrance into God's kingdom, eternal life—these are matters which face people along the path of life. The ruler came to grief when confronted with the demand Jesus addressed to him. Who, then, could hope to be saved? Jesus' listeners, too, were disillusioned and saddened. Jesus said nothing to calm them, as a man might do if he noticed that his words had frightened his audience. " It is impossible for a man." We should not pass over these words too quickly, to draw comfort and consolation from the phrase which follows. First we must feel the ground being taken away from under our feet before attending to the other saying. A man must first admit that of himself he has no hope of being saved; he must first experience this impasse before entering on the way God opens to him. It is only when we have looked into the abyss of our own helplessness that we can grasp at this second saying.

To bring men to salvation is possible to God. This is not merely a conventional formula of encouragement; there is no explicit reference to the " grace " which will make it possible, despite everything. Jesus left his hearers in no doubt that he demands a supreme effort (13:24; 16:16; 14:25ff.). He does not take this back. When a man who is in search of salvation becomes frighteningly aware that it is impossible for him to attain salvation of himself, he has learned the fundamental lesson on the way to salvation. He has become poor. It is possible to God. This saying frees him from fear and gives him confidence. God's kingdom means compassion for those who place all their hope in God.

²⁸*But Peter said: " See, we left what was ours and followed you."*

The apostles had taken the step the ruler could not bring himself to take. They had left what was theirs, their nets, and their boat (5:11), the customs office (5:28), everything that they had (5:11, 28). According to St. Mark, Peter said they had left " everything "; St. Luke says they had left " what was theirs," everything to which they had a right, of which they could dispose, which they could attribute to themselves, including their own personal achievements. They regarded nothing as their own any more; they had nothing on which they could presume.

What is the point of St. Peter's words? According to St. Matthew's version, he held up what he had done as a claim to a reward: "We have left everything; what shall we have in return?" (Mt. 19:27). Peter was looking for a new form of security which was not God. In St. Matthew's Gospel, his question is followed closely by the parable of the laborers in the vineyard (19:30—20:16). It is not any legal claim on a man's part which will gain him admission into God's kingdom; it is God's goodness which is at work in Jesus. St. Luke does not mention St. Peter's request: "What shall we have in return?" Instead, he quotes Jesus as attaching the promise of salvation directly to Peter's words. Peter and the apostles had already put Jesus' words to the wealthy ruler into practice. They stand before the church as the great leaders on the way to salvation.

²⁹But he said to them: "I tell you truly: there is no one who has left house, or wife, or brothers, or sisters, or parents or children, for the sake of the kingdom of heaven, ³⁰who does not receive many times their worth in this life and eternal life in the world to come."

The apostles had left what was theirs—their money, their land, and all their possessions. But that was not all. They had also left all that a person's heart is attached to, their homes and their families. When can a man say that he has left everything? The conditions Jesus prescribed for those who wanted to become his disciples when he was setting out on his journey to Jerusalem occur here once more (9:57–62). The version of this saying quoted by St. Mark (10:29) says nothing about leaving one's wife. In the parable of the guests who were invited to a great supper, one of those invited could not come because he had taken a wife (14:20). The lives of the apostles who renounced their possessions and left their wives are a constant reminder for the church of Jesus' appeal to be detached from everything in order to be at the disposal of God's call and his claim. The disciples renounced their possessions for the sake of the kingdom of God (18 : 29), for the gospel's sake (Mk. 10 : 29), for the sake of Jesus' name (Mt. 19 : 29). God's kingdom which was coming, Jesus who proclaimed and brought it, and the preaching of the gospel, are all intimately bound up with one another. The man who places himself at the service of the gospel preaching, who becomes Jesus' disciple and opens his heart to God's sovereign rule, must be quite sure that he is no longer in love with his possessions. Jesus was journeying towards Jerusalem where death and glorification awaited him.

The course of history is divided into this time, the present world, and the world to come, the time of salvation. The world to come intrudes into the present world. God's kingdom is among you (17 : 20). In the present world, Jesus' disciple receives many times the worth of all that he left; he shares in the fellowship of his brothers and sisters in the faith (Acts 11 : 1; Rom. 16 : 1); he shares their belongings (Acts 2 : 14), while hospitality (1 Tim. 5 : 10; 1 Pet. 4 : 9) and Christian love open the homes of all Christians to him. In the world to come, he will receive eternal life.

Towards the Kingdom of God (18 :31—19 :27)

Jesus now entered on the last stage of the way to Jerusalem. What did this journey mean in salvation history? What did it not mean? The way of Jerusalem was a journey towards death, but also towards the resurrection and the ascension (9 :50). The final prophecy of the passion makes this clear (18 : 31-34). Jesus entered Jerusalem as a saviour and the Son of David. By curing the blind man and calling Zacchaeus to salvation at the very beginning of the last stage of his journey, Jesus made it clear what the events in Jerusalem meant in salvation history (18 : 35-43; 19 : 1-10).

His journey to Jerusalem was not accompanied by the glorious revelation of God's kingdom; it did not mean that God's kingdom was to be established in glory here and now. The glory of the kingdom would be conferred on Jesus when he had gone away. Later he will return in power and glory. The period between his ascension into heaven and his coming in power is a time of trial for his disciples during which they must prove themselves in their missionary activity and in persecution (19:11–27). His entry, which St. Luke presents as an entry into the temple, laid the foundations of the church which would develop between the time of salvation marked by Jesus' life on earth and his coming in glory.

The Consummation Draws Near (18:31–34)

³¹*But he took the twelve aside and said to them: " See, we are going up to Jerusalem and all that was written about the Son of man by the prophets will be accomplished."*

Jesus' death on the cross which awaited him in Jerusalem was a disillusionment and a severe trial even for those who had faith. For many, it seemed a valid and definitive sentence which marked his undoing. The twelve who had accompanied him in all his travels were the only ones on whom he imposed this burden. They had renounced everything to follow him, and so he confided to them what his entry into Jerusalem would mean for him. He wanted to show them the way which the path to glory follows. This was the way they were to follow and proclaim as the way to life.

Jerusalem was now about to experience its greatest hour in salvation history. The Son of man was about to enter the city. It was there that he endured the passion Isaiah had foretold for God's suffering servant; it was there he was taken up into God's power, as Daniel has announced would happen to the Son of man. In Jerusalem, God's servant passed through suffering and death to his glory. " Was it not inevitable that the Christ should have suffered this, and entered so into his glory?" (24:26). Jesus' passion marked his entry into glory; it was the foundation on the basis of which his church is gathered together into one.

What the prophets had written was now being accomplished. At the transfiguration, Moses and Elijah had spoken of the "departure" Jesus would accomplish in Jerusalem (9:31). Throughout scripture, Christ's way is portrayed as a way which leads through suffering to glory, 24:25–27; 24:44). It is this event, the death and glorification of Christ, which gives salvation history its meaning (1 Pet. 1:10f.). God's plan of salvation is fulfilled in Jerusalem; Jesus' longing for its consummation is satisfied (12:50); the task which was given to him was accomplished (13:32; 22:37). It was in Jerusalem that he could pronounce the words recorded by St. John: "It is consummated [accomplished]" (Jn. 19:30).

[32]" *He will be given up to the gentiles. He will be mocked and blasphemed and spat upon,* [33]*and after they have scourged him, they will kill him, and on the third day he will rise again.*"

The prophecy bears the stamp of St. Luke's account of the passion. There is no mention of our Lord's trial before a Jewish court. The Jews gave him up to the gentiles. At a later date, St. Peter reproached them with the words: "You gave him up and disowned him in Pilate's presence" (Acts 3:13f.). "You gave him up in accordance with God's plan and foreknowledge; you nailed him to the cross and killed him by the gentiles' agency" (Acts 2:23). Jews and gentiles alike were guilty (Acts 4:27–29).

The gentiles in their arrogance mocked Jesus and spat on him; in their malice they attacked the all-holy Son of God, whom God himself had anointed as the Messiah-king (Acts 4:27; Is. 53; Ps. 2; Acts 10:38). Jesus' humiliation reached its climax when he was executed on the cross. According to Roman penal law, crucifixion was always preceded by scourging. Jesus was condemned to the most shameful death known to the pagan world.

But this annihilation was not the end; it was only the beginning of his glorification. It is true that Jesus was in the same class as God's spokesmen in the Old Testament; he shared their fate. But it was as the Son of the man that he strode through the portals of death. He was not merely " raised up " (Mt. 20:18); he "rose up." In the Easter event, it was not merely that God acted in Jesus; the Son of man himself had the power to rise from the dead. The supremely independent behavior of the risen Christ is in sharp contrast to the fact that he was given up and put to death.

34And they understood nothing of this [saying]; what he said was hidden from them. They did not know what had been said.

The way Jesus followed remained an incomprehensible mystery to the apostles to the very end. They did not know, they did not understand, how the truth these words expressed could be possible. The path Jesus was obliged to tread is beyond the grasp of purely human reasoning; it is impenetrable, " hidden." Not even scripture which centers around this mystery could unveil it. It was only when the risen Christ opened the meaning of the scriptures to his disciples and lifted the veil himself that this mystery became intelligible. Even the faith which believes that Jesus entered into glory through death is a fruit of the way he followed (see 24:25-35).

THE CURE OF THE BLIND MAN (18:35-43)

35It happened that as he was drawing near Jericho, a blind man sat by the way, begging. 36When he heard the people coming there, he inquired what this was. 37They told him that Jesus of Nazareth was passing by. 38And he cried out, saying: " Jesus, Son of David, have pity on me!" 39Those who were in front rebuked him, telling him to be silent. But he cried out much more: " Son of David, have pity on me!"

99

In Jesus' time, the town of Jericho lay south of the ancient border of Israel. Herod the Great and Archelaus had adorned it with splendid buildings in the Greco-Roman style. Jesus drew near the town. He was surrounded by the people; he was obviously traveling with a group of pilgrims who were going up to Jerusalem for the Passover. Once more, St. Luke uses the word "journeying." It was in Jericho that the ascent to the city began, the city which was the goal of his journey.

There was a group of beggars at the gate of the town and among them sat one who was blind. He heard the crowd passing by. Why were there so many? The answer was merely: "Jesus of Nazareth." Nothing more was said. But this blind man bore witness that Jesus was the Son of David, the royal Messiah who sprang from David's race and would restore the Davidic kingdom (1:32f.). The blind man's profession of faith was accompanied by a cry of distress (Mt. 9:27). The Messiah had been announced by the prophets as a saviour for those who were blind. "The blind will have sight" (Is. 35:5f.); he was anointed and sent to restore the light of their eyes to the blind (4:18; see Is. 61:1f.), to bring the goods news to beggars (4:18). Jesus was the saviour who had been promised. The beggar shouted out his profession of faith and his appeal for help in the hearing of everyone.

The blind man's cry disturbed the silence observed by the people as they continued on their pilgrimage. When they spoke threateningly to him, he cried all the louder. His cry was like the cry uttered by the prophets who were carried away by the power of God's Spirit (Amos 3:8). His faith in Jesus as the Son of David was the result of a divine illumination (see Mt. 16:17) which could not remain hidden. The man who was blind enjoyed a spiritual insight. Many people had seen Jesus' miracles, but remained blind to his true nature. God granted Jesus this profession of faith as he was preparing to go to his death. The blind beggar who was granted an interior insight set the headline for the last stage of Jesus' journey and his entry into Jerusalem, and underlined their true character.

⁴⁰But Jesus stood still and commanded him to be brought to him. ⁴¹When he came close, he asked him: " What do you want me to do for you?" But he said: " Lord, that I may see."

The title " Son of David " was charged with political and nationalist hopes. On a previous occasion, Jesus had forbidden its use (see Mt. 9:30), but now he permitted it and accepted it. His journey to Jerusalem would put an end to these hopes and reveal a different image of the Messiah, an image in keeping with God's plan of salvation. The blind man now addressed Jesus as " Lord " (St. Mark: " Rabbini," " Master "). " Lord " was the title of sovereignty given to Jesus in the Hellenistic churches; he is the supreme ruler who enjoys divine power. Jesus of Nazareth is the Son of David (the Messiah, Christ) and the Lord (*Kyrios*). What the blind man saw on the way to Jerusalem had been announced by the angels at Jesus' birth: a saviour (Jesus), Christ (Son of David) the Lord (2:10). The faithful would later give expression to this profession of faith in a hymn as a fruit of Jesus' journey to Jerusalem: "He lowered himself by becoming obedient to death, death on the cross. God exalted him and gave him a name which is above every other name . . . and every tongue must confess: Jesus Christ is the Lord, to the glory of the Father " (Phil. 2:8–11).

⁴²And Jesus said to him: " Recover your sight, your faith has saved you." ⁴³And he received his sight immediately, and he followed him, praising God. And all the people who saw it gave glory to God.

His miraculous cure confirmed the blind man's profession of faith in Jesus as the Messiah. What God had done for him interiorly became visible exteriorly. His faith had saved him and he followed after Jesus. It was by professing his faith that Jesus Christ is the Lord that he began to be his disciple. However, Jesus had still to complete his journey to Jerusalem for the sake of the people who were blind. " We feel our way along the wall like blind men; we grope our way free like people who are without the light of their eyes. In the brightness of the day, we stumble as if it were twilight. We sit in darkness, like the dead " (Is. 59:10). " The Rising Sun sheds light on those who are in darkness and death's shadow " (1:79).

The blind man believed, although he could not see Jesus. The crowd rebuked him; his shouts disturbed the sacrosanct order of the procession. On the journey to Jerusalem, where salvation history was about to reach its climax in Christ's death and resurrection, the blind man recovered the sight of his eyes. The Jews regarded the blind man as being dead, but here he was raised to life; he was excluded from the community of worship, but now he became Jesus' disciple. Jesus had foretold his passion; yet he found a disciple to follow him in his path of suffering.

Jesus' actions inspired people to praise God. The blind man followed Jesus praising God. By his means, the whole people were moved to give glory to God. The blind man founded a new community of worship by his faith. In this we can see a figure of the church. Jesus' ascension into heaven was followed by the praise the infant church offered to God (24:53).

ZACCHAEUS (19:1–10)

¹*He went into Jericho and was passing through [the town].* ²*And see, there was a man called Zacchaeus who was the head tax collector and a rich man.* ³*He tried to see Jesus, who he was, but he could not do so because of the crowd; he was of small stature.* ⁴*And he ran ahead and climbed a mulberry tree, to see him, because he would have to pass by that way.*

Jesus was passing through and there was a great crowd of people. A small man tried to force his way through the throng, but no one would make room for him, so he ran on ahead and scrambled up a sycamore tree which was growing by the road. The little man was called Zacchaeus: "God remembered"—Zechariah. He was the head tax collector. He farmed the border and market taxes of the area, collecting them by means of agents. Jericho was a customs post in the Arabah and the export town for balsam. As a tax collector, the Jews regarded him as a sinner; as a rich man, he would not take kindly to Jesus' message (18:24).

This was a man who appeared to live solely for money; he had betrayed the loyalty he owed to the people of God; he had brought shame on the honor he enjoyed by belonging to them. Yet he had an ardent desire to see Jesus. The blind man wanted to hear him; Zacchaeus waited to see him. Salvation comes to a man by seeing and hearing. Jesus told the messengers St. John the Baptist had sent: " Go and tell John what you have seen and heard " (7:22). Like the blind beggar, Zacchaeus, too, had to overcome the obstacle presented by the crowd who accompanied Jesus. The blind man cried out; the tax collector climbed up a tree with its wide spreading branches. He forgot about his dignity and was not afraid of the ridicule to which his vantage point might expose him. He refused to be intimidated by the hostile and scornful glances of those who knew him. Making contact with Jesus meant more to him than anything.

⁵*And when Jesus reached the place, he looked up and said to him:* *" Zacchaeus, come down quickly. I must stay at your house today."* ⁶*And he came down quickly and joyfully brought him to his house.*

Jesus was a prophet and he knew men's hearts; he understood Zacchaeus's great longing. As Jesus looked at him, the great today of salvation history dawned for Zacchaeus. Today the scripture was fulfilled for him which promised the gospel to the poor and those who yearned for it (4:21); today the saviour drew near to him (2:11); today he encountered God's " paradoxical " activity in Jesus Christ, that activity which reaps success where no success could be hoped for, humanly speaking (5:26).

Jesus called the tax collector by his name. What his name signified was now about to be accomplished in him; God remembered him and had mercy on him. He took his servant's part, in memory of his mercy (1:54). The imperative, the must imposed by God's saving will which Jesus had to accomplish was realized in his case, too. Everything had to be done quickly; God's visitation has its appointed time (1:39). Zacchaeus came down quickly and Jesus became his guest. He received a hospitable welcome as he entered a sinner's house, to the great delight of his host. God's choice was certainly an unexpected one; a man who was great in a worldly way became little. These were so many indications of what Jesus' ascent to Jerusalem would bring. Once he had been " taken up," everything that happened in Jericho would be multiplied several times over. Again and again, the apostles would have similar experiences on their journeys.

[7] All those who saw it complained, saying: " He has gone into a sinner's house to stay." [8] But Zacchaeus stood there and said to the Lord: " See, I give half of my goods to the poor, and if I have extorted anything from anyone, I give him four times the amount in restitution."

Pious Jews would never sit at the same table with tax collectors or public sinners (15:2). That was why all the people were shocked and complained (5:30; 15:2). Israel complained in the desert when God did not satisfy their demands. God's saving design constantly encounters misunderstanding and complaints. Jesus obeyed God's will and ignored the people's complaints. " It is well for the man who is not scandalized at me " (7:23). This was something to be remembered when he behaved in unexpected ways.

The tax collector grasped the significance of this " today " in salvation history, with the divine offer which accompanied it (Deut. 30 : 15-20). He repented. The sincerity of his conversion was proved by his willingness to fulfill the prescriptions of the law to the utmost. He was not content merely to make restitution of his ill-gotten gains plus an additional fifth of their value, as the law prescribed (Lev. 5 : 20-26); on the contrary, he restored the amount four or five times over (see Ex. 21 : 37). The scribes also directed that a certain sum of money should be given to the poor to show that a person's repentance was genuine. They suggested a fifth of a person's wealth as a first installment, and a similar share of his annual income after that (see Num. 5 : 6f.). The tax collector was willing to do this, too. He mentions this first, because it was not certain whether he had wronged anyone by extortion, the common crime of tax collectors. He listened to the good news of salvation in his heart, and so he fulfilled all the law's demands and even went beyond them. God's love came to him in Jesus, and so he exceeded the law's demands and the scribes' interpretation of it. God made his people a holy people when Jesus took the part of sinners.

⁹But Jesus said to him: " Today salvation has come to this house; he, too, is Abraham's son. ¹⁰The Son of man has come to seek out and to save what was lost."

Redemption (salvation) had come to Zacchaeus's house. What had been announced to the shepherds, whom pious Jews regarded as sinners, at Jesus' birth was now accomplished in the head tax collector by Jesus' word. The shepherds were told: " Today a saviour has been born for you " (2 : 10). What the beginning of the time of salvation had proclaimed was accomplished on the road to Jerusalem. The Jews would never admit that the tax collector was Abraham's son, but his faith and the welcome he gave Jesus showed that he was a true son of Abraham. He " hoped against hope," when God's offer of salvation came to him (Rom. 4 : 17). Jesus extended the concept of descent from Abraham, so that even those who were not descended from him physically could share in the promises made to him.

When he welcomed sinners, Jesus was fulfilling his mission. God sent him to bring deliverance, not destruction; salvation, not condemnation; life, not death. " Christ came into the world to save sinners " (1 Tim. 1:15). What the prophet had foretold for the time of salvation was fulfilled in him: "I will seek those who have strayed; I will lead home those who were scattered. I will bind up what is injured and give strength to those who are sick. I will safeguard what is strong and care for it in the right way " (Ezek. 34:16). In Jesus, God came to his people as the Good Shepherd: " This is what the Lord says: ' So, then, I myself will search for my sheep and look after them ' " (Ezek. 34:1). The message of the parables concerning God's love for sinners was accomplished in real life. Jesus is the saviour of those who are lost.

All the favorite terms and ideas of the " gospel of the poor " are brought together in the story of Zacchaeus's conversion: Today salvation (deliverance); to save what was lost; little, sinner, tax collector; the " must " involved in God's plan of salvation, haste, a welcome into a house, and finally, joy. God's grace and human good will were revealed in overflowing measure in Jericho, a town upon which a curse had been invoked in antiquity (Josh. 6:26), and in the home of the head tax collector who was a rich man and a sinner. Jericho was the town from which Jesus set out to go up to Jerusalem; it was the gateway to the city in which salvation history was to be consummated, and from which deliverance would come.

THE PARABLE OF THE TALENTS (19:11–27)

11*As they were listening to this, he continued and told them a parable; he was close to Jerusalem and they thought that God's kingdom was to be revealed immediately.*

Jesus went up to Jerusalem at the time of the feast of the Passover. Great throngs of pilgrims flocked to the holy city to celebrate the deliverance of the Israelites from Egypt. All their great hopes for the restoration of David's kingdom were roused. The blind man had professed his faith in Jesus as the Son of David and Jesus had not rejected the title. In the encounter with Zacchaeus, he had given it to be understood that he was the Messiah-shepherd whose coming had been promised. After Jesus' death, the disciples admitted that they had hoped that he would deliver Israel (24:21) and inaugurate the messianic kingdom (see Acts 1:6). In such circumstances, the question as to whether God's kingdom would be revealed immediately was perfectly comprehensible. It was already present in a hidden way; perhaps, it would now become visible in all its splendor. This question also occupied the church in its early years. In many circles, people believed there would be only a short delay before the kingdom was revealed in all its glory.

But the Lord kept his church waiting. Some people declared scornfully: " What of his promise that he would come back? From the day when the fathers went to their rest, everything remains as it was from the beginning of creation " (2 Pet. 3:4). The parable of the talents gave the lie to such enthusiastic hopes for an early return of Christ; at the same time, it inspires an eschatological hope.

12He said: " A nobleman went to a distant country, to receive a kingdom and return. 13He summoned his ten servants and gave them ten pounds, and said to them: ' Trade with this until I come back.' 14But his subjects hated him and sent a deputation after him to say: ' We do not want this man to become our king '."

Jericho, where this parable was recited, was in the territory of Archelaus. According to the terms of Herod's will his three sons, Herod Antipas, Philip, and Archelaus, were to divide his territory between them. Archelaus was to have Judea and the title of king.

However, he would first have to get the approval of the Roman emperor Augustus. He went to Rome, but his subjects hated him because of his cruelty. A deputation of fifty Jews succeeded in preventing Herod's wishes from being fulfilled. Augustus gave Archelaus only the title of Ethnarch, until he had proved himself. Jesus' parable seems to have been inspired by contemporary events. The nobleman who went to a distant country was Archelaus. In the parable, the high-born claimant to the throne was a symbol of Jesus who was going up to Jerusalem. He would not receive the kingdom immediately; first he must go to a distant country, through death to heaven. From there he will one day come back again in all his royal power and dignity.

For the time of his absence, the claimant to the throne entrusted his " servants " with a sum of money, so that they could trade with it. The mention of ten servants seems to be purely conventional; they enhanced the nobleman's status. The pound each servant received was not a great sum; a hired laborer could earn it in three months. The " servants " were to give proof of their fidelity in small things (16:10). During the period of separation from his followers, Jesus entrusts the administration of his goods to them. " Who, then, is a faithful steward and a prudent one, whom the Lord will set over his servants, to give them their fixed amount of food at the right time? " (12:42). The period between his ascension and his coming in glory is a period of work, of missionary activity.

His subjects hated the claimant to the throne; they did not want him to be their king. Christ's enemies continue to be active during the time of his absence. They do everything possible to prevent his sovereign authority being recognized. The time of the church is a time of persecution in which the loyalty and perseverance of Christians is put to the test (17:22; 21:12ff.). Jesus is coming in his royal glory—but he is not coming " immediately."

[15]"*And it happened that he came back, after he had received the royal power. He ordered the servants to whom he had given the*

money to be summoned before him, so that he could find out what profit each of them had made with it."

The journey undertaken by the claimant to the throne was not in vain. He came back as king. The servants were called to account. Each one was to be examined concerning the use he had made of the money. Greater responsibility could only be entrusted to the man who had proved himself in small things (16:11). At his second coming, Jesus will demand an account of our administration (12:41ff.).

¹⁶*" The first servant stood there and said: ' Lord, your pound has earned ten additional pounds.' ¹⁷And he said to him: ' That is as it ought to be. You are a good servant. Because you were faithful in the least of all matters, you shall have power over ten cities.' ¹⁸And the second came and said: ' Your pound brought in five pounds.' ¹⁹And to him he said: 'And as for you, you shall be over five cities '."*

St. Luke adduces only three of the ten servants. Reasons of style made it impossible to present them all. Parables are meant to strike those who hear them, not to bore them. The first two servants had administered their money successfully. They were modest enough not to speak of what they had done; it was the pounds which brought them profit. " It is God who gives the increase " (1 Cor. 3:6f.). The recognition they received was for their fidelity in small matters. " The reward due to a man for fulfilling his obligations is itself an obligation." The servants were entrusted with greater responsibilities; they were appointed governors over a number of cities which corresponded to the profit they had made. A disciple who has been a loyal servant will receive a share in Christ's supreme dominion (12:43; 22:30).

²⁰*"And the other came and said: ' See, Lord, here is your pound*

*which I have kept safe in a neckerchief. ²¹I was afraid of you. You
are a stern man and you take what you never deposited; you reap
what you never sowed.' ²²He said to him: ' I will judge you out of
your own mouth, you wicked servant. You knew that I am a stern
man, that I take what I never deposited, and reap what I never
sowed. ²³Why did you not put my money in the bank? Then I
could have drawn it with interest, when I came '."*

The third servant had refused to take any risks with the money entrusted to him. He had kept it safe, hoarding it in a neckerchief
which people wore to protect their necks from the heat of the sun;
he had made no profit with it. The bitter reproaches he made
against his master were inspired by his own bad conscience. He
charged his master with being a cruel tyrant, a rapacious business-
man, and a self-centered egotist. He was determined to play safe,
and so he risked nothing. It may be that we have here a glimpse of
the original meaning of the parable which was meant for the Pharisees. They looked on God as a pitiless claimant.

They were scrupulous in obeying the letter of the law; they
erected a barrier around it which could not be transgressed. They
kept everything, but they risked nothing. The picture Jesus draws
of God is that of a loving and generous Father. He made greater
demands than the law, but he taught that " justice " is a gift God
gives, that his kingdom gives what the law commands; he demanded " everything," because he " gives " everything.

The claimant to the throne was not satisfied merely with having
his money returned to him. He stood by the command he had
given : " Trade with it." The lazy servant had not obeyed this
command. He had even prevented the money itself from earning
interest in the bank without any effort or risk on his part. The Lord
wants his servants to be faithful servants; he wants them to be dar-
ing and energetic, and to work sensibly. The correct eschatological
attitude is not a matter of idle or anxious waiting. Waiting for the

Lord who is coming, who will look for an account, does not paralyze a man; it is a summons to work. If it has a paralyzing effect, this is a sign that it has been misunderstood.

²⁴"And to those who were standing by, he said: ' Take the pound from him and give it to the man who has ten pounds.' ²⁵And they answered him: ' Lord, he has ten pounds.' ²⁶' I tell you: to everyone who has, more will be given. But from him who has nothing, even what he has will be taken away '."

When the king came, he instituted judgment. The pound which the wicked servant still had in his hand was taken from him and given to the man who had risked most and made the most profit. The decision was surprising and even provocative. Security lies, not in keeping everything safe, but in taking risks and earning a profit. In a disciple's life, too, there can be no peaceful possession, no having, without putting what we have to work. The man who wants merely to cling to what he has, and keep it in peace, will lose even what he has.

²⁷" But bring my enemies here, the men who did not want me to rule over them as their king, and kill them in my presence."

The king treated his enemies like an Oriental despot, without favor or mercy. When Archelaus returned without the royal dignity he had hoped for, he took a frightful revenge on his opponents. At his second coming, Christ will act as a judge. The wicked servant will be deprived of what he has, while his enemies will be massacred. The sentence will depend on the measure of a person's guilt (12 : 46–48). The judgment pronounced on the king's enemies was much more severe than that pronounced on the " servant " who failed the test. Christ's second coming overshadows the church's life and activity, as well as the persecutions and the fate it suffers.

IN JERUSALEM (19:28—21:38)

Jesus' Entry into the City (19:28–48)

Jesus entered Jerusalem as the Messiah-king (19:28–40). However, the city rejected this offer of salvation which God made it, and so Jesus foretold its destruction (19:41–44). While in the city, Jesus took possession of the temple and made it the center of his activity and of the new people of God (19:45–48). The foundations of the early church were laid in Jerusalem (see Acts 2:41–47; 4:32–37).

Jesus is Hailed as a King (19:28–40)

²⁸*And when he had said all this, he journeyed on and went up to Jerusalem.*

The false interpretation of what was about to happen had been excluded; Jesus' entry into Jerusalem would not inaugurate the messianic kingdom in all its glory. He continued his journey. The prophet who was " mighty in word and action " journeyed on, surrounded by his disciples; the Son of David went to celebrate the feast of Israel's deliverance. Many of those who went with him had witnessed what he had said and done. They all realized that the hour was approaching when the promises made to Israel would be fulfilled. How this would be accomplished remained hidden from them (18:34).

²⁹*It happened that as he drew near Bethphage and Bethany on the Mount of Olives, as it is called, he sent out two of his disciples,* ³⁰*telling them: " Go into the village facing you; when you come there you will find an ass's foal tethered, on which no one has ever yet ridden. Untie it and bring it here.* ³¹*And if anyone asks: ' Why are you untying it? ' you must say: ' The Lord needs it '."* ³²*The messengers went and found everything as he had told them.* ³³*But*

*when they were untying the foal, its owner asked them: " Why are you untying the foal?" * ³⁴*They replied: " The Lord needs it."*

Bethphage ("the house of the fig ") was situated on the western slopes of the Mount of Olives, while Bethany ("the house of op- pression ") was to the southeast. Anyone coming from Jericho to Jerusalem would come to Bethany first, and then Bethphage. Once more, St. Luke speaks of Jesus' journey from the viewpoint of Jerusalem (17:11); his journey is seen in the light of its goal. This is the only way in which it can be properly interpreted.

It was at Bethphage that pilgrims submitted to the prescriptions concerning ritual cleanliness in preparation for their entry into the holy city. Jesus, too, made his preparations there. He sent two of his disciples ahead, just as he had sent out those who went before him two by two (10:1). This time they were to prepare his coming, not by preaching the word, but by getting what was needed for his entry into the city as a king. It was always their duty to prepare the Messiah's coming.

Jesus needed something to ride on; this had to be an ass's foal. Soldiers rode on horseback, but an ass was the normal animal for the poor and the peace-loving. The prophecy made by Zechariah was fulfilled: " Cry aloud for joy, daughter of Zion. Rejoice, daughter of Jerusalem. See, your king is coming to you. He is just and he brings salvation. He rides humbly on an ass, on a colt, the foal of a she-ass. He will do away with the chariots in Ephraim and the horses in Jerusalem. The archers' bows will be broken. He will command the peoples to be at peace; his kingdom reaches from sea to sea, from the river [Euphrates] to the ends of the earth [in the west] " (Zech. 9:9f.). Jesus chose a foal because it had never yet been used by anyone. Animals destined to be sacrificed could not be used for any ordinary work, because they were set aside for God. In the same way, the animal on which Jesus, the Messiah-king, rode had to be a foal on which no one had ridden.

113

Jesus knew with absolute certainty where such an ass's foal could be found and he disposed that its owners should hand it over to him. He possessed superhuman knowledge and authority over its owners. God's holiness, together with a divine knowledge and power were revealed in him; they accompanied him, as he went his humanly incomprehensible way.

35And they brought it to Jesus. They threw their clothes on the foal and made Jesus mount it. 36As he went along, they spread their clothes out on the road.

"They made him mount it." This is the only time this word is used in the New Testament and it recalls a noteworthy event in the Old Testament in the account of which the same word occurs: "King David gave them [Zadok the priest, the prophet Nathan, and Benaiah son of Jehoiada] an order: 'Take your master's servants with you. Make Solomon my son mount my own mule and bring him down to Gihon. There Zadok the priest and Nathan the prophet must anoint him king of Israel. Then sound the trumpet and cry out: "Long live king Solomon." Then come back here in his train. He is to come and sit on my throne and take my place as king. I have appointed him prince of Israel and Judah'" (1 Kings 1:33-35). The blind man in Jericho proclaimed that Jesus was the Son of David, and it was as David's royal Son and the Prince of Peace that he made his entry into Jerusalem. Even the way his disciples spread their clothes like a carpet on the road before Jesus was part of the ritual surrounding the coronation of a king. When Jehu was called to be king, "they all took off their clothes quickly and laid them on the bare earth at his feet. Then they sounded the trumpets and cried: 'Jehu is king'" (2 Kings 9:13). The disciples' behavior was in keeping with God's plan of salvation; they paid homage to Jesus as the Messiah.

37When he was approaching the descent of Mount Olivet, the whole

crowd of disciples began to praise God joyfully with loud voices
for all the wonders they had witnessed. ³⁸*And they cried: " Blessed*
is the king, he who comes in the Lord's name. Peace in heaven and
glory in the highest."

A person approaching the descent of the Mount of Olives from
Bethany sees Jerusalem spread out before him. At the sight of the
city and the temple in all its splendor, the crowds who accompanied
Jesus were filled with faith and enthusiasm. It was expected that the
Messiah would enter the city from the Mount of Olives (Zech.
14:4). The people remembered the wonders they had witnessed
during Jesus' ministry, " how God anointed him with the Holy
Spirit and with power, and how Jesus went about doing good and
curing all those who were held in subjection by the devil, because
God was with him " (Acts 10:38). God himself visited his people
in Jerusalem to bring them salvation (7:16).

Their cry of homage summed up the reasons the crowd had for
rejoicing. Pilgrims who approached the temple were greeted by
the priests from inside the sanctuary with the blessing: " Blessed
is he who comes in the Lord's name " (Ps. 118:26). The formula
of blessing became a cry of homage which was addressed to Jesus.
He was the king appointed by God, on whom God had conferred
all power. God had bestowed his blessing on him and the people
who welcomed him as a king showered praises on him, as they
greeted him and escorted him into the royal city of Jerusalem. The
messianic king made his entrance into Jerusalem; God's promises
were fulfilled.

A great hour in salvation history had struck. The people who
escorted Jesus were conscious of what it involved. Their acclama-
tions expressed it: " Peace in heaven and glory in the highest."
Here we have an echo of the message the angels proclaimed on the
first Christmas night (2:14). The messianic king of peace entered
Jerusalem and assumed the sovereign power that was his. This was

a sign that God had prepared peace for men; he manifested the glory that was his as God. For the moment, this peace and glory is confined to heaven. But what is disposed in heaven will one day become a reality on earth. The prayer the Jews offered was assured of a hearing: "He who makes peace on high will make peace for us and the whole people of Israel." Jesus' entry into Jerusalem as the king of peace did not result in the kingdom of peace being established immediately; first he had to die and be taken up into heaven. It is only when he comes again that there will be peace on earth (19:11). Three landmarks in salvation history are here brought together: The birth of the king of peace, his entry into Jerusalem for his passion and glorification, and his second coming, when he will accomplish the definitive inauguration of God's kingdom.

³⁹*Some Pharisees among the crowds of people said to him: " Master, tell your disciples to stop this." *⁴⁰And he answered saying: " I tell you: if they keep silent, the stones will cry out."*

There were also Pharisees among the crowd who payed homage to Jesus. On a previous occasion (13:31), they had warned Jesus against Herod, and now they gave him another warning. High politics was involved here. What would the Roman forces of occupation say? The Pharisees laid great stress on the title with which they addressed Jesus: " Master," " Teacher." He was a teacher and he taught with authority; he was entitled to call himself that, but never " king " or " Messiah." They suggested that he should tell his disciples to be quiet. Jesus himself had often enjoined silence on those who followed him. But now the time for silence was past. It was God's will that he should allow himself to be honored as the messianic king.

Jesus accepted the cry of homage addressed to him and his disciples' profession of faith in him as the Messiah, just as he had accepted the appeal for help from the blind man in Jericho who honored him as the Son of David. This profession of faith could not be silenced. Its inevitability is underlined by a proverb which contains an echo of a prophecy of Habakkuk: "Even the stone cries out from the wall, the rafters in the building answer him" (Hab. 2:11). This proverbial saying seems to be a prophecy. If Jesus' disciples were reduced to silence, because his own people rejected his kingship, then the stones of the ruined city of Jerusalem would cry out in witness of the fact that Jesus' claim to be the Messiah had been rejected unjustly. Jerusalem would be reduced to a heap of rubble, not because it was dangerous to confess Jesus as the Messiah, but because the Jews had refused to have Jesus as their king; they failed to recognize the hour of salvation history; they did not accept the offer God made.

Jesus' Lament for Jerusalem (19:41–44)

⁴¹*And as he drew near, he looked at the city, and he wept over it,* ⁴²*saying: "If only you had known on this day, even you, what would promote your peace. But now it has been hidden from your eyes."*

Jerusalem lay spread out in all its glory before Jesus' eyes. He knew that the city would be rejected and destroyed. God's words to Jeremiah were fulfilled in Jesus: "You must tell them [the false prophets] these words: 'My face is bathed in tears day and night; they never stop. The virgin daughter of my people has collapsed completely and suffered a disaster which cannot be remedied'" (Jer. 14:17). Jesus wept over the city.

The sentence of punishment was about to be pronounced on Jerusalem; Jesus could no longer ward it off. He could only say: "If only you had known what would promote your peace." His tears confessed his powerlessness. He had cast out demons and healed the sick; he had raised the dead and converted tax collectors and sinners. His power was limited by the opposition mustered by this city. Jesus' tears and his powerlessness conceal a profound mystery.

In the ancient church, this was so shocking for a Christian's faith in Christ's power that many people were reluctant to regard this as a true account. God hides his power in Jesus' redeeming powerlessness and love. He takes man's free decision so seriously that he prefers to weep helplessly in Jesus than to deprive man of his freedom. Jesus' tears were a last appeal for repentance which he addressed to this obdurate city.

The day of Jesus' entry into Jerusalem as the Messiah brought to a climax the long history of God's offers of salvation to Jerusalem. Peace, the messianic salvation the Jews longed for, which the prophets had promised for Jerusalem the " City of Peace " and for which the people of God prayed so earnestly, was now about to be given to it. All Jerusalem had to do was to recognize that Jesus was the eschatological Prince of Peace sent by God. This was what his disciples had stated in their cry of homage; the blind man in Jericho and Zacchaeus, the head tax collector, had recognized this. But Jerusalem refused to recognize it. This was the city which murdered the prophets and stoned those whom God sent to it for its salvation (13 : 34). The people of Jerusalem closed their hearts against God's words: " They are without counsel; they have no insight " (Deut. 32 : 28).

The city did not accept God's offer of salvation. Instead of paying homage to Jesus as the Messiah, it rejected him and nailed him to the cross. The significance of the hour in which he made his entry was hidden from its eyes—God. Jerusalem's refusal to believe and its stubborn rejection of Jesus were every bit as much a part of the " must " involved in God's design as Jesus' death. However, this did not prevent Jesus' lament from being a genuine lament, or Jerusalem's guilt from being real guilt. When he wept over the doomed city, Jesus acknowledged God as God and admitted the justice of his disposition. When he saw in the course of his ministry that those who thought themselves wise refused to accept his message, while those who were insignificant believed it, he said: " I give you praise, Father, Lord of heaven and earth. You have hidden this from those who are wise and clever, and revealed it to children. Yes, Father, this was what pleased you " (10:21).

Jerusalem did not acknowledge Jesus as the Messiah and it was stricken with a spiritual blindness which made Jesus' wish vain. Judgment had already been passed. The period of grace had expired; now the sentence of punishment must run its course. Jesus could only say: " If only you had known it." The words God once spoke to Jeremiah were verified here too: " You have forgotten me and turned your back on me. So I raised my hand against you and destroyed you. I was tired of showing pity " (Jer. 15:5).

43" *The days will come upon you and your enemies will throw up earthworks around you; and they will encircle you and press on you from every side.* 44*And they will raze you to the ground, you and your children; and they will not leave one stone upon another in you, because you did not recognize the time of your visitation."*

Here Jesus speaks as a prophet of doom. The conjunction " and " occurs five times; its tone is sinister; it shows that Jerusalem's distress will reach its climax in the total destruction of the city. The enemy camped outside the city; they forced their way in and wiped out the population. Not one stone of the city remained on another. The proud city was erased from the map. The prophetic tone of Jesus' warning made it clear that Jerusalem's fate was sealed.

Here once more Jesus alludes to the reason for this sentence. Jerusalem had not welcomed the decisive hour of God's gracious visitation; through its own fault it had failed to recognize or to acknowledge his overflowing goodness in granting it this hour. The time of salvation Jesus inaugurated began with the words: " Praised be the Lord, the God of Israel. He has visited his people and brought them salvation . . . By this means [the mercy of our God], the Rising Sun will visit us [the Messiah], to give light to those who crouch in darkness and death's shadow, to direct our feet into the way of peace " (1 : 67–79). At the climax of Jesus' Galilean ministry, the people acknowledged that God had visited them with the fullness of his grace (7 : 16). Jerusalem, on the other hand, steeled itself against recognizing God's gracious visitation which was granted to it, when the Prince of Peace entered the city. Jesus was a sign which called for a decision.

Jesus Takes Possession of the Temple (19:45–48)

45He went into the temple and began to throw out those who were selling there. 46He said to them: " It is written: ' My house will be a house of prayer.' You have made it into a robber's den."

Jesus went straight into the temple; the temple was the goal towards which his entry led. Jerusalem owed everything it was to the temple on Mount Zion. The temple in its turn received all its glory from the divine presence. By his solemn entry, Jesus gave this presence a new meaning. The words of the prophet Malachi were fulfilled : " The Lord for whom you long comes without warning to his temple, and the messenger of the covenant whose presence you desire " (Mal. 3 : 1). Judgment was to come on this day : " Who can endure the day on which he comes, who will be able to stand fast when he appears? He is like a refiner's fire, or a fuller's lye " (Mal. 3 : 2). But it was also to be a day of salvation : " Then the sacrifice of Judah and Jerusalem will be acceptable to the Lord, as in the days of old and the years long past " (Mal. 3 : 4).

The temple cleansing is described in only a few words. No strong emotion is attributed to Jesus. Yet even these few words are sufficient to indicate the power with which he performed this prophetic action. He " began to throw out the sellers." It was enough for him to begin. Such business transactions were unbecoming in God's house. The temple was a house of prayer (Is. 56:7). The traders, and the Jewish authorities who allowed this traffic and profited by it, had made it a " thieves' hideaway " (Jer. 7:11). Jesus continued the prophets' work, not only by what he said, but especially by what he did. He achieved something which had been prophesied for the messianic era: " On that day, there will be no more traders in the temple of the Lord of Hosts " (Zech. 14:21). God's service was restored to its rightful place, to the exclusion of the service of mammon. According to St. Mark, Jesus referred to the temple as a "house of prayer for all nations " (Mk. 11:17). St. Luke says nothing about this worldwide destination of the temple. The temple would no longer be a place of prayer for the gentile nations, but the infant church in Jerusalem gathered there to pray. That was why Jesus sanctified the temple by his presence and his messianic activity, before it was destroyed. Jesus' church is connected with the Old Testament people of God. Salvation history is accomplished in a process which God leads to its goal.

47a*And, day by day, he taught in the temple.*

When he was twelve years old, Jesus remained behind in Jerusalem. There he sat among the doctors of the law in the temple, listening to them and asking them questions. All those who heard him were amazed at his intelligence and at the answers he gave (2:46f.). Now he himself taught in the temple. On that occasion, he had displayed a profound consciousness of his own being: " Did you not know that I must be in the place which is my Father's?" (2:49). Now he acted with authority as the Messiah and the Son of God (20:44). After his ascension and the descent of the Holy Spirit, his apostles would continue the work Jesus had begun in the temple; they taught in the temple. A bridge reaches from Jesus' coming into the temple as a child, over his entry as a king before his passion and glorification, to the teaching activity of the apostles in the temple after the coming of the Holy Spirit. The great moments in the birth of the church are the incarnation, Jesus' death and exaltation, and the descent of the Holy Spirit. His childhood and the coming of the Spirit are seen in the light of his death and exaltation.

The temple's purpose was realized to the full and it achieved its greatest glory before it was destroyed. The Messiah taught in it and gathered his people about him. As long as the Jews had not rejected the gospel definitively, the old place of worship retained some connection with the new form of worship inaugurated by Jesus. This connection was intended to be a bridge between Israel and the new church of the gentiles. However, by speaking up for the new spiritual worship, St. Stephen made it clear even in his day that the destruction of the sanctuary built by human hands would come soon (Acts 7:48ff.). His words were treated as blasphemy and they led to his execution. Some years later, the Jews' increasing obduracy set the final seal on Jerusalem's fate. The Jews excluded Christians from their ranks; in this way, they broke definitively with Jesus' church.

47bBut the chief priests and the scribes tried to destroy him, as did the leaders of the people. 48But they found nothing they could do. The whole people adhered to him, listening to him.

By cleansing the temple, Jesus had made himself an enemy of the spiritual leaders of the Jews. The high priests and the priestly aristocracy had an interest in the trading which took place in the precincts of the temple. The high priest who held office was the president of the supreme council (the Sanhedrin), the highest authority the Jews had. This was composed of the priestly aristocracy, the scribes, and the lay nobility. The leaders of the Jews were determined to destroy Jesus. After the descent of the Holy Spirit, they would also do their utmost to prevent the apostles from completing their task of building up the church.

But the people adhered to Jesus. The multitude (" the whole people ") was on his side. They listened to Jesus' word. When the apostles began to build up the church, it was the same. The people gathered around Peter and John (Acts 3:11), and it was to the people they spoke (4:1). The people had great respect for the infant church (5:13). In them, the real people of God, the true Israel, was visible; they were ready to welcome God's message in Jesus. It was from this people that the new people of God, the church, would be formed. For fear of the people, the council was afraid to proceed against Jesus openly and with violence (Acts 5:26). In Jesus, the Lord of the nascent church, the church sees an image of its own fate.

The Lord of the Nascent Church (20:1–26)

Jesus reveals himself as the Lord of the nascent church in the temple. He has authority from God (vv. 1–8); the authority of the supreme council is at an end (vv. 9–19). Jesus' authority does not contradict the authority of the Roman emperor (vv. 20–26).

Jesus' authority (20:1–8)

¹*It happened on one of these days, while he taught the people in the temple and preached the gospel, that the high priests and the scribes approached him, together with the elders.* ²*They addressed him saying: " Tell us, by what authority do you do this and who is it that gave you this authority?"*

Jesus had taken possession of the temple, and now he filled it with his preaching. His teaching consisted in proclaiming the gospel of salvation, that salvation which had now dawned. " Today salvation has come to this house " (19:9). The preaching of the gospel conferred salvation. Jesus surpassed all the other teachers in Israel;

they taught, but they did not proclaim salvation. He surpassed the prophets; they promised salvation, but they did not bring it or confer it. Who was he, that he could claim that his preaching marked the fulfillment of God's great promises?

When the supreme authority among the Jews, which was composed of the acting high priest, the chief priests, the scribes and the elders of the people (the nobility), questioned Jesus about his authority, they were acting quite legally. They had questioned John the Baptist in the same way (Jn. 1:19ff.), and they would later put a similar question to Jesus' disciples (Acts 4:5ff.). Jesus acted as a teacher; yet he had never attended the scribal schools; he had never had his learning and his formation confirmed by the laying on of hands. The people regarded him as a prophet, but the demands he made were much greater than those the prophets made. Who was he? At the back of the question concerning his authority stood the question whether he was the Messiah. The council avoided this question, until it was impossible to avoid it any longer (22:70).

³*But he answered them, saying: "I, too, want to question you about something: ⁴John's baptism, did it come from heaven or from men? Answer me!"*

The disputations which Jewish teachers were accustomed to hold proceeded by question and counter-question. Jesus took up the question put to him by the council; he did not contest their right to question him about his authority. His counter-question was not an attempt to shirk the issue; it was not meant to put his opponents on the defensive. It was intended to make them think. John preached an appeal for repentance on the banks of the Jordan; he baptized and announced the coming of God's kingdom. With him, a new era had dawned for Israel. Jesus continued the Baptist's work, although he did not baptize (Jn. 4:2); he appealed for repentance and proclaimed the good news of the dawn of salvation. What did the council think of John's baptism? Of the role he played, his mission, and his preaching? The answer to the question concerning the Baptist's authority would throw light on the authority Jesus enjoyed. John's whole mission was to prepare the way for Jesus.

⁵They considered this among themselves and said: " If we say: ' From heaven,' he will say: ' Then why did you not believe him?' ⁶And if we say: ' From men,' the whole people will stone us. They were convinced that John was a prophet." ⁷And they answered that they did not know where it came from.

The members of the Sanhedrin were not looking for divine truth; they were interested only in themselves. Consequently, they could not come to a decision. No matter which way they answered, they would lose themselves. If they declared that John's baptism came from God, they would logically be forced to have faith in him; so they would " lose " themselves in God. But if they said it came from men, their lives would be in danger. The people believed that the Baptist had been sent by God and they would lynch the unbelieving members of the Sanhedrin as blasphemers. But if the councillors were no longer prepared to stand up for divine truth, if they obstructed it, how could they lead the people in God's name? With that, they abandoned all claim to exercise authority themselves.

⁸And Jesus told them: " Neither will I tell you by what authority I do this."

Like John's baptism, Jesus' counter-question was an invitation to repent and to believe his preaching that the time of salvation had come. It recalled his whole life from the time John baptized until now (Acts 10 : 37–39); his whole life bore him witness that God was with him (Acts 10 : 38). The members of the council shut their

125

minds to the realization that the Baptist was sent to prepare the time of salvation which dawned in Jesus; they shut their minds to the realization that God was with Jesus. Consequently, they were incapable of understanding the authority by which Jesus taught and preached the gospel when he appeared in the temple. Jesus answered their question even as he refused to do so. However, the way he answered made it clear that his answer was not accepted by his opponents. The Baptist was sent by God and the testimony he bore Jesus continued to be important in the church. He summed up the entire witness of the Old Testament. The church's consciousness of itself as the new people of God is based on the authority Jesus enjoyed.

The End of the Sanhedrin's Power (20: 9–19)

⁹*But he began to tell this parable to the people: "A man planted a vineyard and let it out to some vinedressers and went on a journey for a long time."*

A distinction is made between the people and their leaders; Jesus spoke to the people. The people had good will; they represented the Old Testament people of God and in them the people of God of the New Testament could already be seen. Jesus now took over their leadership. From the time of Isaiah the prophet, a vineyard had been a symbol of Israel. The man who planted the vineyard was God. The owner let out his vineyard to some vinedressers. The upper valley of the Jordan and, very likely, the northern and western shores of the sea of Galilee, together with a great part of Galilee itself, were divided up into huge estates which were in the hands of foreigners. These lived abroad, far from their estates; the local farmers were their tenants. The owner spent a long time traveling and left the vinedressers free to do as they pleased; he had complete confidence in them. The vinedressers represent the leaders of the people. The parable is an account of God's dealings with his people. These involved a whole series of revolts on the part of their responsible leaders against the demands God made of his people.

10"And when the time came, he sent a servant to the vinedressers, so that they could give him some of the fruit from the vineyard. But the vinedressers sent him away empty-handed, after they had beaten him badly. 11And he sent another servant; but they sent him, too, away empty-handed, after they had beaten him badly and insulted him. 12And, once more, he sent a third servant. But they threw him out also, after they had inflicted injuries on him."

According to the law, the lease was recalled after five years (Lev. 19: 23–25). Wine was not the only fruit of a vineyard; fruit trees and even corn were often planted in them. The tenants' behavior became increasingly unjust and malicious. The first two servants were merely sent away, but the third was thrown out. The first two were badly beaten, while the second one was also insulted, and the third was injured. An atmosphere of revolt existed among the tenant farmers of Galilee. Groups of zealots and partisans had aroused the farmers to oppose their absentee landlords, particularly as they included Romans who were especially detested. The owner in the parable showed unlimited and unrealistic patience. Why did he go on sending servants? Why did he not intervene forcibly? The parable abandons real life to give a drastic emphasis to God's patience. This is what God, not man, is like. This shows how patient and how docile he is in his efforts to bring men to salvation. The servants stand for the prophets whom God sent to the leaders of the people; the fate they met was the prophets' fate.

13"But the Lord of the vineyard said: ' What am I to do? I will send my son, my only son, to them. Surely they will have respect for him?' 14But when the vinedressers saw him, they had a discussion among themselves and said: ' This is the heir. Let us kill him, so that the inheritance will be ours.' [15a]*And they threw him out of the vineyard and killed him."*

The owner of the vineyard now took counsel with himself to see what he should do next. He will send his own son. But this is his only son whom he loves dearly, the sole heir. Worry and anxiety warn the owner, but the hope that the limits of brutality have been reached is stronger. Perhaps they would respect him. However, it was still a risk; this last attempt would reveal the tenants' malice in all its ugliness. The parable here takes leave of real life. Would the owner who had only one son expose him to these fanatical tenants? Even if a certain hope remained that they would respect his son, somber experience would prevent him from taking the risk. His hesitation, expressed in the word " surely," should make us reflect on the incomprehensible decision the owner made. God sent his Son, his only Son, whom he loved dearly (3:22; 9:35). What God did to bring his people to salvation is beyond our human comprehension; it transcends anything a man could do.

When they saw the son, the vinedressers, too, discussed among themselves what they should do. They presumed that the owner had died and that his son was coming to take possession of his inheritance. If they killed him, the vineyard would be ownerless property. They were the first there and they could legally take possession of it. Their thinking was an extraordinary combination of legality and wickedness. This may seem surprising, but it was just such an outlook which led to Jesus' death. He was put to death by the very people who kept watch to see that the law was fulfilled.

The son was thrown out of the vineyard and put to death outside it. The explanation of the parable is here woven into the text of the parable itself. Jesus was put to death outside the city of Jerusalem. He knew what was before him. Previously he had spoken of his death only before his apostles (18:31); now he foretold it before the people, even though it was veiled in the form of a parable. The members of the Sanhedrin murdered the Messiah because they were unwilling to give up the fruits of the vineyard which God demanded. Throughout the course of salvation history, God had led his people and fitted them for their task; now he expected that they would recognize the Messiah whom he had sent, who was his own Son. But they refused Jesus this recognition; they were selfish and they wanted to keep the vineyard for themselves. They refused to bow to Jesus' rule (Mk. 15:10).

^{15b}*" What will the Lord of the vineyard do to them now? ¹⁶He will come and destroy those vinedressers and give the vineyard to others." Those who heard this said: " Never! That must not be."*

The owner's patience and forbearance were at an end. Jesus himself announces the sentence of punishment. God will give the leaders of the Jewish people over to destruction (Mt. 23:30–33). The people of God will be handed over to others, to the new pastors of the new people of God.

The people who heard Jesus' words were shocked. They were appalled; they could not believe that God would inflict such a sentence. The people respected the Sanhedrin and dealt reverently with them. A long time would still have to pass before the people who adhered to Christ would abandon the old institutions. The history of the early church bears ample witness to this (Acts 1—15). The infant church was still closely bound up with the social and religious organization of Judaism. When he was brought before the court, St. Peter addressed the Sanhedrin with the words: " Leaders of the people and elders " (Acts 4:6).

¹⁷*He looked at them and said: " What is the meaning, then, of the words which are written: ' The stone which the builders rejected has become the keystone '?"*

Jesus understood the amazement the people felt, but he had only told them the truth. God's design is unalterable. He confirms what he had said in the parable by a quotation from scripture. The greeting with which the people had honored Jesus as the Messiah was taken from Ps. 118 [117] v. 22. This same psalm also mentions the stone which the builders rejected, but which later became the keystone crowning a new building. The members of the Sanhedrin regarded themselves as Jerusalem's builders: "The great Sanhedrin is the builder of Jerusalem." Jesus is the stone. The supreme council rejected him as a useless stone and gave him up to death. But God raised him up and glorified him. Jesus is the builder of a new house of God which is the church, and it is he who crowns the edifice (Mk. 14:58). It was not the members of the Sanhedrin who built up the people of God; it was Jesus who built them up, by his death and resurrection (Acts 4:11).

¹⁸" *Everyone who falls on that stone will be dashed to pieces, and it will destroy anyone on whom it falls.*"

The prophet Isaiah had said with reference to God: "He will be a stone people trip over, a rock to make them stumble. He will be a pitfall and, indeed, a snare for the inhabitants of Jerusalem. Many of them will stumble and fall; they will be dashed to pieces, trapped, and taken prisoner " (Is. 8:14f.). Daniel speaks of a kingdom which will dash all other kingdoms to pieces and bring them to an end. This kingdom itself will stand firm forever (Dan. 2:44f.); it is represented by a stone. "Surely you saw it yourself! The stone which was loosed from the mountainside without the help of human hands dashed to pieces iron, bronze, pottery, silver, and gold " (Dan. 2:45). The stone is Christ; he is a touchstone (2:34). Salvation and condemnation depend on him. The man who runs into him will be shattered. When he comes again as a judge, Jesus will " dash him to pieces." Jesus claimed supreme authority over Israel, as the Christ, as the Son of man, and as the Son of God (see 22:67ff.).

¹⁹*At that very moment, the scribes and the high priests tried to lay hands on him, and they were afraid of the people. They knew that it was against them that he told this parable.*

The scribes and the chief priests realized that this parable revealed the plans their hatred had inspired. There is no mention here of the lay nobility. Their hearts were closed to Jesus' word, and so their hatred was intensified. Only fear of the people prevented them from taking extreme measures.

A rift was now apparent among the Jews. The people and their leaders were divided. The early years of the church would be marked by the same phenomenon (Acts 5:24f.). How much longer would the people be able to prevent the members of the Sanhedrin from giving full vent to their hatred? They were not conscious of all that was involved in this drama. This is clear from the answer they made to the parable (20:16).

The Emperor's Authority (20:20-26)

²⁰*And they had kept him under surveillance. They sent spies who pretended to be honest, to catch him in what he said, so that they could hand him over to the authorities and the governor's power.*

The scribes and the high priests (20:19) were determined to destroy Jesus. This would have to be done behind the people's back. Jesus would have to be involved in a dispute with the Roman authorities who were represented by the procurator Pontius Pilate (vv. 26–36). The members of the Sanhedrin remained in the background; they acted through spies who pretended to be anxious to fulfill the law with painful exactness. The ground was being prepared for Jesus' trial—and the difficulties in which the infant church would have to prove itself.

²¹*And they questioned him, saying: "Master, we know that you speak and teach correctly. You teach God's way in truth, without*

regard for personalities. ²²*Is it permitted to pay taxes to the emperor or not?"*

The secret agents faked a question of conscience. They approached Jesus as a doctor of the law, as is clear from the title they gave him: " Master." They asserted their confidence in him: " You speak and teach correctly." They acknowledged his unwavering objectivity : " You have no regard for personalities "; you do not defer to those who enjoy political power; you are not influenced by fear or favor. They praised his fear of God: " You teach God's way in truth," the moral conduct God demands. As a teacher, Jesus fits the description the Teacher of Wisdom gives of himself : " All the words of my mouth are right; they contain no falsehood or perversity. They are all intelligible to those who have insight; they are clear to those who seek knowledge " (Prov. 8 : 8f.).

Having prepared the ground in this way, the spies put their trick question. In 6 A.D. Quirinius the governor of Syria had held a taxation census and reorganized the system of taxes and customs in Palestine. Taxes and customs duties went to the emperor. The reaction all over the country was embittered. The ultra-nationalist Zealots called for the refusal of such taxes on religious grounds. Foreign domination had to be resisted. God would be prepared to help only when the people themselves had done everything they could. Numerous people probably asked themselves in their own conscience whether their patient subservience to the rule of foreigners involved falling away from God. Did a person who paid taxes to the Roman emperor thereby acknowledge pagans as the rulers of the people of God? Those who were behind the spies were realistic politicians. They saw no reason to resist and so they paid taxes without the slightest scruple.

²³*But he knew their cunning trick and he said to them:* ²⁴*" Show me a denarius. Whose image and inscription does it bear?"* They

said: " Caesar's." ²⁵And he said to them: " Then give to Caesar
what is Caesar's and to God what is God's."

The spies' tactic was a cunning trick; they were hypocritical (Mk.
12 : 15) and malicious (Mt. 22 : 18). Under cover of a pious difficulty
of conscience, they laid a trap for Jesus which they were sure he
could not escape. Political passions were especially inflamed on feast
days. The crowds who hailed Jesus so joyfully regarded the Messiah as a saviour from political oppression (24:21). The Romans
kept a close watch on everything that went on. No matter how
Jesus answered the question which was put to him to test him,
the result was bound to be fatal for him. If he said that it was
lawful to pay taxes, he would have to fear the Zealots' fanaticism
and the people's apostasy. If he said it was not lawful, the governor
would take action against him. One way or the other, those who
sent the spies stood to gain.

Jesus did not answer the question by launching into a learned
discussion. His enemies themselves would have to cooperate if the
problem was to be solved. Jesus made them show him a denarius.
It was immediately apparent that his " conscientious " interrogators
carried such coins with them. A denarius was a silver coin which
carried on the obverse a portrait of the emperor Tiberius (14–37
A.D.). He was naked, as befitted a god, and wore a laurel wreath
as a sign of his divine dignity. The inscription ran : " Tiberius
Caesar Augustus, son of the divine Augustus." The reverse showed
the Roman high priest and a portrait of the emperor's mother sitting on the throne of the gods. In her right hand, she held the long
olympic scepter and in her left an olive branch, which gave her the
aspect of an earthly incarnation of heavenly peace. The spies who
were so zealous for the law carried this coin with them, with all its
symbols of the deification of the power of Rome.

In antiquity, the principle adopted was that a king's territory
coincided with the area in which his coins were legal tender. This

principle was accepted by the Jews. The man who accepted a coin and made use of it recognized the authority of the one who was responsible for having it struck. The Jews who used Caesar's coins accepted his rule; consequently, they also had the duty to pay taxes. Therefore, they already had the answer to the question they put to Jesus. Jesus merely drew the conclusion : " Then " give to Caesar what belongs to Caesar, everything to which he had a claim, according to the legal theory of the time. Jesus accepted the political domination of the Romans.

Once Jesus had pronounced these words, he immediately relegated them to the second place. The whole purpose of his preaching was God's kingdom; he told his disciples that their only care should be to " seek his kingdom " (12:31). God's kingdom was already present in everything he said and did. When they asked him whether a man should pay taxes to the emperor or not, his enemies had pretended to be anxious for God's honor and the proper observance of the law. They failed completely to realize that this God was present in the person whom they were questioning, and that he made far more important and urgent demands than the one which worried them. Give to God what is God's. Here and now God asserted his kingdom's claim in the midst of the world; his kingdom limits the demands the state is entitled to make and relegates them to the second place.

[26]*They could not catch him out in anything he said before the people. His answer filled them with wonder and they were reduced to silence.*

Jesus' interrogators were reduced to silence; their effort was in vain. His answer filled them with admiration. St. Luke took the account of this dispute from St. Mark, but he rewrote the introduction and the conclusion extensively. The question was important for him. The church was growing and it was caught between the need to acknowledge God's supreme rule in Christ and allegiance to the Roman state. The unbelieving Jews tried to rouse suspicion against Christians on a political level (Acts 17:5; 18:12; 24:1). Christians had to be able to explain the true state of affairs to the Roman authorities. Like Jesus, they were loyal to the state; their first and greatest interest was religious.

Fundamental Truths of the Christian Life (20:27—21:4)

After revealing himself as the Lord of the nascent church, Jesus initiates the people who adhered to him in the most important beliefs held by the new people of God; belief in the resurrection of the dead (vv. 27-40), and in Jesus as the Lord (vv. 41-44). He also inculcates the necessity of surrender to God (20:45—21:4).

The Resurrection of the Dead (20:27-40)

27Then some Sadducees came to him, people who say there is no resurrection, and they questioned him, saying: " Master, Moses wrote for us: ' If a person's brother who was married died and his wife is childless his brother must take the woman in marriage and raise up posterity to his brother '."

The Sadducees were a political and a religious class of the aristocracy rather than a party. They included the wealthy noble families and the priestly aristocracy. They were never able to win the support of the ordinary people. In theological questions, they represented the conservative tendency which did not accept the development of the Jewish religion which had its beginning in the second century before Christ. They accepted scripture alone, and rejected the " traditions of the ancients." Their denial of the resurrection of the dead created a sharp distinction between them and the Pharisees and other adherents of rabbinical piety.

135

Jesus shared the conviction of the Pharisees and the ordinary people that the dead will rise again. For this reason, a number of Sadducees wanted to ridicule him. They tried to prove from scripture that faith in the resurrection is nonsense. The law concerning levirate marriages was as follows: " If brothers live together and one of them dies without leaving a son, the dead man's widow must not marry with a stranger outside the family. Her brother-in-law should come to her, take her as his wife and do a brother-in-law's duty by her. Her first-born son must be called after the brother who died, so that his name will not disappear from Israel " (Deut. 25:5f.). What followed from this law, with reference to faith in the resurrection?

²⁹" *There were seven brothers; the first married a wife and died childless;* ³⁰*and the second* ³¹*and the third took her, and* [*eventually*] *all seven. They left no children when they died.* ³²*The woman died last of all.* ³³*At the resurrection, then, whose wife will the woman be? All seven were married to her.*"

The law, therefore, made no allowance for the resurrection of the dead. It could not be the cause of a grotesque situation such as the Sadducees described. God spoke in the law, and according to the law the resurrection of the dead was impossible. But scripture can be misinterpreted and abused. Jesus is the key to the proper interpretation of it—he and his word.

³⁴*But Jesus said to them: " The sons of this world marry and are given in marriage,* ³⁵*but those who are made worthy to attain that eon and the resurrection of the dead neither marry nor are given in marriage.* ³⁶*For they cannot die any more. They are like the angels, sons of God, because they are sons of the resurrection.*"

The Jews' faith in the resurrection included the belief that after the resurrection those who had risen would continue to live a life similar to that on earth; they believed that it was only then that life would be accompanied by an abundance of all that seemed desirable. A celebrated scribe held that: " Only then [after the resurrection] will women bear children every day." The joy they felt in children would be filled to overflowing. It was against this concept of the resurrection that the Sadducees' arguments were directed. But Jesus did not share the Jews' faith in this respect. Once a person has risen from the dead, he does not marry and is not given in marriage. Life after the resurrection is not a continuation of our earthly life.

Once a person has risen from the dead, he belongs to a new world, to the world to come, not to this world. The views of history adopted by Jewish apocalyptic writers involved two eons, that is, two worlds or ages—the present world and the other world. The present eon was an eon of injustice, oppression, instability, and sinful corruption; it would be followed by the new eon to come, an unending era in which all corruption would be banished, disobedience would be uprooted, and infidelity destroyed. There justice would be practiced and truth would find a home. The New Testament, too, adopts this vision of history. The sons of this age are subject to sin and corruption. On the other hand, those who by grace and by God's choice belong to that other age receive eternal life and resurrection from the dead.

Marriage suits this present world. In the eon to come it is no longer necessary; there people will never die again. Marriage is regarded as a means towards the preservation of the human race (Gen. 1:28). But if everyone is immortal, there will be no more need for marriage. The Sadducees' " proof " was not to the point. Marriage comes to an end with this present eon.

Those who live in the eon to come are immortal, because they are like the angels. They share in the angels' existence. They enjoy this privilege because they are sons of God. The angels are described in scripture as " sons of God " (see Job 1:6; 2:1). They share God's glory, God's power, and God's splendor (Acts 12:7). Those who have risen from the dead receive the gift of divine sonship (1 Jn. 3:2; Rom. 8:21). They are given glory (Rom. 8:18) and a " spiritual body " (1 Cor. 15:44). " That is the way with the resurrection of the dead. The seed is sown in corruption; it is raised up incorruptible. It is sown as something insignificant, but it is raised in splendor. It is sown in weakness, and raised in power. A material body is sown, but it is a spiritual body that is raised up " (1 Cor. 15:42ff.).

Those who rise from the dead have the power never to die any more. At that time, pious pagans in the Greek world longed for a life of happiness in a godlike state which would never be threatened by death. This was what they hoped to attain by means of their mystery cults and "knowledge" ("Gnosis"). They saw nothing desirable in the resurrection of the body. The body was regarded as a burden, as the prison and the tomb of the soul. The resurrection involves more than mere immortality; the dead will arise incorruptible and we "will be different" (1 Cor. 15:52). It is not merely the soul which will have life; the whole man, body and soul, will live for ever.

If a man rises from the dead, it is because he has been made worthy of the eon to come. The resurrection is an unmerited gift of God's grace, just like God's kingdom (2 Thess. 1:5). But the resurrection will not be restricted solely to those whom God has chosen and made worthy; all men will rise again, both good and bad. St. Paul was familiar with the hope that both just and unjust would rise again (Acts 24:15). But only the just will rise to a life of glory (14:14). It was of these that Jesus was thinking when he said they were made worthy of the eon to come.

[37]" *Moses, too, disclosed that the dead would rise, at the burning bush. There he calls the Lord: ' The God of Abraham and the God*

of Isaac and the God of Jacob.' [38]*But God is not [the God] of the
dead; he is the God of the living. For him, all men are alive."*

Like the Sadducees, Jesus appeals to a saying of Moses in the discussion on the resurrection. In the story of the burning thorn bush,
Moses describes God as saying: " I am the God of Abraham, the
God of Isaac, and the God of Jacob " (Ex. 3:6). God, therefore,
revealed himself to Moses first and foremost as the God the patriarchs adored. However, Jesus understood these words in a deeper
sense. When God described himself as the God of the patriarchs,
he meant to imply that the patriarchs still adored him as their God.
Therefore, they were still alive; otherwise they could not have
adored him.

God is the God of the living; for him, all men live. Even a man
who is dead is alive; the God of the living does not surround himself with those who are dead. Men live for God; their whole essence
consists in living only for the service and glory of God. God calls
them into existence for this purpose; that is why he wants them
to continue to live. Jesus' words do not make it clear how a man
continues to live after death and despite death. He says nothing
about life in the intermediary state between a person's death and
his resurrection, or what his " immortality " consists in; he says
nothing about the way life continues after death, or about the
resurrection. He merely states one basic doctrine: for him, all men
live. They live because they exist for him. The man who lives for
God is truly alive.

[39]*Some of the scribes answered, saying: " Master, you have spoken
well."* [40]*They did not dare question him about anything any more.*

Jesus was a teacher who spoke well; the scribes bore him this testimony. The Sadducees were afraid to ask him any more questions;
the scribes (and Pharisees) acknowledged the wisdom of his teach-

ing. Jesus was a teacher before whom even the most skilled teachers gave way. He stood before the people and before the church as the great teacher. It was from him that they received the teaching concerning the resurrection of the dead. This separated Christians from the Pharisees, from the Sadducees, and from pagans. Christian preaching announces the news of " Jesus and the resurrection " (Acts 17 : 18).

Christ is the Lord (20:41–44)

⁴¹And he said to them: " How is it that they say Christ is David's Son? ⁴²David himself says in the book of the Psalms: ' The Lord said to my Lord: " Sit on my right hand, ⁴³until I make your enemies a footrest for your feet "." ⁴⁴Therefore, David calls him Lord. How is he his Son?"

This time Jesus himself takes the offensive. Psalm 110 was attributed to David and was interpreted as referring to the Messiah who was to come. It involved a mystery. The words the Psalm attributes to God (" The Lord said ") refer to the Son of David (the Messiah) as David's Lord. This calls for reflection.

The Christ (the Messiah) is the Son of David. It was as such that he had been promised by the Old Testament. "A shoot sprouts from the stump of Jesse . . . The Spirit of the Lord comes down on him " (Is. 11 : 1f.). It was for him that Israel prayed : " Raise up their king again, the Son of David " (*Ps. Sal.* 17 : 23). The blind man at Jericho addressed Jesus as the Son of David and acknowledged him as the Messiah (18 : 38). Did this title express everything that the Messiah was?

The mysterious words of the Psalm call him " David's Lord." The Messiah is superior to King David. He is the Lord of Lords (Rev. 17 : 14). God himself gives him a place on his right hand, and shares his universal sovereignty with him. He makes his enemies a foot stool on which his feet rest. He grants him victory and crushes all opposition.

St. Peter takes up this picture of the Messiah in a sermon and explains it: " Let me speak freely to you about our father David . . . He was a prophet and he knew that God had sworn him an oath that he would put one of his descendants on his throne. In saying this, he was speaking in prophecy of the Messiah's resurrection . . . God has raised up this Jesus and we are all his witnesses. Exalted at God's right hand, he has received the promised Holy Spirit from the Father and poured him out, as you see and hear. David never went up to heaven. Yet he said: ' The Lord says to my Lord: " Sit at my right hand until I make your enemies a foot stool for your feet ".' Let the whole house of Israel know, then, that God has made this Jesus whom you crucified Lord and Messiah " (Acts 2:29–36; see 4:25ff.). At the beginning of the Epistle to the Romans, St. Paul claims in the words of an ancient hymn that he is an apostle of the gospel " which was proclaimed beforehand by his prophets in sacred scripture. It deals with his Son who became a descendant of David according to the flesh, but was appointed God's Son in power by the spirit of holiness after his rising from the dead, Jesus Christ our Lord " (Rom. 1:1–4). The church is founded on the profession of faith: " Jesus Christ [the Son of David] is the Lord " (Phil. 2:11).

The Poor Widow (20:45—21:4)

A number of sayings which are directed against the Pharisees are contrasted sharply with a brief reference to a poor widow. The basic moral and religious attitude of the nascent church is described positively and negatively.

⁴⁵*As the whole people were listening, he said to his disciples:* ⁴⁶*"Beware of the scribes. They love going about in long robes. They look*

eagerly for greetings in public places, the first seats in the syna-
gogues, and the places of honor at banquets. ⁴⁷*They eat up the*
houses of widows and recite long prayers for appearances' sake.
They will be judged all the more severely."

Jesus here addresses his disciples in the presence of the people, the
people of God. They were to take the scribes' place. The foundations of the new people of God were being laid.

The scribes were avaricious and ambitious. The robes of office
they wore and the place they occupied in the synagogue service
were meant to be accompanied by a religious and reverential spirit.
Yet they used them as means to their own ends in their ambitious
efforts to win the approval of men. Exchanging greetings and sharing a meal should have been marks of loving fellowship, but they
only served as an occasion for trying to capture the first place. Their
avarice tainted actions which should have been done in a spirit of
helpfulness and piety. Scribes who knew the law used to offer legal
assistance to widows who had no standing in court without their
husbands (Ex. 22:21). In return, they accepted gifts; so they ate up
the houses of these poor widows. Their narrow-minded selfishness
led the scribes to reject Jesus, whose very existence consisted in living for others (Mk. 10:45).

God's sentence will be more severe for the scribes than for other
people. As lawyers, they knew God's will better, and as teachers
of virtue they were responsible for others. God never rejects anyone;
new teachers will take their place, when the new people of God
has been built up.

^{21:1}*As he looked up, he saw wealthy people putting their gifts in*
the offering boxes. ²*But he saw a poor widow putting in two mites.*

In the women's court of the temple, opposite the treasury, which
was accessible to everybody, there were thirteen trumpet-shaped

money boxes. These were for offerings prescribed by the law as well as voluntary offerings. Jesus was sitting there, too, sitting as a teacher did. He looked up and saw the people putting their gifts in the offering boxes. They gave them first to the priest on duty who asked them how much the offering was and what it was intended for. Then he examined the money, and indicated the appropriate container where it was to be put, according to the purpose for which it was destined. Jesus watched what was going on. He saw wealthy people bringing their gifts, and a poor widow only offered two of the smallest gold pieces.

³*And he said: " I tell you truly: this poor widow has put in more than any of them. ⁴They all put in gifts out of the abundance of their wealth, but she, in her penury, has put in her whole livelihood."*

The widow at the treasury was poor and also despised. She was like the woman of whom we are told she could only bring in a handful of meal to the oblation and for this reason was greeted contemptuously by the priest on duty. In Jesus' view, the poor widow had given more than those who were rich. Her offering was small, but at the same time it was great; she gave everything she had. She placed her life in God's hands without worrying anxiously (12:22–31). She was one of those to whom Jesus addressed the beatitudes (6:10); she lived by his word: " Seek his kingdom [God's kingdom] and this [your livelihood] will be given to you " (12:31). She represented the people of God who were told: " Do not be afraid, little flock. It is your Father's gracious design to give you the kingdom " (12:32). The people of God are poor and without legal standing, but they give the little they have. They put their trust in the Father, not in wealth and power. This was the way the mother church at Jerusalem lived: "All those who had received the faith held together and shared everything in common. They sold their possessions, all they had, and divided the proceeds with everyone according to their needs. Day after day they came together with one mind in the temple; they broke bread in the houses and took their food in happiness and simplicity of heart, praising God and enjoying the respect of all the people " (Acts 2 : 44–47).

The church's life is inspired by three fundamental truths which Jesus committed to it as it set out on its journey through the ages : the dead will rise again; Jesus is the Christ and Lord; the church is the community of those who are insignificant, poor, and despised, and yet are great in God's eyes because they sacrifice everything they have, humbly and secretly, and put their trust in God.

The Eschatological Discourse (21:5-38)

Like St. Mark (13), St. Luke closes Jesus' final ministry in Jerusalem with an eschatological discourse (an apocalypse). Despite numerous similarities, the two writers often differ widely in their accounts of this discourse. For this reason, many exegetes presume that, besides St Mark, St. Luke used another source. However, the differences can be explained by the way St. Luke edited his source. He passes over some points to avoid repetition (for example, he omits Mk. 13:21–23 because he mentions the same thing in 21:8 and 17:21), and others because of theological scruples (for example, Mk. 13:32). Prophecies which had already been fulfilled are changed in the light of the event (compare Mk. 13:14 with Lk. 21:20; Mk. 13:19f. with Lk. 21:23f.).

It is difficult to explain the way in which St. Luke describes the destruction of Jerusalem (19:43f.).; 21:20, 24) unless we admit that when he wrote his gospel this was already a matter of past history. The number of those who agree that St. Luke wrote his gospel after the year 70 A.D. is constantly increasing. "St. Mark in his gospel looks on Christ who was to come, but describes him as he had already come because, having come, this was the way he revealed it to him. This sentence can also be put another way: St. Mark describes Christ who had come as the One who was to come. Lastly, it can be put like this: St. Mark attests Christ who was present by looking forward to his second coming and present-ing him with the aid of means which referred to him who had come." As an evangelist, St. Mark payed no attention to any genuine before and after, in the sense of a historical sequence of events. St. Luke was dif-ferent. He was able to look back on a number of prophecies which had already been fulfilled (vv. 5–24). The Son of man's coming had not yet taken place (vv. 25–28). The period of time between the ascension and his coming is the time of the church, during which the church prepares for his coming (vv. 29–36). St. Luke read his source (Mk. 13) with the eyes of a person who had already been enlightened by the historical event; he interpreted it in the light of the experience of a later age. The events which had occurred showed him that Jesus was right, and that his prophecies had been fulfilled. This was a guarantee that what was still in the future would also come true. The church today continues to live in this eschatological hope; it is bound to live in it. For this reason, it is not quite accurate to speak of St. Luke's "primitive Catholicism."

Prophecies which have been Fulfilled (21:5–24)

PRESSING QUESTIONS (21:5–9)

⁵*When some remarked about the temple that it was adorned with beautiful masonry and votive offerings, he said:* ⁶*" You see all that? The days will come in which one stone will not be left on another. It will all be thrown down."*

The temple which was still being built in Jesus' time (20/19 B.C.— 63 A.D.) was one of the seven wonders of the ancient world. Its white marble stonework gleamed splendidly; its votive offerings were a glorious sight, especially the golden vines over the gate to the sanctuary. The saying went: "Anyone who has not seen Jerusalem in all its glory, has seen no joy in his whole life. Anyone who has not seen the sanctuary in all its array, has never seen a delightful city."

Jesus answered the admiring voice which came from the crowd

with a prophecy of doom; the temple will be destroyed (19:43). God was not interested in beautiful stonework or costly votive offerings; what he looked for was a people whose lives would make it clear that God lived among them. Jesus repeated the threatening prophecy made by the prophet Micah which was now about to be fulfilled: " Listen, you chiefs of Jacob, you leaders of Israel, you who abhor what is right and twist what is straight . . . Her leaders grant justice for the sake of presents; her priests teach for a reward; her prophets prophesy for money. And in so doing they trust in the Lord: Is not the Lord with us? No harm can come near us in any way. Because of you, Zion will be ploughed up like a field. Jerusalem will be reduced to a heap of rubble and the temple to a wooded hill " (Mic. 3).

⁷But they questioned him saying: " Master, when will this be? What is the sign that it is about to take place?"

The question here concerns only the date of the end of the temple. According to St. Mark, Jesus' listeners also asked when the end of the world would come (13:4). St. Matthew formulated the question more accurately: " When will this be and what is the sign of your coming and of the end of the world?" (Mt. 24:5). The destruction of Jerusalem, the coming of the Son of man, and the end of the world are here bound up with one another. St. Luke separates them. The destruction of Jerusalem was not one of the events which would mark the end of time. When he wrote his gospel, it had already occurred, but the end of the world had not come yet. Every prophecy is obscure until it has been fulfilled. In St. Luke's gospel, we can read the eschatological discourse as St. Luke read it. For us, too, some of the prophecies it contains have already been fulfilled, but we are waiting for the others to be fulfilled.

⁸He said: " See to it that you are not led astray. Many will come in my name and say: ' It is I,' and: ' The time has come.' Do not run after them. ⁹When you hear of wars and revolts, do not be anxious. These must take place, but the end will not come immediately."

No answer is given to the question about the date of the destruction of Jerusalem and the sign which would precede it. A word of warning is addressed to Christians who looked forward longingly to the coming of Christ. Their ardent desire for the fulfillment of their yearning made them susceptible to voices which might lead them astray. St. Paul, too, was forced to warn the Christians at Thessalonica : " We beg you, brothers, with regard to the coming of our Lord Jesus Christ and our being united with him, do not let yourselves be suddenly thrown into confusion or overcome with terror by some spiritual revelation or by some message or letter allegedly coming from us to the effect that the day of the Lord is near. Let no one lead you astray in any way " (2 Thess. 2 : 1ff.).

Many would come, claiming the title of Messiah; they would quote with reference to themselves the words in which Jesus expressed his self-revelation : " It is I." By this they meant that they were the final saviour sent by God to usher in the restoration of all things. In the days of the Roman procurator (44–46 A.D.), Theudas appeared and " claimed to be someone special " (Acts 5 : 36). After him, Judas the Galilean arose and won a considerable following among the people (Acts 5 : 37). Jesus' prophecy unmasked these " saviours " as deceivers. Others proclaimed : " The end of time has come." They, too, disguised their message with Jesus' words. The over-eager expectation of Christ's immediate coming and the end of this eon must be discouraged. " The Lord is taking his time " (12 : 45). The claimant to the throne traveled to a distant country, to obtain the royal title for himself (19 : 11).

It is not easy to see through these disturbing messages. Those who preach them are many and even their number could make a seductive impression. They hide behind Jesus' words. The message they preached bears a certain resemblance to his: " It is I "; " The time has come." Like him, they gather a number of disciples about them who follow after them. In the midst of all this confusion and deception, the Lord's word is like a warning beacon. These men are impostors; their end is apostasy and perdition. Jesus' words begin and end with a serious warning: " Do not let yourselves be led astray; do not run after them."

In Jewish apocalyptic literature, wars and revolts were prophesied for the end of the world, together with a spate of contradictory rumors about them: " The days will come when I, the Most High, will deliver those who are on earth. Then the dwellers on earth will be greatly agitated, so that they will plan wars against one another, city against city, district against district, people against people, kingdom against kingdom " (4 Ezra 11 [13] : 29–32). The prophets of Christ's imminent coming may have interpreted contemporary events as signs that the end was approaching. Nero's death was followed by revolts led by Galba, Otho, and Vitellius (68–69 A.D.). The Jewish war began in 66 A.D. Jesus' warning was directed against those who proclaimed that the end was near. Wars and revolts are no reason for being worried that the end may be near. Even these frightful scourges of humanity are taken up into God's plan. Like the present eon, they are passing, but they must keep Christians alert for the eon that is coming and lead them to repentance (Rev. 16:11). Wars and revolts are not a sign that the end is coming immediately. These words of Jesus deprive the teachings of all the " adventist " sects of any foundation.

The Signs Which Foretold the Destruction of Jerusalem (21:10–11)

[10]*Then he said to them: " Nation will rise up against nation and kingdom against kingdom. *[11]*There will be great earthquakes and*

famines and epidemics and frightening events on all sides. And there will be great signs from heaven."

These verses mark a fresh beginning in the discourse. They announce signs. The words are obscure. St. Luke seemingly interprets them as signs of the destruction of Jerusalem and the temple. He could look back at these events and he knew that the disaster had been announced by signs. Jesus' prophecy that there would be signs had been fulfilled.

The signs mentioned affected every aspect of man's situation. Everything which went to make his life secure was shaken. Peace and harmony among nations were destroyed by wars; the stability of the earth was disturbed by earthquakes; men's lives were threatened by famine and epidemics; the order of the heavenly bodies was disturbed by terrifying portents. We have no idea in what contemporary events St. Luke saw this prophecy fulfilled. Was he thinking of the Roman war of revolt? Or of the confused situation in Palestine before the outbreak of the Jewish war? He may have had in mind the earthquakes which were reported from Phrygia at this period. St. Luke was aware that there had been a famine during the reign of the emperor Claudius (Acts 11:28). According to a Jewish tradition, a sword-like star appeared over the city of Jerusalem in the year 66 A.D., and a comet was visible in the sky throughout the year. Six days after the outbreak of the Jewish war, a vision of chariots was seen charging at full speed across the heavens. At Pentecost in that year, the priests in the temple heard a voice at night saying: "Let us go away from here." St. Mark regarded these signs as the "beginning of the travail" which accompanied the "rebirth of the world" (Mt. 19:28), as God intervened to restore it. Although he read this in his source, St. Luke says nothing about it. He interpreted these signs, not as the beginning of the woes which will mark the end of time, but as signs of the imminent destruction of Jerusalem. He explained the prophecy in the light of the historical event. The course of history is not determined exclusively by causes which are imminent in the world; it also depends on God's design. Even when we look at it in this way, history still contains many mysteries.

THE CHURCH WILL BE PERSECUTED (21:12–19)

[12]" *Before all this, they will lay their hands on you and persecute you. They will hand you over to the synagogues and to prison. They will bring you before kings and governors for my name's sake.*"

The events foretelling the destruction of Jerusalem would be preceded by a persecution inflicted on Jesus' disciples. St. Luke arranges events in their historical order; first the church was persecuted, as we read in the Acts of the Apostles; then followed the events which preceded the destruction of Jerusalem which are interpreted as portents of what was to come; last came the Jewish war, with the destruction of Jerusalem and the temple.

Jesus' disciples were persecuted by both the Jewish and the pagan authorities. " While Peter and John were speaking to the people, the officer in charge of the temple and the Sadducees descended upon them . . . They laid hands on them and put them in prison until the following day " (Acts 4:1–3; see 5:18; 8:3; 12:4). The magistrates at Philippi had Paul and Silas " stripped of their clothes and scourged. After they had inflicted numerous lashes on them, they were thrown into prison " (Acts 16:22f.). St. Paul was brought before the tribunal of King Agrippa II (Acts 26:1), of Gallio the governor of Corinth (Acts 18:12), of Felix (Acts 24:1f.), and of Festus (Acts 25:1) at Caesarea. Jesus' prophecy was borne out by historical events. Christ's disciples must not regard the fate history inflicts on them as a somber or oppressive destiny. The Lord has known from the first what they would have to suffer and he has given it a place in God's plan of salvation.

The disciples will endure persecution, condemnation, and punishment for the sake of Jesus' name. It was in the name of the Lord Jesus that they were baptized, after they had professed their faith that Jesus is the Lord (Acts 8:16). At that moment, they became one with those "who invoke the Lord's name" (Acts 9:14). It was by invoking this name that St. Peter cured a man who was ill (Acts 3:6). "There is no other name under heaven given to men by which we can be saved" (Acts 4:12). In their preaching, the apostles proclaimed and taught the name of Jesus Christ (Acts 4:17f.; 5:28; 8:12). It was because they preached this that they were punished, but "they left the council full of joy because they had been found worthy to suffer humiliation for the sake of Jesus' name" (Acts 5:41). The name Jesus was a symbol of the active presence of the glorified Christ.

¹³" This will result in your being able to bear witness. ¹⁴Take it to heart, therefore, that you must not worry in advance how you are to defend yourselves. ¹⁵I myself will give you eloquence and wisdom, so that all your adversaries will not be able to withstand or refute it."

The disciples' greatest anxiety, their most ardent wish, must be to proclaim Jesus' name. Persecution would give them numerous opportunities to bear witness to Christ. Courts of justice were made to serve the preaching of the gospel, while prison cells expanded the church's missionary activity. The Christians of the mother church at Jerusalem were forced to flee the city to preserve their lives. In this way, they carried the gospel to Judea and Samaria (Acts 8:1-4), as well as to Phoenicia, Cyprus, and Antioch (Acts 11:19; 15:3). Peter, John, and Stephen appeared before the Sanhedrin; Paul appeared before governors and brought the news of Christ to circles which would otherwise have been closed to it. St. Paul could tell the Christians at Philippi that his imprisonment was helping the spread of the gospel: "It has become known to the whole praetorium and all the others that it is because of Christ I am in chains" (Phil. 1:12f.).

The disciples received a promise which they were meant to impress indelibly upon their minds for the time of persecution. They had no need to be anxious about the speech they would make in court in their defense; they were not to study their speech beforehand, so that they would not let Christ down when they appeared in court. Christ himself would give them eloquence and wisdom. God promised Moses that he would be with his lips and teach him to say what he should (Ex. 4:12); in the same way, Jesus will equip his disciples to profess their faith and bear him witness before his enemies. They will not have to rely solely on human rhetoric and wisdom; their speech will be endowed with divine power, with God's own wisdom. The Holy Spirit will teach them what they are to say in that hour (12:12). History had proved that this promise was kept faithfully. When the members of the council saw how eloquently Peter and John defended themselves and realized that they were uneducated men, they were amazed (Acts 4:13). The Hellenized Jews who disputed with Stephen were no match for the wisdom and the spirit with which Stephen spoke (Acts 6:10). It was not the disciples who were reduced to silence, it was their adversaries. The words of this prophecy radiate the optimism which the gospel's victorious course inspired.

[16]" *You will be given up by parents and brothers and relatives and friends, and they will kill [some of] you.* [17]*You will be hated by everyone, because of my name.*"

The members of their own households, their own relatives and friends, would betray Christ's disciples. They would not be safe even among their own friends and families. When they professed their faith, their profession was based on faith in Christ and on nothing else. St. Luke presents the original prophecy: "They will be killed" (Mk. 13:12), in such a way that it is clear it has already been fulfilled: "They will kill [some of] you." When he wrote his gospel, some of Christ's disciples had already been put to death for their faith, among them Stephen (Acts 7:54–60) and James (Acts 12:2).

Fidelity to Christ brought his disciples into conflict with Jews and gentiles alike; they clashed with the worldwide Roman empire, and with society and its accepted customs. They were hated by everyone. Christians incurred " the hatred of the human race." This was the way the Roman historian Tacitus summed up the common attitude towards Christians. They were hated because of Christ's name. A Christian believes in the message that is preached " concerning God's kingdom and the name of Jesus Christ " (Acts 8:12). Christ and his message were rejected; in the same way, Christians, too, were rejected. " If the world hates you, you must realize that it hated me before it hated you " (Jn. 15:18). God manifests his glory in the way Jesus' disciples bear their witness (Phil. 2:11). Martyrdom is an act of worship (Phil. 2:17f.).

18" *Not a hair of your head will be lost.* 19*It is in your endurance that you will preserve your lives.*"

Christ's persecuted disciples are not abandoned to the arbitrary power of their enemies. God looks upon his persecuted church and extends his hand over it. Here too the proverb holds good: " Not a hair on your head will be lost " (1 Sam. 14:45). Some would be killed but many others would escape from the gravest dangers through God's protective providence. St. Peter was miraculously rescued from prison (Acts 12:6ff.), while St. Paul was able to accomplish his extraordinary missionary activity despite the hostility and persecutions he so often encountered (Acts 13ff.; 2 Cor. 11:23–31). After the stoning of St. Stephen, " a great persecution came upon the church at Jerusalem. With the exception of the apostles, they were all scattered throughout Judea and Samaria . . . Those who had been dispersed went about and preached the good news of the word " (Acts 8:1–4).

The time of the church is a time of persecution, and it will last a long time. Final redemption comes only with the advent of the Son of man, but this will not happen immediately. Endurance, steadfastness, and perseverance will be needed; Christians must be able to " remain under " (" *hypomene* " = " endure ") all that persecution inflicts on them and God has disposed for them. A man will save his life and attain salvation, not by resorting to violence in a spirit of vehement passion, or by renouncing the faith, but by enduring patiently. " If a man must go into captivity, let him go; if a man must die by the sword, let him be killed by the sword. It is in this that the saints' patience and faith are manifested " (Rev. 13:10). God allows nothing to happen to his faithful which cannot be turned to their good (Rom. 8:28).

THE DESTRUCTION OF JERUSALEM (21:20–24)

[20]" *When you see Jerusalem hemmed in by armies, then you must know that the time is near when it will be laid waste.* [21]*Then those who are in Judea must flee to the mountains. Those who are in the middle of it must go out of it. Those who are in the country must not go back into the city.* [22]*These are the days of vengeance, in which all that has been written will be fulfilled.*"

In his source, which was St. Mark's Gospel, St. Luke read : " When you see the abomination of desolation standing where it should not be, . . . then the inhabitants of Judea should flee to the mountains " (Mk. 13:14). The final events will begin to take place when the abomination of desolation is set up. Troops sent by Antiochus IV Epiphanes (175-164 B.C.) desecrated the sanctuary in Jerusalem and the citadel. They abolished the perpetual sacrifice and set up the ruinous abomination (Dan. 11:31); this was an altar or statue to the god Zeus. In the same way, a ruinous abomination will stand where it should not be before the end of time comes. What this involves is a mystery. " Whoever reads this must use his intelligence " (Mt. 24:15). A text of St. Paul tries to answer the question in the following way: " No one must lead you astray in any way. The apostasy must come first, and the lawless one will be revealed, the son of perdition, the adversary who exalts himself above all that God and the worship of God stand for. He will usurp a place in God's temple and claim that he is God " (2 Thess. 2:3f.). In the symbol of the two beasts, the Apocalypse manifests a similar eschatological expectation. The first beast is a political power which blasphemes God and demands adoration, while it persecutes those who have the true faith (Rev. 13:1-10). The second is a reality of the religious order. They fight against the Lamb (Christ) and work sham miracles. In this way, they lead men to adore the first beast (Rev. 13:11-18). This power is the " anti-Christ " (see 1 Jn. 2:22)

Even though he makes a distinction between the destruction of Jerusalem and the end of the world, St. Luke takes up the mysterious reference to the abomination of desolation and interprets it in the light of events. The Roman army which surrounded Jerusalem was the abomination which led to its being left desolate. It may be that this interpretation does not exhaust the meaning of this mysterious expression. The Apocalypse of St. John reveals another aspect which involves the worldwide Roman empire and its emperors who set themselves up in place of God. The war the two beasts waged against the Lamb was a veiled reference to the situation of the church in St. John's time. The church was being persecuted by the Roman empire and was having a hard struggle.

When the Roman army surrounded Jerusalem (19:43f.), it was meant to be a God-given sign to Christians that his judgment was about to be inflicted on the city. There was no hope of escape and resistance would be in vain. The city was about to be given up to its enemies. Christians were not to suffer the city's fate; they could escape by fleeing. Those who lived in Jerusalem had to leave the city when the enemy approached. In former times, those who lived in the open country used to take refuge in the city which was strongly fortified; now, this would be pointless. Jerusalem was about to fall. The country in the immediate vicinity of the city was in the same danger. The only thing to do was to flee to the mountains. In the mountains were numerous hiding places, inaccessible cliffs and caves. In the general collapse of the Jewish people, Jesus' prophetic words saved his disciples who believed in him.

The time of vengeance and retribution was coming on the city; the time of grace was past. The doom which the prophets had threatened for it was about to be accomplished. In scripture, the destruction of Jerusalem is regarded not merely as a political event, but as a divine judgment.

[23]" *It will be too bad for women who are pregnant or have children at the breast in those days. There will be great distress in the country and anger against this people.* [24]*They will fall at the point of the sword, and they will be carried off as prisoners of war among all the nations. Jerusalem will be trampled underfoot by the gentile nations, until the times of the gentile nations have expired."*

The whole country would suffer great distress; God's sentence of punishment was inflicted on all its inhabitants. What would otherwise be a source of joy would now become a sad misfortune. Pregnant women and nursing mothers would endure misery and suffering. In the harrowing example of pregnant and nursing women, Jesus describes the distress the forthcoming sentence would bring;

at the same time, however, he indicates the sorrow he felt for the city (19:42ff.). Even as a prophet of doom, Jesus is not a fanatical zealot who has no sympathy for those who are about to be destroyed. He is a brother of those who are condemned; he merely submits, in a spirit of obedience, to God's plan and his word.

Jesus' prophecy was fulfilled in the Jewish war (66–70 A.D.). St. Luke interprets it and fills in details in the light of what has happened. The fulfillment of the prophecy is confirmed by the Jewish historian Josephus Flavius. According to his figures, which are not entirely free from exaggeration, one million one hundred thousand Jews were killed and ninety-seven thousand carried off into captivity. The city was laid waste and the temple burnt to the ground. The whole country was occupied by the conquerors. When St. Luke was writing his gospel, the state of occupation still continued. Jerusalem was trampled underfoot by the gentiles.

The terms of the prophecy reëcho the words used by the prophets. The inhabitants of Jerusalem would fall at the point of the sword. This is a reminiscence of Jeremiah: " They will fall by the sword of their enemies . . . I am giving the whole of Judea into the power of the king of Babylon. He will lead them off to Babylon and he will slay them with the sword " (Jer 20:4). Jerusalem would be trampled by the gentiles. Daniel had said the same thing. " The vision concerning the daily sacrifices, the wickedness of the despoiler, and the surrender of the sanctuary which is trampled by the army—for how much longer will it be fulfilled?" (Dan. 8:13). The prophets' word and the destruction of Jerusalem by the Babylonians prepared the way for its definitive fall. The divine patience has reached its limits. The threat contained in the parable of the wicked vinedressers was about to be executed. Scripture was given to us to comfort us, exhort us, and warn us (1 Cor. 10:11).

The length of time for which Jerusalem has been made over to the gentiles has been fixed by God, who has also set a limit to it. When the time granted to the gentiles has expired, the general judgment will be held and God's kingdom will be definitively inaugurated. The time granted to the gentiles runs from the destruction of Jerusalem to the coming of the Son of man. History has made it clear that in this period the gentiles enter the church. The time during which Jerusalem is trampled down by the gentiles is also the time in which God offers the gentiles the salvation he promised Israel.

As God's chosen instrument, St. Paul enjoyed a special insight into the historical development of God's plan of salvation and the goal he pursues in history. Consequently, he could write: " Therefore, my brothers, I do not want to leave you in ignorance concerning this mystery. Otherwise, you might think yourselves clever. Blindness has affected a part of Israel, until the full number of the nations has entered; then all Israel will be saved " (Rom. 11 : 25f.). It seems that a similar hope is implied in the words: " Jerusalem will be trampled until the time granted to the gentiles is fulfilled " (see 13 : 35). Despite the rejection of the gospel by the Jews, God's fidelity is still effective.

The Coming of the Son of Man (21:25–28)

SIGNS IN THE COSMOS (21:25–26)

[25]" *There will be portents in the sun, the moon, and the stars. On earth, the nations will be anxious, at a loss in the face of the roaring and tossing of the sea.* [26]*Men will be wasted away with fear as they await the events which are to come upon the earth. The powers of heaven will be shaken.*"

The discourse now turns from the prophecies which could already be seen to have been fulfilled to the events which will mark the end of time, which are still to come. A clear distinction is made between the destruction of Jerusalem and the end of time. However, nothing is said about the length of the period granted to the gentile nations.

The end of time will be announced by great cosmic events. Before the Son of man comes, the whole universe will be thrown into disorder. Its three great spheres will be shaken. These are thought of in accordance with the three-storey idea of the world current at the time. In the firmament, there will be portents in the sun, the moon, and the stars. St. Luke apparently is not very interested in describing these portents more closely, as St. Mark does: " The sun will be darkened, the moon will not give its light, the stars will fall from heaven " (Mk. 13:24). On earth, people will be overcome with anxiety and despair. The sea which is held in check by God's power (Job 38:10f.) will be abandoned to its chaotic impulses. According to the idea of the world current in antiquity, the universe was held in check by spiritual forces which had their home in heaven; they maintained order in the world and guided it. These heavenly powers will be shaken, so that everything will be reduced to chaos.

The nations, the gentiles, all mankind, will be attacked by anxiety and a feeling of helplessness; mortal fear and terror will grip them. " When numbing fear grips the earth's inhabitants they will feel great distress and immeasurable anguish " (*Apoc. of Baruch* 25:3). What could a man build upon when even the most immutable laws no longer held good? The ground fell away beneath their feet. People will ask themselves what all this means, what it indicates. As a result of what Christ said, his disciples know the meaning of these events. They are signs that he is coming. Christ's words apply to the whole world. Humanity is divided into two great camps; one, the " people," is overcome with fear; the other, Christ's disciples, looks forward to this hour with eager expectancy. Without Christ there is only fear; with him there is confident hope.

The various portents are described in terms which have a long tradition behind them. In a prophecy concerning the disaster of

Babylon, we read: "The Lord is coming without mercy. He is fierce and blazing with anger. He turns the earth into a desert and wipes out sinners in it. The heavens and Orion in it do not shed their light. The sun is dark when it rises. The moon does not let its light shine" (Is. 13:9f.). In a sentence of condemnation for Edom, the same prophet says: "All the hills are destroyed. The heavens roll up like a scroll. His whole army withers, just as leaves wither on a vine, or on a fig tree. The Lord's sword is laden with anger and it hangs in the sky; it falls on Edom, to punish the people whom he cursed" (Is. 34:4f.). In a sentence of doom for Egypt, we read: "I will cover the heavens when you are obliterated, and clothe its stars in darkness. I will conceal the sun with a cloud, and the moon will not give her light any more. I will extinguish all that gives light in heaven because of you. I will bring darkness on your land" (Ezek. 32:7f.). God's intervention in history, when he intervenes to punish cities and states, is described against a background of gigantic cosmic disturbances. These seem to be merely a graphic representation of God's power and majesty as he comes for judgment. The universe trembles as he arises to visit the earth. When we are told that the whole cosmos will be shaken at the coming of the Son of man, we can be sure this is intended only to introduce the Son of man to whom God has entrusted all power in heaven and on earth. As he strides through the universe at his coming, the powers of heaven will tremble, overcome with reverence and dismay. However, prophecies are always obscure until they are fulfilled. Who would dare to claim that his explanation was final?

The Appearance of the Son of man (21:27-28)

27" Then they will see the Son of man coming on a cloud with great power and glory."

The Son of man will become visible. People will be able to see him

160

with their own eyes. No one will be able to disregard this event. Moreover, it will be clear to all who see him that it is he.

The Son of man's appearing is described in traditional images. This was the way Daniel had seen him in his visions at night. "Then, on the clouds of heaven, there appeared one who was in the form of a Son of man. He went up to the One who was from of old [God]; he was brought before him. He was given authority and majesty and royal dignity; all nations, peoples, and languages serve him. His sovereign rule is an eternal rule which will never pass away. His kingdom will never be destroyed" (Dan. 7:13f.). The Son of man will come on a cloud; a cloud was God's chariot. When God reveals himself, he does so in power and great glory. The Son of man, therefore, shares God's sovereign power. The traditional imagery is intended to indicate Christ's divine majesty. All such images are only a feeble, stammering expression of his ineffable glory. Jesus comes now, not in the "weakness" which characterized his earthly life, but in the majesty and glory of his exaltation. Who could give an exhaustive description of this?

28"*But when this begins to happen, stand up and lift up your heads. Your deliverance is near.*"

The church goes bowed like a person who has a heavy burden to carry. It holds its head down like a person who is hated, persecuted, and denied all honor. When the signs begin which precede the final event, the faithful must take heart. What holds a threat of destruction for others means that they are about to be raised up. It is only when the Son of man comes that the church will cease to be a church that is oppressed, tried, and bowed low.

When the Son of man appears in his glory, it means that deliverance is near. Persecution and intimidation will be at an end. Hopes which had been laughed to scorn will be fulfilled. The suffering church will become the church of joy. The words the Baptist's father sang, as the time of salvation drew near, can now be sung as having been fulfilled: "Praised be the Lord, Israel's God. He has visited his people and brought them redemption" (1:68).

The church stands erect, with all its members assembled. The coming of the Son of man marks the day when the church's harvest is reaped. According to Mark, the Son of man will send out his angels to gather his elect from the four winds (Mk. 13:27). There is no mention of this in St. Luke. The time of the church, between Christ's ascension and his second coming, was a time for missionary activity, a time for assembling all the nations. Now is the time when the assembled church will reach its full achievement and receive the fullness of redemption.

Eschatological Attitudes (21:29–36)

BEWARE OF BEING LED ASTRAY (21:29–33)

²⁹*And he told them a parable: " Look at the fig tree and all the trees. ³⁰As soon as the buds open, you know yourselves, when you see it, that summer is near. ³¹So, too, when you see this happening, you are to know that God's kingdom is near."*

When the Son of man comes in the world's last crisis the faithful will stand erect. Now it can be said truthfully that the kingdom is near. Those who said this before were deceivers (21:8); they did not tell the truth. Then there will be no need for anyone to announce the coming of the kingdom; its very proximity will make it clear to everyone. This is illustrated with a brief parable. When the fig trees and the other trees come into bud everyone knows that winter is over and the summer is near. There is no spring in Palestine; summer follows winter directly. No one in his right mind needs the help of another to know that summer is near when he sees the trees blossoming.

The coming of the Son of man, the redemption, and God's kingdom are closely connected. " The end will come when Christ hands over the kingdom to God the Father, once he has destroyed every force and power [which is opposed to God]. However, he must continue to reign until all his enemies are put under his feet . . . Because he has subjected everything to him . . . When everything has become subject to him, the Son himself will become subject, in turn, to him who subjected everything to him, so that God may be all in all " (1 Cor. 15:24–28).

32" I tell you truly: this generation will not pass, until all this has taken place. 33Heaven and earth will pass, but my words will not pass."

Though the time between the ascension and Jesus' second coming may be long, this generation, the human race, will experience everything that the full achievement of the divine plan of salvation involves, the Son of man's appearing, the final deliverance, and the definitive inauguration of God's kingdom. All this will take place without the slightest doubt. What Jesus states so definitely is not meant to indicate a date; it is meant to assure us that his prophecy will be fulfilled. If he refers to the human race as this generation, it is intended to remind us that men are evil and cannot hope to endure God's sentence of themselves. They need to remind themselves that the end of the world will come. Eschatological preaching always involves an appeal for repentance.

It may often seem as if God's promises were merely fine words. The faithful of every age have complained that God was slow in coming to their help. With this, the greatest of his promises, it could scarcely be otherwise. Patience and endurance are difficult when there seems to be no end to a person's wait. The trustworthiness of Jesus' promise is there, to counteract any semblance of untrustworthiness on God's part. The universe which seems eternal will pass; Jesus' words will never lose their force. The end of time will come, and this throws light on our present life. When it will come makes no difference; but we cannot be indifferent to the fact that it is coming.

BE SOBER AND KEEP WATCH (21:34–36)

³⁴"Attend to yourselves, that your hearts may not become dulled by intemperance and drunkenness and the cares of life, so that day takes you unawares ³⁵like a trap. It will come upon all those who live on the face of the earth."

The Son of man is coming, even though those who had expected that he would come soon were disappointed and the moment of his coming is delayed. We cannot afford to imitate the unfaithful servant who said in his heart: " My lord is taking his time about coming " (12:45). He will come suddenly, without warning, swift as the springing of a trap in which the unsuspecting and overconfident bird is caught. People need to attend to themselves. The day on which the Lord comes will be a day of judgment (17:31). It is then that man's final destiny will be sealed. It is both a day of judgment and a day of deliverance. Everyone must be ready for it.

Intemperance and drunkenness dull a person's heart to the thought of what is to come; exaggerated care about food or drink prevents a person from seeing what awaits him clearly. It is from the heart that a person's moral and religious decisions come, and he must not close his heart to the final events. A man who is interested only in enjoying his earthly life has neither the time nor the desire to think of " that day." " The night is well on its course and the day is near. Let us put away the works of darkness and put on the weapons of light. Let us live honorably as in the day, not in feasting and drinking bouts, not in lust and dissoluteness, not in disputes and jealousies " (Rom. 13:12f.).

The day of judgment will come upon all the inhabitants of the earth. It will affect all those who live on the face of the earth. The words seem unnecessarily repetitious but they arouse our attention. These were the words Jeremiah used to proclaim the universality of the judgment: " See, I am beginning by punishing the city which bears my own name, and shall you, then, go free? No, you will not remain unpunished. I am summoning a sword against all those who live on the earth " (Jer. 25:29). A Christian cannot afford to say: " I am Christ's disciple. This day cannot do me any harm." The sentence inflicted on Jerusalem is a warning that the world, too, will be sentenced.

[36]" *Be alert, therefore, and pray at all times that you may have the strength to escape all that is coming and stand fast in the Son of man's presence."*

The Son of man is coming; of that there can be no doubt. When he comes, he will settle accounts with his servants, both true and faithless (12:41–48). He will demand an account from those who multiplied the pound entrusted to them, and also from those who kept it safe without putting it to any use (19:12–27). A Christian must be alert; he must be ready to welcome the Lord. The Son of man is coming but no one knows the day or the moment when he will come. " Keep watch, then, you do not know the day when the Lord will come " (Mt. 24:42). Christ's disciple is aware of the decisive events which are to come; he cannot give in to drowsiness. His whole life will be guided by the need to keep awake for the Lord and be prepared for his coming. The exhortation to be ready is one of the most basic and most characteristic elements of the message Jesus preached.

Watching is associated with praying: the man who prays is awake for God; anyone who keeps a religious watch will devote himself to prayer. " Pray always in the Spirit, with every kind of prayer and entreaty. Keep awake for this with all perseverance "

(Eph. 6:18). It is necessary to pray at all times; no one knows the day or the moment when the Lord will come. The early church associated watching and praying with the celebration of the eucharistic meal: " Preserve in prayer. Keep watch in it at the Eucharist " (Col. 4:2). This exhortation combines the three things: praying, watching, and the eucharistic meal. The celebration of Christian worship in the form of a vigil was an expression of Christian watchfulness. Vigils were an imitation of what Christ himself had done when he celebrated the Paschal feast (22:15).

Christ is coming as a judge. Will we escape all that is coming, including the sentence of condemnation? Will we be able to stand fast in the Son of man's presence? Will we find in him an all-powerful advocate? Watching and praying will enable us to escape the threatening sentence of condemnation and stand fast before the judge.

The last discourse Jesus pronounced before the people in the temple was at an end. Its last word was: " The Son of man." He went on to his passion, but he will return as the Son of man. The last words he spoke before the Jewish council were: " From now on, the Son of man will sit at the right hand of God's power " (22:69). Jesus' coming as the Son of man to whom God has given all power will be a sign that the claim he made was just, that the message he preached was true, and that the promises and threats he made will be kept. His way led from the people in the temple and from his enemies in the council to his passion and death; but this led him to the Son of man's glory. The Son of man has the last word.

The Last Days of Jesus' Ministry (21:37–38)

37During the day, he taught in the temple, but at night he went out and spent the night on the Mount of Olives as it is called. 38And all the people used to come early to him in the temple, to listen to him.

St. Luke's account of Jesus' ministry in Jerusalem is framed between two similar verses (see 19:47f.). Jesus finished what he had begun. Nothing could come between him and his ministry. He was teaching—day by day—in the temple. Teaching was his work. He was always active and never stopped. By his teaching, he made the temple God's dwelling place among his people, where he could bring them salvation.

Jesus spent the nights outside the city on the Mount of Olives. The earlier passage about his ministry in the temple was followed by the words: " The chief priests and the scribes, together with the leaders of the people, tried to destroy him " (19:47). He spent the nights outside the city to escape his enemies. His ministry was accomplished in the face of opposition from those who wielded power; the darkness was closing in. The time had not yet come in which Jesus was handed over to those who wielded power, in accordance with his Father's will.

The people stood by Jesus, all the people. Once more the ordinary people appear as the people of God. The future church was visible in them. " They adhere to Jesus, listening to him." They were to be found in his presence in the early morning listening to him, joyfully and perseveringly. The new people of God centers around Jesus; they adhere to him; they are guided by his teaching. They are to be found in his presence, listening to his message. And all this despite the hostility of those in authority against Jesus!

THROUGH SUFFERING TO GLORY (22:1—24:53)

The church's situation in the world is marked by persecution. How can it stand firm? Only in the power of the way Jesus followed through his passion and death to glory. Jesus is present to his church in the new paschal meal which he bequeathed to it as a legacy (22:1-38). He is its model in its martyrdom, before the Jewish and pagan tribunals, on the way to death, and in his death (23). As the risen and glorified Lord, he remains close to it (24).

The Paschal Meal (22:1–38)

The Great Moment Approaches (22:1–13)

JUDAS BETRAYS HIM (22:1–6)

¹The feast of the unleavened bread, the paschal feast as it is called, was approaching.

Together with Pentecost and the feast of tabernacles, the feast of the unleavened bread, the paschal feast as it is called, was one of the three pilgrimage-feasts and a high point of the liturgical year. It recalled the greatest event of Jewish history, the exodus from Egypt. Then God punished Egypt and spared his people (Ex. 12:26f.). The recollection of their liberation from Egypt kept the hope of future deliverance alive. Consequently, it frequently happened that political movements sprang to life at the time of the paschal feast (13:1ff.) and religious passions were enflamed (Acts 12:1-4). The Jews expected their future liberation to come from the Messiah. It was thought that he would come on the night of a paschal feast. At the most important stages of Israel's history, there was a vivid awareness of the significance of this feast, with its memory of their deliverance and of the exodus which was actualized in the yearly paschal celebration. This was true of their stay in the wilderness of Sinai (Num. 9) and the invasion of Canaan (Josh. 5); of the time of the reform of Hezekiah in 716 B.C. (2 Chron. 30) and of Josiah in 622 B.C. (2 Kings 23:21ff.). It was also true of the period of the restoration after the exile, about the year 515 B.C. (Ezra. 6:19–22). The return from the exile is described by Deutero-Isaiah as a new exodus (see Is. 63:7—64:11), while gathering together those who were dispersed (Is. 49:6) is regarded as the specific task of the suffering servant (Is. 53:7). Together with the paschal lamb, the servant of Yahweh was intended to serve as a type of the Messiah who was to come. Now salvation history was about to reach its climax.

The events which the evangelist is about to describe give the old paschal feast a new content and meaning. A new exodus from the land of slavery and a new entrance into the promised land is beginning. Christ himself is the paschal lamb (1 Cor. 5:7). Those who have received baptism are like the people of God who were delivered by the blood of an immaculate and untarnished lamb and then set out on their journey with their loins girded (1 Pet. 1:13–21). The old paschal meal was transformed into the eucharistic meal which looks forward to the eschatological feast of salvation. The midst of time has come.

Since the days of the apostles, the church has celebrated a Christian Pasch every year. The paschal celebration of the early church took place at the same time as the Jewish ceremonies. The Jews had expected that the Messiah would come on the night of a paschal feast; in the early Christian paschal feast, Christ's second coming formed the center of the celebrations. Instead of the Jewish paschal meal, Christians kept a vigil. They fasted and read the account of the exodus (Ex. 12), referring the paschal lamb to Christ. At cock crow they celebrated the sacred meal which united them with the Lord. The whole mystery of the redemption is summed up in the idea of death and resurrection. The paschal celebration was, of course, an intensified and solemn form of the eucharistic celebration which characterized Sunday, the Lord's day. Sunday is a miniature Easter feast. It was from the story of Christ's passion and resurrection that the Christian celebration of Sunday and Easter originated. The way St. Luke wrote his account was influenced by the way Christians celebrated the Pasch. The words: " It was the day of unleavened bread, the paschal feast as it is called," throw light on everything St. Luke says, and it is in this light that what he said must be understood.

2And the chief priests and scribes tried to find some way of doing away with him; they were afraid of the people.

The drama of Jesus' death was beginning. The powers behind it were the chief priests and the scribes. It had been decided that Jesus would have to be destroyed. The only thing which prevented them from resorting to open violence was the people; ever since the day of his entry into Jerusalem the people had constantly given fresh proof of their attachment to Jesus. All attempts to drive a wedge between Jesus and the people had failed. So his enemies were forced to think how Jesus could be killed without arousing the people.

From the beginning of Jesus' ministry, the people gave his message their allegiance; they were hungry for salvation (6:17). They listened to his words (7:1) and acknowledged that Jesus was a great prophet through whom God visited his people with his grace (7:16). When Jesus cured the blind man, they praised God (18:43). Even when the leaders of Israel came out against Jesus, the crowd adhered to him and listened to him (19:49). The attitude of the people was such that the members of the Sanhedrin dared not attack him openly. They feared the people, and were afraid they might stone them in a fit of rage if they questioned the Baptist's God-given mission (20:6). The people grasped the significance of Jesus' ministry. This makes it all the more frightening that their own shepherds should have deprived them of their true shepherd and saviour (Mt. 9:36).

³But then Satan entered Judas who was called Iscariot and was one of the twelve. ⁴He went and discussed with the chief priests and the temple officers how he could hand him over to them. ⁵They were delighted and made an agreement with him to give him money. ⁶He agreed and looked for a favorable opportunity to betray him, away from the people.

After the temptation in the desert, the devil left Jesus, until the time appointed by God (4:13). Now the time during which Satan's power was bound was over, and power was given to him once more. The passion bears the stamp of Satan's influence. Judas, the man from Carioth, was his instrument; his place of birth distinguishes him from the other apostle of the same name who was also called Thaddaeus (Lebbaeus).

Judas was one of the number of the twelve (6:16), one of Jesus' intimate companions. He had been initiated into his way of life, and now he was to be used to promote the schemes of his enemies. He was one of the circle of those who were closest to Jesus, whom he had chosen for himself; this is a deep mystery certainly. He belonged to the patriarchs of the new people of God, and had been chosen after Jesus had spent a whole night praying (6:13). This could easily be a stumbling block for the faith. St. Luke explains this mystery as the work of Satan who leads men astray and is God's great opponent.

Parties to the agreement with Judas were the chief priests and the temple officers who had charge of the temple guard. From the moment Jesus entered Jerusalem as the Messiah and purified the temple of the trading which dishonored it, the priestly aristocracy were hostile to him; the heads of the supreme authority among the Jews were against him. The chief priests and the temple officers were also in the forefront of the struggle against the infant church in Jerusalem (Acts 4:1—5:24).

How could Jesus be delivered up to the Jewish authorities away from the mass of the people? The agreement they made with Judas was intended to solve this problem. The decision to put him to death could be carried out; there was no need to fear the people any more. " They were delighted." When Jesus was born, the angel said: " I announce a great joy to you . . . Today the saviour has been born to you " (2:10f.). As the scheme to kill him was about to be put into execution, we are told: " They were delighted." God's joy is not man's joy.

A contract was made with Judas. " They made an agreement with him." Judas would betray Jesus, and he would receive a sum of money. His avarice exposed Judas to the danger of turning traitor (Jn. 12:6). It drove him to the infamy of making a profession of treachery. "Avarice is the root of all evil. Many people have given themselves up to it and have abandoned the faith. They have exposed themselves to many bitter torments " (1 Tim. 6:10).

The traitor went about his task in the service of those who had commissioned him with cool deliberation. He looked for a favorable opportunity. Judas was under Satan's influence, but he acted deliberately and on his own responsibility. His plotting marked the beginning of the story of the passion, but it also marked the beginning of the church. The key word is " to give up." Judas gave up Jesus to the Jewish authorities (22:4, 6, 21f., 48); the Sanhedrin gave him up to Pilate (24:20; see 18:32); Pilate gave him up to the Jewish crowd (23:25). He was given up to the soldiers to be executed (Mk. 15:15). Like Jesus his disciples will be given up to courts of justice by their closest friends (21:12). St. Paul was given up to the gentiles (Acts 21:11; 28:17). This phrase outlines the whole history of the passion and its explanation. Jesus was given up for our sins (Rom. 4:25). This giving up was not merely something accomplished by human agents; ultimately, it was God himself who gave him up, as he planned and executed our salvation. Christ's passion was the work of men who were under Satan's influence, but it accomplished God's plan of salvation.

PREPARATIONS FOR THE PASCHAL MEAL (22:7–13)

⁷The day of unleavened bread came, on which the paschal lamb had to be killed. ⁸He sent Peter and John on an errand, telling them: "Go and prepare the paschal meal for us to eat." ⁹But they asked him: "Where do you want us to prepare it?" ¹⁰He said to them: "See, when you enter the city you will meet a man carrying a jar of water. Follow him into the house he enters. ¹¹And say to the owner of the house: ' The Master told us to ask you: " Where is the room where I can eat the paschal meal with the disciples?" ' ¹²He will show you a large upper room furnished with couches. Prepare it there." ¹³They set out and found everything as he had told them.

The ritual for the feast prescribed that the paschal lamb should be killed on the first day. This was done in the temple after the evening sacrifice (about 2:30 p.m.). It was then eaten at the festive paschal meal in the evening. The meal St. Luke is about to describe must be seen in the light of the paschal celebration.

Jesus took the initiative, which corrects the impression given by St. Mark (Mk. 14:12), and sends the disciples to prepare everything they needed for the paschal meal. He arranged this meal and made it possible for them to hold it in virtue of his apostolic authority. He would also give the Old Testament Pasch a new meaning.

The apostles sent were Peter and John. After Pentecost, they were the most active of the apostles. They had a special part to play in the foundation of the church, in its proclamation of the word, and in the celebration of the sacred meal.

The paschal meal had to be eaten within the walls of the city. Every house in Jerusalem was under obligation to put any rooms which were available at the disposal of pilgrims who wanted to celebrate the feast there. In return, the owner of the house received the skin of the lamb. Before his entry into Jerusalem, the Messiah knew where a mount could be found on which he could make his entry and he disposed of it with full authority. In the same way, he knew where there was a room ready for his paschal celebration, and he claimed it for himself authoritatively. The paschal meal which was being prepared was bathed in the light of Jesus' authority and the knowledge he had of the future.

The room he chose for the meal was an upper room, the room normally reserved for guests. It was furnished for the feast. The paschal meal was eaten reclining on couches, in the attitude of free men, not like slaves. The festival atmosphere was an expression of joy at their deliverance. Upper rooms, decorated with bright lights, remained the place where the early church celebrated the new paschal rite (Acts 20 : 6f.).

The Meal (22:14–20)

St. Luke gives us here an artistic diptych in which the Christian Pasch (vv. 19-20) is contrasted with the Jewish rite (vv. 14-18). The paschal lamb and the cup of the old rite give way to the bread and wine of the new rite.

THE OLD PASCH (20:14–18)

[14]*And when the time came, he reclined at the table and the apostles with him.*

The time fixed by the law for the paschal meal was the period immediately after sunset (Ex. 12:8). This time had come. This was also the time fixed by God's will for Jesus' passion and glorification to begin. Christ left the world when this time came. He acted of his own free choice and in obedience to the Father.

The old rubric according to which the paschal meal had to be eaten hastily and in a state of readiness to leave on a journey was no longer observed. The meal had taken the form of a Greek festive banquet. The twelve apostles (6:13) were Jesus' companions at table. Together with him they formed one community. Not less than ten and not more than twenty persons had to be present for the paschal meal. In this community, Jesus took the place of the father of the house. As they celebrated the paschal meal, the Lord was present; he was the centre of the company.

15He said to them: " I have longed with great longing to eat this paschal meal with you before I suffer. 16I tell you: I shall never eat it again until it finds its full realization in God's kingdom."

St. Luke describes the old paschal meal with its essential elements, the paschal lamb and the wine-cup, in just a few words. The picture he gives of it is influenced by the celebration of the Christian Eucharist.

The ritual paschal meal of the Jews which, according to St. Luke's brief indications, Jesus celebrated followed a strict pattern. The father of the house opened the celebration with an expression of praise for the feast day. Then he took a cup of wine and pronounced a blessing over it: " May you be praised, Yahweh, our God, King of the world. You created the fruit of the vine." The wine in this first cup was then drunk. The participants washed their right hands and ate the first course. The first dish was made up of bitter herbs dipped in a strongly spiced sauce. This was chewed meditatively. A second cup was poured and placed on the table without being drunk immediately. The son then asked the father of the house how it was that this night differed from every other night in the customs observed at table. At that, the father gave him a lesson on the meaning of the paschal celebration and the significance of the various foods (the " Paschahaggada "). These words of explanation had to include a reference to the Passover (" because God passed over our fathers' houses in Egypt "), the unleavened bread (" because they were delivered so quickly that the dough did not have time to be leavened "), and the bitter herbs (" because the Egyptians had made the lives of our fathers in Egypt very bitter "). After these words, the first part of the Hallel was sung (Ps. 113f.). This ended with the paschal hymn: " As Israel went out of Egypt, the people of Jacob from an alien race, Judah became his sanctuary and Israel his domain " (Ps. 114:1f.). Then the second cup was drunk. They washed their hands once more and the main course began. The father of the house took the un-leavened bread and pronounced a blessing over it: " May you be praised, Yahweh, our God, King of the world. You make the earth produce bread." Then he broke the bread and gave the pieces to those present who ate them with bitter herbs and stewed fruit. Then the paschal lamb was eaten. When the meal was ended the father of the house said a prayer of thanksgiving for the meal over the third cup (" the cup of blessing "). This was an expression of hope for the coming of the Messiah: " Oh Lord our God, our eyes are turned towards you. You are God, the King of mercy and grace. The Merciful One! May his royal dominion be always and ever upon us. The Merciful One! May he send us the prophet Elijah, to bring us the gospel, to bring us help and comfort. The Merciful One! May he honor us with the days of the Messiah and the life of the world to come, he who magnifies his King's salvation and shows favor to his Anointed, to David and his descendants for-ever." When this cup had been drunk, the second part of the Hallel was sung (Ps. 114 [115]—118). This includes the words: " Death's cords bound me. The fear of the realm of the dead filled me. I felt afraid and distressed. Then I invoked the Lord's name: 'Lord, save my life.' The Lord is full of kindness and justice; our God is full of mercy. The Lord protects the simple; when I was weak, he saved me . . . How shall I repay the Lord for the way he saved me? I will take up the cup of salvation. I will invoke the Lord's name " (Ps. 116:3–6, 12f.).

The paschal meal was about to receive a further consecration which would give it its true meaning. Jesus had longed for it with great longing. The hour which he always had before his eyes in the course of his ministry had now come: " I have come to cast fire on the earth, and what do I wish other than that it should be kindled already. But I have to receive a baptism, and how oppressed I am until it is accomplished!" (12:49f.). " See, I will cast out devils and heal the sick today and tomorrow, but on the third day I will come to my end " (13:32). Jesus' mission would be accomplished only when he had met his death. The Last Supper marked the beginning of his passion and his glory; it prepared the way for the sacrament of baptism and the descent of the Holy Spirit. Easter, Pentecost, and the last things all combine to shed light on Jesus' death. His death brought salvation to the many. The early church celebrated the eucharistic meal in an atmosphere charged with eschatological hope (Acts 2:46). The meal Jesus was preparing to share with his followers, the twelve who were with him, was a farewell meal. His words referred to the proximity of his death: " Before I suffer." The recollection of this farewell meal remains bound up with the thought of Jesus' death.

As always, Jesus looks beyond the present to God's kingdom. For him, death is not the end. The present with its encroaching darkness is placed firmly in the light of the future. Eating the paschal lamb aroused the hope that the Messiah would come and that the participants would share in the life of the future world. This prophecy, too, was now being fulfilled. It is fulfilled first of all in the church, in the eucharistic meal; it will receive its definitive fulfillment when Christians share in God's supreme dominion, which is symbolized by a meal (22:30).

17And he took a cup, pronounced the thanksgiving prayer, and said: " Take this and share it among you. 18I tell you: from now, I will never drink of the fruit of the vine again until God's kingdom comes."

When the paschal lamb had been eaten, everyone drank from the " cup of blessing." This was connected with the thanksgiving prayer. Jesus handed the cup to his companions and invited them to drink. He did not drink himself; otherwise there would have been no need to tell them to drink. When the father of the house drank, it was a sign to the others to drink, too. Together with the cup, Jesus offered his companions joy and a blessing.

The drinking cup, too, looked beyond the present moment. Jesus would drink it anew. His death was followed by glory in God's kingdom. In the early church, people used to recall Jesus' two sayings over the paschal lamb and the drinking cup when they gathered for a meal in the Lord's absence. The Lord's saying kept the hope alive that God's kingdom would come, and that those who hoped would share in the meal of which Jesus had spoken.

Seen in the light of the words Jesus spoke over the old Pasch, the new food and drink he was about to give his disciples must be regarded as the Lord's parting gift, as he went to his death. They are a feast to commemorate the new deliverance; a meal shared with the risen Lord; a promise of new life, of a new and final banquet, in God's kingdom.

THE EUCHARISTIC MEAL (22:19–20)

19And he took bread and pronounced the thanksgiving prayer. He broke it and gave it to them, saying: " This is my body which will

178

be given up for you. Do this in memory of me." [20]*He did the same with the chalice, after the meal, saying: " This chalice is the new covenant in my blood which will be shed for you."*

The new Pasch was being instituted. Jesus' body takes the place of the paschal lamb; the chalice with his blood takes the place of the paschal cup filled with wine. However, not every trace of the old Pasch was blotted out. The words: " He gave thanks," and: " after the meal," remain like isolated boulders left from a former age. After the paschal lamb had been eaten, Jesus used the third drinking cup, the " cup of blessing " (1 Cor. 10:16), to present his new gift. The thanksgiving is mentioned at the beginning of the eucharistic meal although, historically, its place was before this cup was drunk. The word " thanksgiving " is a sort of title set over the whole description. The paschal meal as Jesus renewed it is the great thanksgiving the church offers with Christ, the " Eucharist." All this makes it clear that the account of the institution of the eucharistic meal was not intended to be an exact historical account of what took place at the Last Supper. On the contrary, St. Luke relates the events in such a way that his account could serve as a norm and an indication how Christians should celebrate the sacred meal. The rite they followed had its source in Jesus (see 1 Cor. 11:23).

Jesus is the center of the new Pasch. It is from him that the gift, the rite, and the message it involves, come. Rising from the couch, he took the bread into his hands; he spoke the formula of blessing, broke the bread, and shared it with those who were present. He did the same with the chalice which was filled with red wine mixed with water. The words he spoke as an accompaniment to the rite explained what his gifts were. They presented them as a saving gift which was rooted in his death.

The gift Jesus gave his disciples was his body and his blood. The body was his living body, himself; the blood was the source of life, his life, his own self. By means of the two gifts, his body and blood

179

were presented as separate entities. In this way, they alluded to his death. Jesus gave himself to his disciples as a memento of his death. " As often as you eat this bread and drink the chalice, you announce the Lord's death until he comes " (1 Cor. 11 : 26).

The words with which Jesus inaugurated the meal filled the whole evening with the thought of his violent death. The gifts he gave were his body which would be given up, and his blood which would be shed in death. Jesus took this death upon himself on behalf of the disciples to whom he gave these gifts. His body would be broken and given up—for you; his blood would be shed—for you. Jesus' death would benefit them; it would be a saving death for them. By his death, a martyr wins grace and the remission of sins for the people. Because of his atoning death, divine providence comes to Israel's aid in its affliction. In the same way, Jesus won reconciliation and forgiveness by his death. His death is an atoning death, a martyr's death. His blood brings reconciliation (Lev. 17 : 11).

The words " for you " are addressed to the disciples to whom Jesus gave his body and blood. These words apply to the disciples what the atoning death of the servant of Yahweh would confer on the many. The suffering servant was a man of sorrows; he was familiar with suffering (Is. 52 : 3). He bore our sufferings, and took our sorrows on himself. It was for our sins that he was wounded, for our wickedness that he was bruised. He was punished to bring us salvation; by his weals we were saved. The Lord laid on him the guilt of all our sins (Is. 53 : 4–6). Jesus is the servant of Yahweh who offers himself as a sacrifice of atonement for men. His death is a sacrificial death of atonement.

The chalice Jesus gave his disciples was " the new covenant in my blood." It contained the blood which would be poured out to seal the new covenant. The old covenant God made with his people on Mount Sinai had been abrogated, because the people of God had been unfaithful. But God is faithful and merciful, and he promised his people forgiveness and a new divine economy: " See, the time is coming when I will make a new covenant with the house of Israel and the house of Judah. It will not be like the covenant I made with their fathers, when I took them by the hand to lead them out of Egypt, a covenant which they broke, although I was their Lord. No, this will be the covenant I will make with the house of Israel in those days; I will put my law in their hearts and inscribe it on their souls. So I will be their God, and they shall be my people. No longer will they teach one another, saying: ' Recognize the Lord,' because they will all know me, from the least to the greatest. I will forgive them their guilt; I will not remember their sins any more " (Jer. 31 : 31–34). In his blood, Jesus confers on his disciples the blessings of the new divine dispensation; he gives them a foretaste of the salvation that is to come, intimate fellowship with God, reconcilation with him, and the forgiveness of sins.

By means of the cup of salvation, Jesus showed that he was the mediator of the new covenant. Through him, the servant of Yahweh who interceded for the many and atoned for their sins with the sacrifice of his life, the new divine economy was inaugurated: " I, the Lord, summoned you in my goodness. I took you by the hand and watched over you. I made you the mediator of the covenant for the people, a light for the gentiles, to open the eyes of the blind, to lead prisoners out from captivity, and those who sit in darkness from their dungeons " (Is. 42:6f.). "At the time of grace, I listened to you. On the day of salvation, I came to your aid. I protected you and made you the mediator of the covenant for the people, to restore the land, to divide up hereditary land that is waste, to tell those who are in captivity: ' Come out,' and those who live in darkness: ' Come to the light.' They will graze on the roads, and find pasture on the bare hill tops. They will not be hungry or thirsty; the scorching wind and the sun will not touch them. The one who has pity on them will be their leader; he will make them take their rest by springs of water. Shout for joy, heaven! Be jubilant, oh earth! You mountains break into a cry of joy. For the Lord has brought his people comfort. He has taken pity on the poor among them " (Is. 49:8–13). The message Jesus preached in Nazareth at the beginning of his ministry finds its fulfillment and its completion in the holy meal (4:17–20). What he proclaimed by his word was accomplished in his body and blood and is given to us in this meal.

Jesus was not content merely to give expression to the saving power of his death; he gave it to his disciples when he gave them his flesh and his blood as their food: " He broke the bread and gave it to them." He did the same with the cup. The saving effect of his death is no longer appropriated by faith alone; it is appropriated by receiving this food and drink into one's body. Great as it is, the symbolism of bread and wine can never be sufficient in itself to express all that the Eucharist contains. " The giving of the bread and wine which is emphasized so strongly needs to be understood in the most realistic sense possible." Jesus performs this act of giving in the shadow of the paschal meal. The paschal lamb was eaten after it had been sacrificed; the sacrifice was followed by a sacrificial meal (Ex. 24:11).

Jesus accompanied his words over the bread with a command to repeat the rite: " Do this in memory of me." This also applied to the chalice (1 Cor. 11:24f.). Jesus' disciples were to " do " the whole rite of the evening meal as he had performed it in bread and wine in memory of him. Whenever they did this, Jesus himself would be present, he who establishes the new divine economy in power by his death. The old paschal meal, too, was more than a mere memorial rite accomplished in the context of a family celebration. In it, God's saving action in the past, in the exodus, became present as a source of grace for those who shared the meal. At the same time, it was the basis of their hope that they would also share in the salvation which was to come. Each individual was meant to feel personally involved in Israel's deliverance. " In every age, a man is bound to look on himself as having escaped from Egypt. Consequently, we are bound to thank, to praise, and to acclaim . . . him who accomplished these marvels for our fathers and for all of us. He led us out of slavery to freedom, out of sorrow to joy, out of mourning to a feast day, out of darkness to a great light, and out of subjection to the yoke of deliverance. We will sing Alleluia in his presence."

This was the way the Jews felt when the memory of the Passover was being celebrated. This was also the way Jesus' disciples felt at the farewell meal which the Lord placed in the light of the paschal meal. The new Pasch Jesus instituted was in no way inferior to the old. His saving action is present when this meal is celebrated in memory of him. The commission Jesus gave his apostles to repeat this meal is the source of the church's life and strength; it is the law which inspires its conduct. Jesus accomplished the Pasch, the Passover from the cross to the resurrection, in his own person. In the Eucharist, he makes all those who receive this bread and wine in a spirit of faith pass over in an ever greater measure from the death of sin to his new life.

A Farewell Discourse (22:21-38)

Various parting words of Jesus which are based on traditional material are included in the account of the meal. Greek, Old Testament, and Jewish literature contain similar last words of famous men. Plato wrote Socrates' spiritual testament in the form of a farewell discourse. The book of Deuteronomy reads very much like Moses' last will and testament. The book of Tobit contains a number of exhortations addressed by Tobit's dying father to his son. Jesus' farewell discourse as it is recorded by St. Luke and St. John forms part of the same literary tradition.

Four verbal compositions occur here which are arranged with rigid fidelity to the laws of style: the prophecy concerning the traitor (vv. 21-23), an exhortation and a promise for the apostles (vv. 24-30), the prophecy of St Peter's fall (vv. 31-34) and, finally, a further exhortation and promise for the disciples (vv. 35-38). Jesus has a word for the first and the last in the list of the apostles, and for all the apostles together. In the twelve who were present at the Last Supper, the church sees itself, as it assembles to carry out the Lord's command. The golden age of Jesus' life on earth provides the church with a norm for its future worship.

The Traitor (22:21–23)

21" *Yet, see, the hand of the man who is betraying me is with me on the table."*

The discourse concerning the great legacy of the Eucharist breaks off (" Yet "). Something unexpected and incomprehensible is about to be said (" see "): one of those who shared the meal with him was about to betray Jesus to his enemies and give him up. Despite this infidelity, the Lord did not allow himself to be offended to such an extent that he refused to bequeath to the church the legacy in which he makes his saving action present. " In the night on which the Lord Jesus was given up, he took bread " (1 Cor. 11:23). This was the way the oldest account of the institution began. St. Paul reminds the church in Corinth of it to prevent them from tolerating behavior in their midst which was incompatible with the memory of Jesus' death.

Sitting at table with a person is a sign of a common fellowship of loyalty and friendship. David complains about his unfaithful table companion: " Even my closest friend, upon whom I relied, who took bread with me, lifts his heel against me " (Ps. 41 [40] :10). There is an echo of this complaint in Jesus' words. Everything that happens to Jesus is part of God's design which is expressed in the words of scripture. Sharing Jesus' meal, which occurs also in the celebration of the Eucharist, involves an obligation of fidelity to the Lord of the meal who is Jesus himself. Apostasy from the church means violating one's loyalty to the Lord and to those who sit in his company at his table.

²²" The Son of man, indeed, goes his way as it is decreed for him. But it will be too bad for the man by whom he is being betrayed."

Jesus knew who his betrayer was; he was not surprised. Judas was about to give him up. But this betrayal was only a superficial element in the story of his passion and death. It was God who fitted this betrayal by one of those who were with him into his life and decreed it beforehand. This was part of Jesus' mission. He was the Son of man who must pass through suffering and death to glory. He is now seated at the right hand of God's power as a reward for his obedience (22:69).

God's decree did not relieve the traitor of his responsibility. It will be too bad for that man. This threatening woe announced Judas' reprobation at the judgment. The Son of man is a judge. In the face of Jesus' word, all efforts to excuse Judas are in vain. Sharing Jesus' table and being his disciple do not of themselves guarantee salvation. Jesus demands a personal decision in favor of his word and his person (13:26f.). The memory of the Lord, fidelity and salvation, infidelity and the sentence of condemnation, are all connected (1 Cor. 11:23-24). The celebration of the Eucharist confronts us with a number of personal choices.

²³And they began to argue with one another which of them it might be who would do this.

Their astonished argument and their questions underlined the abominable character of Judas' treachery. It was something inconceivable; the faithful disciples were horrified. In their questioning, the disciples examined themselves. Anyone who partakes of the eucharistic meal must examine himself: "A man should examine himself and then eat of the bread and drink from the chalice. Anyone who eats and drinks unworthily, eats and drinks judgment for himself. He makes no distinction between the body of the Lord [and ordinary food] " (1 Cor. 11:28). " What is holy is reserved to those who are holy."

A DISPUTE CONCERNING PRECEDENCE (22:24–30)

²⁴*But a dispute also arose among them about which of them was to be regarded as the greatest.* ²⁵*And he said to them: " The kings of the gentiles dominate them, and those who use violence against them insist on being called benefactors.* ²⁶*But you are not to be like that: the greatest among you must become like the youngest; he who leads must be like one who serves."*

The disciples' dispute about precedence took place in the context of the Last Supper; it had reference to the Son of man's departure, and it occurred in the presence of his saving death. It is in the light of this event that it must be considered. Our whole life takes place in the light and power of Jesus' presence. It is influenced by his saving death and his work of atonement, by the Last Supper and the future banquet at the end of time.

The significance of precedence within the community of Jesus' disciples is very different from its significance among the unbelieving pagans. There, those who had power to deprive others of their power did so, so that none but they might have power, and they could rule absolutely. Ironically, these " rulers " insisted on being called " benefactors." Since Augustus, the Roman emperors bore the title: " Saviour and benefactor of the whole world." The urge to dominate is often disguised as friendship or philanthropy. A man's conscience can see almost instinctively what a just social order demands.

Rank and importance among Jesus' disciples demand that a man should serve others. The words: " Greatest " and " youngest," " leader " and " servant," imply a certain organization in the church. They refer to an order of precedence, a "hierarchy." Jesus did not plan his church without giving some of its members a place over others, and others a place under them. Those who enjoy rank and importance in the church must realize that they are servants, not masters. God's sovereign rule is beginning. All standards based on a human norm are reversed; man's whole scale of values is altered.

27"Who is greater, he who reclines at table, or the servant? Is it not he who reclines at table? But I am like a servant in your midst."

At the Last Supper, Jesus himself was a servant. Like the faithful steward, he gave his disciples food at the appointed time (12:42). He gave himself as their food and drink; he went to death for his disciples, and became "a ransom for the many" (Mk. 10:45). He promised that at the future eschatological meal he would gird himself and make his disciples who had kept watch for his coming recline at table while he served them (12:37). It is Jesus who is the Lord of this meal; it is he who provides it. Yet by an extraordinary reversal, he is also the servant who serves it.

In the church at Jerusalem, there was a time when the twelve waited on the tables of the poor (Acts 6:2). This service was then taken over by seven men on whom the apostles imposed hands in prayer (6:6). The leaders of the church, those who presided at the table, waited on the poor and needy at the common meal. In doing this, they may have been thinking of Jesus who told the apostles, at the miracle of the loaves and fishes in the desert: "You give them food to eat" (Mk. 6:37). He had them make ready for the meal and distribute it among the people (Mk. 6:39, 41). He sent Peter and John to prepare the Last Supper, and he spoke of the way he himself would wait on his disciples at the eschatological meal. A servant of God is also a servant of his fellow men.

The order observed in divine worship also became the order

which governs the church and the lives of Christians. The law of service binding on all those who enjoy authority, learning, talent, wealth, or influence, draws its obligation and its force from the eucharistic meal. The life of Christians in common bears the mark of this law, whether it is a question of a common meal, of the family community, of a community of work, of the community in the state, or of the community of nations. St. Paul exhorts the Christians at Philippi in the following words: "If, therefore, encouragement in Christ, if loving consolation, if fellowship in the Spirit, if sincere affection and sympathy [mean anything to you], fill up my joy by being unanimous in your outlook. You must not maintain a quarrelsome or vainglorious attitude. On the contrary, you should regard others as higher than yourselves in all humility. None of you should think only of his own interests; each of you must remember the interests of others as well. You should all have the attitude between yourselves which you [are bound to have] in Christ Jesus" (Phil. 2:1–5). Then he quotes an old eucharistic hymn which celebrates Jesus' emptying of himself in his incarnation and death and his life in the form of a slave (Phil. 2:6–11). In Christ, having power means serving others.

28" *It is you who have persevered with me in my trials.* 29*And, as my Father has appointed the kingdom for me, I appoint for you* 30*that you should eat and drink at my table in my kingdom, and that you should sit on thrones, judging the twelve tribes of Israel."*

At this farewell meal, Jesus looked back over his life. In the course of his ministry, he had met with inability to understand on the part of his disciples, with lack of faith and misunderstanding on the part of the people, with hatred and persecution on the part of the authorities. And now he was about to be rejected and put to death. All his life long, he had been a " sign which was contradicted " (2:34). On the mount of the transfiguration, Moses and Elijah, the great symbols of suffering in the Old Testament and the saviours of the people of God, had appeared together with him (9:30). With them as with all men of God, he shared a life of trials in his destiny of suffering. Why was it that God's great design and the mission he gave Jesus was manifested in powerlessness, and not in power? Why was God's sovereignty revealed in the helplessness of the suffering Christ who was persecuted and crucified? His disciples were scandalized at this, and it was for this reason that the people abandoned him. But the twelve stood fast and remained loyal to him, although they, too, shared in his trials. " After many of his followers had left him, Jesus asked the twelve: ' Do you, too, want to go?' But Peter said: ' To whom should we go? You have the words of eternal life ' " (Jn. 6:67).

The path of suffering Jesus trod ended in the glory of the kingdom his Father gave him. Jesus was aware of his Father's plan; he knew from scripture that he was to pass through suffering to glory (24:26) and that the Father had promised him the kingdom and supreme dominion, and appointed them for him. The bitter days of his passion would be followed by a festive meal, the symbol of God's sovereignty (14:15ff.); his rejection and destruction would be followed by his exaltation on a throne, the symbol of the authority he enjoyed as a king and a judge (Mt. 25:31). The apostles had stood by him in his time of trial, and so he makes a valid legal disposition whereby they will share in his glory. The words " with me " characterized their lives here on earth, and the same phrase would characterize their future. By his death, Jesus became the mediator of the covenant (*diatheke*); here he mediates (*diatithemai*) the reward God's covenant bestows when it is fully accomplished. Because of their loyal adherence to the crucified, the apostles will share Jesus' table in glory and be judges over the people of God.

As we celebrate the Eucharist, we look forward to the time when we will sit at Jesus' table and share his sovereignty. But we also recall that the kingdom which is to come will be given only to those who have followed Christ faithfully in their lives, despite the attacks made on their faith. These three things, the celebration of the Eucharist, following Christ in suffering, and sharing his sovereignty, are all connected by the words " with him." The eucharistic meal unites us with him; enduring his destiny of suffering should unite us with him; and the final event will give us a share in God's sovereignty with him. In an early Christian hymn which was probably sung during the celebration of the Eucharist, we read: " If we have died with him, we shall also live with him. If we persevere, we shall reign with him. If we disown him, he will also disown us. If we become unfaithful, he will remain faithful. He cannot disown himself " (2 Tim. 2:11ff.).

SIMON PETER (22:31–34)

³¹" *Simon, Simon, see, Satan has demanded to be able to sift you all like wheat.* ³²*But I prayed for you, that your faith may not fail. And you, when you have repented, must strengthen your brothers."*

Jesus' word is final; it cannot be shaken. By addressing Simon twice, he stresses the fact that his word can be trusted, even though what he is about to say may come as a terrible surprise (" see "). The temptation to fall away does not leave even the apostles untouched. Who, then, could imagine that he is secure?

Satan appears before God as the prosecutor of the human race. He acts as a " state attorney " on God's behalf. God recognized that Job was virtuous and a good man; he was a man who feared God and stayed far away from evil. But Satan said to God: " Does Job not have good reason to be God-fearing? Do you not cherish his house and all he has most carefully? Do you not bless the works of his hands? Just stretch out your hand to touch what is his! Perhaps then he will curse you to your face " (Job 1:8–11). Satan is an enemy of God's loving plan of salvation for Israel (Zech. 3:1–5).

He did not want to be absent from the scene, as Jesus was about to accomplish the plan he had made in his love for the new people of God. Satan's power was bound. He had to beg God to allow him to use his power.

Satan's attack was directed against the apostles. Their faith in Jesus must be shaken. He would sift them like wheat. Wheat was tossed in a sieve to separate the chaff from the corn; it was shaken from side to side and thrown about in every possible way. When the passion came, and Jesus and his disciples were given into Satan's power, his disciples would be exposed on all sides to violent temptations to fall away. Satan hoped that the disciples would fail, so that he could bring a charge against them before God. God does not take his apostles and his church out of persecutions and temptations. He does not take them out of the " world " (Jn. 17:15).

Jesus opposed Satan's efforts by his intercession; the power of his prayer brought Satan's plans to nothing. Jesus was his disciples' advocate. He prayed only for Peter, and not for the others, although all of them were to be sifted. Simon, therefore, was given a place apart among the twelve. He was the leader and he acted as spokesman for the twelve and for the early church (Acts 1—12). He was also to be the support of their faith. Jesus prayed that Peter's faith might not fail. It was not any human power, " flesh or blood," which revealed to him that Jesus was the Messiah (Mt. 16:17). In the same way, he stood firm in the faith, not by any human power, but by God's gift which Jesus won for him by his prayer. Jesus implored his Father that Peter would keep the faith, nothing more and nothing less. In the work of our salvation, it is faith in Jesus that is decisive. The church's faith is founded on the faith Peter showed.

The " privilege " Simon enjoyed by comparison with the other disciples was given to him for the others. It was given to him for his brothers, for Jesus' disciples, for the " brotherhood " of the church (Mt. 18:15–17), for the apostles and the faithful. Peter was to strengthen them by the word of faith, a word which comes from faith and leads to faith, when their faith was endangered. Jesus' cross which was Satan's work, and was fully exploited by him, could so easily become a stumbling block for the faithful.

Even Simon Peter would abandon the right road and disown the Lord. He would need to be converted; he was on the verge of falling away. Faith was all that he had left, because Jesus' prayer was heard. His faith led him to repentance and, once he was converted, it was his task to bring back the brothers to the faith, " lovingly and loyally " (2 Sam. 15 : 20). The leaders of the churches are bound to strengthen the brothers in the faith : " Have a care for yourselves and for the whole flock in which the Holy Spirit has appointed you bishops. You are to lead the churches, which he [Jesus] won for himself by his own blood. I know that when I am gone, ravenous wolves will force their way in among you. They will not spare the flock " (Acts 20 : 28). The obvious place for such exhortations must have been the liturgical assembly of the early church. The eucharistic meal demands the spoken word. Jesus intercedes for his church as its high priest and victim, but the leaders of the church must be prepared to undertake the responsibility for their brothers' faith. Jesus' parting words which were included in the account of the Last Supper indicate the rite for the celebration of the eucharistic meal in the Christian community. The Eucharist is part of the church's living organism.

³³But he said to him: " Lord, I am ready to go to prison or to death with you." ³⁴But he replied: " I tell you, Peter, the cock will not crow today until you have denied three times that you know me."

St. Peter could not bear the thought of having his loyalty questioned : " When you have been converted . . ." He protested, showing the reverence he felt for Jesus in the title " Lord." Jesus was the

Lord who had complete power to dispose of him. He declared his determination: "I am ready." He presumed on his strength and his fidelity and was prepared to risk the worst, prison and death. The sincerity of his love was revealed in the words "with you." But he had not listened to what Jesus was saying when he said that only his prayer would save him from falling into the abyss.

Jesus' prophecy revealed what would become of Peter's protestations of loyalty within a few hours after the great day had begun. He would deny three times that he knew the Lord. What was left then of all his protestations: Lord—with you—to death? Those who have to exhort others in the church can only do it in the full consciousness of their own weakness. "Brother, if anyone commits some fault, as one who is filled with the Spirit, you must carry him in a spirit of gentleness. In so doing, have a thought for yourself, so that you, too, may not be tempted" (Gal. 6:1). "The man who believes that he is standing firm must take care that he does not fall" (1 Cor. 10:12). Even the eucharistic meal does not make us secure against infidelity.

Peter was the first among the apostles. We find it hard to bear the realization that his worth as a human being was not in keeping with the position he held. St. Luke improved on the portrait of St. Peter which he found in Mark. According to Mark, Peter protested his fidelity twice, despite what Jesus had said; according to Luke, he did this only once. Mark writes: "You will disown me"; St. Luke writes: "You will deny that you know me." According to Mark, Peter placed himself above the other disciples; St. Luke suppresses this. Luke, but not Mark, makes St. Peter say that he was prepared to go to prison with the Lord, because he did go to prison later (Acts 12:3ff.). It is good for us to have St. Mark and to know from him that even Peter was extremely given to weakness, sin, and falling away. Only Jesus' prayer kept him safe. If the "triumphalism" found in the church is aware of this, it ceases to be real "triumphalism."

³⁵And he said to them: " When I sent you out without a purse or knapsack or sandals, did you want for anything? " They answered: " No." ³⁶Then he said to them: " But now, the man who has a purse must take it, and also a sack of provisions. Anyone who has not got a sword should sell his cloak and buy one."

Jesus had sent out the apostles in a state of poverty and powerlessness (10:4); yet they had not wanted for anything. God's " year of salvation " (4:19) assured them of security, of the people's affection and protection (8:2; 10:7). At that time, they came back from their mission rejoicing (10:17). But now times had changed; everything was different. The peace they had enjoyed in God's protection was at an end. The disciples' sheltered existence was a thing of the past. Now they must provide for themselves and arrange their own defense. No hospitable door would open to them. The disciples and the word they preached would meet with rejection; hostile encounters awaited them. The time of the church, as it is described in the Acts of the Apostles, was beginning. It began with Jesus' passion, in the shadow of which these words were pronounced. Now Satan was permitted to carry on his hostile activity. Jesus' apostle is exposed to temptations; he must struggle, and this struggle will last until the Son of man comes (21:28).

As the peace Jesus brought disappeared, the disciples' equipment took a different form. Now they would need a sword. They would need one so badly that they would have to sell even their most essential possession to buy it if they did not have one. A cloak in those days was something to clothe a man by day and cover him by night. This was a metaphor Jesus used to describe the time of crisis; it was not a call to struggle by force of arms, or to wage a messianic war such as the Zealots advocated. Jesus refused to allow himself to be defended with a sword (22:49ff.). In its time of difficulty and struggle, the church must arm itself with spiritual arms, with endurance and readiness to die, and with prayer. These are the weapons which it must acquire at any price.

³⁷" *For I tell you: the saying of scripture must be fulfilled in me: ' He was counted among the evildoers.' As far as I am concerned, the end is coming."* ³⁸*But they said: " Lord, see, here are two swords." And he said to them: " It is enough."*

Hostility towards the apostles followed on the rejection of Christ. They were persecuted because he was persecuted (Jn. 15:20). He was declared an evildoer and condemned as a criminal. He suffered the fate reserved for God's suffering servant (Is. 53:10), who did not struggle but bore his suffering patiently and so won through to victory. God's will which is revealed in scripture must be fulfilled in him. His passion was something decreed by God, not imposed by men. He accepted it as God's will, in a spirit of obedience. This prophecy looks forward, not only to his passion and death, but also to his victory—after a severe trial. Jesus' life was nearing its end. God's will, the commission God had given him, was fully accomplished. His life was being brought to its consummation; his taking up into heaven awaited him (Jn. 19:30).

The disciples did not understand Jesus' words. He had spoken of persecution and martyrdom; this made them think of a battle which would be fought with swords. Galileans used to carry daggers; they loved freedom and were fond of fighting. Their staccato way of speaking expressed their fierce determination and their fighting spirit. But what use would they be here?

The words with which Jesus broke off the conversation are mysterious. They are filled with the sorrow of one who is misunderstood and stands alone. They seem to be almost ironical. Yet to an even greater extent they bear the mark of Jesus' sadness at his disciples' failure to understand him and at the unhappy way things were about to turn out for his disciples. The path the Messiah had to tread led through suffering to glory; this is an impenetrable mystery. The prophet Isaiah alluded to this in his hymn concerning the suffering servant: " His appearance was inhumanly disfigured; his form was no longer like that of a man, so that he will fill many nations with amazement. Kings will seal their lips in his presence when they see what had never yet been told them, when they learn what they had never yet heard. Who gave credence to what we were told? To whom has the Lord's arm been revealed?" (Is. 52:14—53:1).

The mention of a sword brings Jesus' parting words and the Last Supper to an end. The bequest Jesus left behind would equip his disciples for the time of struggle which was coming. He was going away from his followers, but he confided the results of his ministry to his church for all time, his own self, the new divine economy of the covenant, and the forgiveness of sins . . . All this is summed up in the eucharistic meal. By means of his parting gift, he remains united with the community of his disciples and confers on them without interruption the saving fruits of his violent death until the table they share reaches its full achievement. The way to God's kingdom consists in appropriating the fruit of Jesus' passion to one-self.

The eucharistic meal was given to the church for a time in which it is exposed to hostile attacks. In this meal, Christ gave his church a pattern to be followed in the community life and the private lives of Christians. He himself is present in the church as the saviour who interceded for the first head of the church, that he might be able to strengthen his brothers. By means of the one who presides in the community, Jesus offers his church his word of power and exhortation.

In the time of the church, Satan is permitted to exercise his power as far as God wills and allows it. But this new presence of Satan is counteracted by Christ's presence and the presence of the fruits of his work. Satan's power is set at naught by Jesus' high priesthood. The eucharistic meal is an event in which Christ is present, interceding and offering himself. But this does not do away with temptation or with the need for effort; perseverance in following Jesus is still necessary. However, it gives those who fight with him a guarantee of victory.

Sharing in the eucharistic meal is the focal point of the church's religious life; it is its strength on its way, the source of its eschatological joy, and the law of its life. The eucharistic meal enshrines the lasting results of all that Jesus did for his disciples, now that he was about to leave them. The time of struggle to come would not find his disciples all alone. Jesus sits as the Lord at the Father's right hand; his disciples would receive the Spirit. They have the sacred banquet.

Given Up to the Jews (22:39-71)

Jesus had told his disciples: " They will lay their hands on you and persecute you. They will hand you over to the synagogues and to prison; they will haul you before kings and governors " (21:12). These words were fulfilled in Jesus himself first of all. He is the archetype of the persecuted church. In the witness he bore, Christians can see how they should prove themselves in martyrdom. St. Paul writes to Timothy: " I call upon you before God who gives life to all men and before Christ Jesus who bore witness before Pontius Pilate, a glorious confession " (1 Tim. 6:13).

Jesus Prays on the Mount of Olives (22:39-46).

[39]*He went out and withdrew, as was his custom, to the Mount of Olives. His disciples followed him.*

Since his entry into Jerusalem, Jesus had taught each day in the temple. In the evening, he used leave the city to spend the night on the Mount of Olives. This time, he had celebrated the paschal meal and spoken his parting words in his host's upper room. The first Christian church at Jerusalem met in the temple and in the houses of its members (Acts 2:46). The church took what Jesus did as its norm of conduct.

Even on this occasion, Jesus did not vary his custom of spending the night on the Mount of Olives, although he knew what awaited him. He did not evade the moment (22:53) his Father had appointed for the beginning of his fatal journey; he was firmly determined to undergo the passion (9:51). Death came to him, not as a tragic fate, not as a form of violence imposed on him by men which he could not escape, but as the will of the Father which he accomplished in a spirit of obedience (Jn. 10:18).

His disciples, too, followed him. They still appeared as true followers who traveled about after their master wherever he went (9:57).

⁴⁰*And when he reached the place, he said to them: " Pray, that you may not fall into temptation."*

On the Mount of Olives, Jesus sought out the place he had always gone to on previous nights, and which was also known to Judas. He was utterly devoted to God's will and he went to meet the approaching danger. His only care was for his disciples. Now the hour of temptation was at hand. He would be arrested and his enemies would have him in their power. This would leave them bewildered; it would endanger their faith. Satan would make every effort to make them fall away. Temptation yawned before the disciples like an abyss, to lure them to destruction. It spread like a net before them, to entrap them.

To avoid being exposed to temptation, his disciples had need of God's help; this could be assured by prayer. The petition Jesus had taught them to make in the Our Father must now be pronounced: " Lead us not into temptation " (11:4).

⁴¹And he tore himself away from them, about a stone's throw; then he knelt down and prayed saying: ⁴²" Father, do you will it? Make this chalice pass me by! Yet may your will, not mine, be done."

Jesus tore himself away from his disciples, as if he was constrained by some power or other. The power was God's plan, the " must " which was imposed upon him. The same word is used in the passage where we are told that St. Paul tore himself away from the presbyters at Miletus to take the road to Jerusalem where suffering and imprisonment awaited him (Acts 21 : 1). Jesus is the model for his disciples who are martyred.

The Lord prayed alone in the Father's presence. He went a stone's throw away from his disciples, but remained close enough to be seen. He wanted them to be able to see him and hear him, and he wanted to be able to call them. In this moment of crisis, he prayed kneeling, whereas it was usual to stand up at prayer (18 : 11). He repeated the words insistently and devoutly. As he was being stoned to death, St. Stephen fell on his knees to pray, like Jesus on the Mount of Olives (Acts 7 : 60). Peter did the same before he raised Tabitha from the dead (Acts 9 : 40), as did Paul when he was taking his leave of the presbyters at Ephesus, after he had told them that they would not see his face again (Acts 20 : 36). Together with his companions, St. Paul also knelt down on the beach at Tyre, when the disciples warned him in the power of the Spirit that he should not go up to Jerusalem (Acts 21 : 5). When they were confronted with the power of death, they all prayed kneeling down. Martyrdom can be overcome only by prayer. Jesus is the model of martyrs.

Jesus' prayer began with the address " Father." All Jesus' prayers begin with this intimate, trusting, and childlike form of address. Even when he used the words of the Psalms to pray (23 : 46), he adapted them to this title. In so doing, he assimilated expressions of prayer which were not his own into his own unique relationship with God, which he expressed in the word *"Abba."* It was his infinitely loving Father who imposed his passion and a martyr's death on him.

The prayer Jesus offered was a genuinely human prayer. He prayed that the chalice, the symbol of suffering and martyrdom, the sign of God's avenging judgment, might pass him by. God offered Jesus the chalice from which he must drink his avenging judgment as the representative of the human race (see Is. 51:22). Jesus is the suffering servant and a martyr. He took his passion and death upon himself to atone for the sins of the nations and as their representative.

Human nature trembles in the face of violent death. But Jesus was resigned to his Father's will and he prayed that God's will alone might be done. His whole prayer was framed in words expressing self-surrender. It began with such a word: " If it is your will," or: " Do you will it?" It closed with the prayer that God's will might be accomplished. Once again, we hear an echo of the " Our Father," although Luke did not find the petition: " Your will be done " (Mt. 6:10) in the source he used. Like Christ, a Christian must pray: " *Abba*," " Father, your will be done, lead us not into temptation." The " Our Father " is Jesus' prayer; it is the prayer of martyrs, the prayer of Jesus' disciples, a prayer for the critical moments of life, and for the hour of death.

[43]*An angel from heaven appeared to him and strengthened him.* [44]*And he was involved in the decisive contest and he prayed still more insistently, and his sweat was like drops of blood falling to the ground.*

Jesus' prayer was heard, not in the sense that the chalice passed him by, but in the sense that he prayed still more earnestly and was given strength to accept the chalice. God hears the prayers we offer when we suffer; he hears them by giving us strength to accept his will. He opens our hearts for his plan of salvation, in a spirit of faith.

Three times in Jesus' life we are told that a heavenly proclamation came as God's answer to his prayer: at his baptism, at the transfiguration, and on the Mount of Olives. These three events were among the great moments of the Lord's life; they were connected with his passion and glorification. God prepared Jesus, his " well beloved," his " Chosen One," to carry out his plan of salvation which included the " must " involved in his passion and death; he was to attain his glory by means of a struggle to the death.

Angels comforted the martyrs and confirmed them in their struggle to the death. The Lord's angel came to the aid of the three young men in the furnace: " He descended into the furnace together with Azariah's companions and he drove the flames out of the furnace. He made the heart of the furnace as cool as when the wind blows which brings the dew " (Dan. 3:49f.). When Daniel learned by a revelation what was to happen his people in the last days, he had to be strengthened by an angel: " Then that figure which looked like a man touched me once more and gave me strength. He told me: ' Do not be afraid! God loves you! May it be well with you. Be strong, have courage!' As he spoke to me like this, I felt an increase of strength and said: ' Now, my lord, speak, for you have given me strength ' " (see Dan. 10:1–19). Jesus was to accomplish God's plans for the human race, but he could do this only by the Father's power. God gave him strength by means of the angel; angels assisted him in his work (2:19; Acts 1:9f.).

Strengthened by the angel, Jesus entered the decisive contest. It was not fear of death, but fear for victory which oppressed him. This was the decisive contest on which the salvation of the world depended, and it was a hard contest. After the temptations in the desert, Satan left him alone for a time (4:13). But now he pressed him hard once more, to turn him from the path pointed out for him by the Father.

Jesus summoned up all his strength and overcame his repugnance; so he gave his consent to his Father's will. The effort forced sweat from his pores which fell to the earth like drops of blood.

[45]*And he stood up from his prayer and came to the disciples and found them asleep, overcome with sorrow.* [46]*He said to them:*

" Why are you sleeping? Rise up and pray, so that you may not fall into temptation."

As he chose the chalice of suffering in that great hour when he accomplished the salvation of the world on the Mount of Olives, Jesus' first and last care was for his disciples. He found them asleep. St. Luke adds the words: "overcome with sorrow," to excuse them. They gave themselves up passively to what was in store for them and slept. Jesus did not reproach them; instead, he worried about them. He was their servant. "Why are you sleeping?"—Now, at this hour, when temptation and affliction were coming? It is necessary to pray always, and never give up. Constant prayer will prepare the church to meet all the attacks to which it is exposed during the period before Jesus' second coming.

Mark describes Jesus' agony on the Mount of Olives in the starkest terms. Luke plays down its more shocking and terrible aspects. He says nothing about the fear Jesus felt or the way he trembled, or about the sorrow which made him ready to die. He makes no mention of the loathing which filled him. Mark says Jesus fell to the ground; St. Luke tones this down: "He sank to his knees." Jesus' prayer is calmer; he merely asks modestly if it were possible that the chalice of suffering could pass him by. Luke mentions only one period of prayer and one exhortation addressed to the disciples. Mark portrays his prayer as being answered only by silence; Luke tells us Jesus received an answer in the appearance of an angel. Even in this difficult hour, Jesus preserves his human greatness. In his abandonment, he draws strength from the prayer he offered to his Father. Despite his distress, he cared for his disciples with perfect human understanding. St. Luke raises Jesus above the unique situation on the Mount of Olives and portrays him as a model for martyrs and for all those who, in times of crisis, must choose in favor of God's will, while bearing the responsibility for others.

Jesus is Arrested (22:47–53)

[47]*As he was still speaking, see, a great crowd came there. The man*

*called Judas, one of the twelve, marched at their head. He came
close to Jesus to kiss him. ⁴⁸But Jesus said to him: " Judas, do you
give up the Son of man with a kiss?"*

Suddenly, a crowd appeared there, not just a motley troop assembled by chance, but a section of the forces of law and order which
took orders from the Sanhedrin and was commanded by the temple
officers. They were in the service of the Jewish authorities; they
carried out arrests, brought those who were charged before the
court, kept guard over those in prison, and executed the sentences
imposed by the Jewish court. Even as Jesus was speaking to his
disciples, the whole situation was completely altered. He was surrounded by his enemies, and hemmed in by distress. This would
be the church's situation in the world. The hour of darkness only
waits until it is given its chance.

The group was led by Judas. One of the twelve! He knew Jesus
intimately. He was given up for the first time by one of those who
were closest to him (see 21 : 16). Judas drew near to kiss him. Even
before he kissed him, Jesus branded his treachery as a shameful act.
His words were also intended to make him think and bring him
to repentance. He addressed Judas by name, the name by which
he had called him to become an apostle. A kiss was a sign of a
pupil's reverence for his master; Judas made it a sign of betrayal
(Mk. 14 : 44). Judas betrayed the Son of man; the person he betrayed
would one day judge him (22 : 22). Even as his enemies surrounded
him, Jesus dominated the scene by his goodness and majesty.

⁴⁹*When those who were around him saw what was going to happen,
they said: " Lord, must we use our swords?" ⁵⁰And one of them
struck at the high priest's servant and cut off his right ear. ⁵¹But
Jesus answered and said: " Leave off! That is enough." And he
touched his ear and healed him.*

There is an echo here of the mention of a sword at the Last Supper.
The disciples had not understood the meaning of Jesus' words then;

consequently, they could not understand what was happening now either. Even to his closest and most intimate friends, those who were around him, Jesus' powerlessness remained an enigma and a mystery. They professed their loyalty to him openly; they showed him respect and obedience; they addressed him as " Lord," but they could not understand that the Lord's path led through the cross to glory. Their efforts to defend him were ridiculous; they revealed their good will, but also underlined the insufficiency of their faith. More is demanded of Jesus' disciples than any merely human loyalty (14:26f.).

Jesus forbade them to have recourse to the sword. He had nothing in common with the Zealot movement which wanted to establish God's kingdom by force, or with the Jewish partisans who wanted to put an end to the foreign domination of their country by force of arms. He would have nothing to do with political or military means. He used the power at his disposal to heal the man who had been wounded, to do good to his enemies. He remained the Lord and saviour: the Lord even of this hour of darkness; the saviour even of his enemies.

⁵²But Jesus said to those who had come for him, to the chief priests, and the temple officers and the elders: " Have you come out with swords and clubs, as if you were coming for a robber? ⁵³I was with you every day in the temple and you did not raise your hands against me, but this is your hour, the hour of the power of darkness."

The troop which came to arrest him was under the command of the supreme council. Those who constituted it are enumerated solemnly. They represented the élite of the people, to whom the greatest blessings they enjoyed were entrusted: the law, the temple, the people of God. All these institutions looked forward to Christ and now they had him arrested. The guilt of Jesus' death was borne by the leaders of the Jews. By their crime, they did away with the reason for their own existence and destroyed themselves (20:8).

Jesus protested against being treated as a common thief, like a criminal who hates the light, or a man of violence who must be captured with swords and clubs. Jesus pursued the same goal as the members of the Sanhedrin, God's truth, the observance of the law, and the service of the temple. He was a teacher in religious questions. His enemies could have had convincing evidence at any time that he looked for nothing else; his teaching was given openly in the temple. The members of the council did nothing to interfere with him. They discussed disputed questions of a religious nature with him. Jesus' solemn declaration of this was important for the church. The church is not a secret society bent on creating religious differences and political upheaval. It does not reject what God has accomplished in salvation history; on the contrary, it brings it to its full accomplishment in Jesus.

The members of the Sanhedrin would have had no power over Jesus if God had not given it to them. It was he who was behind what was happening. That this hour, their hour, had come was not their doing; it was God who permitted it. They were acting as instruments, not as God's instruments, but as the instruments of Satan. The hour in which they put their plans into effect was the hour in which the power of darkness, Satan, was permitted to exercise its influence. The darkness is Satan's kingdom. The supreme council did not believe in Christ; consequently, they became subject to Satan's rule. They did not serve Jesus, and so they became the servants of the devil.

Disowned and Insulted (22:54-65)

DISOWNED BY PETER (22:54-62)

⁵⁴*When they had arrested him, they led him away and brought him to the house of the high priest. But Peter followed at a distance.*

It was no longer Jesus himself who acted now; his enemies acted with him as they pleased. They arrested him, led him away, and brought him in. He had grasped the chalice; the Father had given him up into his enemies' hands. The power of darkness and its instruments had their way. He obeyed, was given up, and was handed over.

Jesus was brought to the house of the high priest Caiaphas where the Sanhedrin met. The evangelist is content with the general picture. Jesus' behavior, what he said and what he did not say, was far more important to him than its historical setting. He was interested in what the highest authorities in the land had to say about the Lord, and in what was said about him in their presence.

When Jesus went to the Mount of Olives, his actions were still determined by his own will; he went out and made his way to the hill, while his disciples followed him. Now he was led, he was brought into his enemy's house; only Peter followed him, and then only at a distance. Peter still stood by the resolution he had taken, he alone—he followed at a distance. The way was being prepared for his denial; his apostasy had begun.

55But when they lit a fire in the middle of the courtyard and sat around it, Peter took a seat among them.

Early in the year nights in Palestine are cold. The guard who had brought in Jesus warmed themselves at the fire. Peter followed Jesus to the courtyard of the palace. He sat among the crowd whose knowledge of Jesus was confined to the charges his enemies brought against him. Among them he was in danger. Temptation surrounded him, just as the darkness surrounded the light of the fire.

56But when a maid saw him sitting in the glow of the fire and had taken a close look at him, she said to him: " This man, too, was with him." 57But he denied it and said: " Woman, I do not know him." 58After a short time, another person looked at him and said: " You, too, are one of them." But Peter said: " Man, I am not." 59After about an hour had passed another person insisted and said: " Indeed, this one too was with him. He is a Galilean." 60aBut Peter said: " Man I do not know what you are saying."

Three tempters emerge from the group surrounding Peter, a woman and two men. The first two attacks follow one another in quick succession. Then there was an interval of an hour, which was followed by an even more serious attack. The tempters' insistence increased each time: " This man, too, was with him "; " you, too, are one of them "; " indeed, this one, too, was with him." First a remark was made concerning him; then followed an attack on him. Finally, the whole crowd was roused against him. First, the maid merely looked at him; then he was addressed directly, and finally he was examined attentively and unmasked as a Galilean. The word " Galilean " sounds like an accusation that he was a Zealot or a rebel. The net in which Peter was caught closed about him gradually. Peter is a warning to every member of the church.

St. Peter's passionate protestation at the Last Supper, which he had expressed in the words " with you " (22:23), was the subject of the three attacks. It was for this that Jesus had called him and the other apostles, that they might be with him (Mk. 3:14). The idea of being " with him " was meant to show the apostles light. Following Jesus is a visible manifestation of faith in him; it demonstrates openly that a person listens to him. It has a symbolic function, of which a disciple's preaching activity in which he affirms his faith in words is only a part (22:28). All of Christ's disciples share in the reality expressed in the phrases: " with him," " one of them." It is precisely with reference to this that Christ's disciples are tempted.

Peter's denial became progressively worse: " I do not know him "; " I am not one of them "; " I do not know what you are saying." Peter wanted to have nothing to do with Jesus, with his disciples, or with his affairs. The gulf between them grew. Peter went further and further away from him, abandoning the idea of being " with him " more and more.

[60b]*And immediately, as he was speaking, the cock crew.* [61]*And the Lord turned around and looked at Peter. And Peter remembered the Lord's word, how he had told him: " Before the cock crows, you will disown me three times."* [62]*And he went out and began to weep bitterly.*

Day was beginning to dawn when Peter denied the Lord for the third time and the cock crew. Jesus was being led through the court-yard. He looked at Peter. Peter repented. Jesus' prayer had been heard.

Peter was led to repent by the crowing of the cock which reminded him of Jesus' prophecy, by Jesus' glance which gave him confidence, and by the recollection of Jesus' word which had now been proved true. Behind these three factors stood the Lord; he is twice mentioned by name. Jesus is the Lord—even in this darkness. Meeting him in the symbols of nature, in the Lord's word, and in the actions performed in his memory (the eucharistic meal and the sacraments) leads a person to the light.

The time of the church is threatened by the powers of darkness. But the church must know that the Lord is superior to all that threatens it and to human weakness. The church will be a threatened church until the Lord comes again. For this reason, too, it will always be a church of sinners. On the other hand, the church knows that the Lord is its high priest. He will intercede for it if only Christians remember the presence of the Lord and his word, and the presence of Peter who was converted.

INSULTED BY THE GUARD (22:63–65)

[63]*And the men who were guarding him insulted him.* [64]*They covered his face and said: "Prophesy, who is it that struck you?"* [65]*And they said a lot of other things, blaspheming.*

The members of the guard played " blindman's buff " with Jesus, a game which was also known in antiquity. In this way, they challenged his claim to be a prophet and scorned him. The temptation the devil put before him was repeated: " If you are God's Son . . ." (4:3.9).

St. Luke makes no mention of Jesus' other humiliations (Mk. 14:6). He prefers moderation and conceals what is inhuman. He condemns everything they did as blasphemy. Jesus is more than a prophet (9:20f.). He is God's self-revelation (5:8); in him, God himself visited his people (7:16). Having to endure blasphemy is part of the church's destiny of suffering. " I know your distress and your poverty, but you are rich. I know also the blasphemies of those who call themselves Jews, but are not; they are rather Satan's synagogue " (Rev. 2:9).

Before the Sanhedrin (22:66–71)

St. Luke's account differs from that of Mark, which St. Matthew also followed. The most striking difference is that Luke transfers the judicial process to the morning, at daybreak. Moreover, the process does not seem to have been a real trial; no witnesses were called, there was no adjuration by the high priest, and no sentence. Jesus was questioned only about his identity as the Messiah. From this a number of scholars conclude that Luke follows a source which was peculiar to him, according to which Jesus was not tried by the Sanhedrin and was never condemned by the Jewish authorities. The Mark/Matthew tradition, they say, introduced a trial before the Sanhedrin for apologetic reasons. They wanted to lay the whole blame for Jesus' death at the door of the Jewish authorities and exonerate the Romans. Therefore, the Sanhedrin merely had Jesus arrested; they questioned him briefly and turned him over to the governor, so that he could have him executed for high treason.

However, this reconstruction of the events falls away for the simple reason that it cannot be proved that Luke used a source which differed from the Mark/Matthew tradition and was peculiar to him. His presentation of the facts (22:54–71) can be satisfactorily explained as the result of his editing of the text of Mark which he had before him. Luke merely wanted to record the concluding phase of Jesus' trial before the Sanhedrin —which certainly took place in the morning. In this he emphasizes the question of Jesus' identity as the Messiah and his open admission of his identity. He wanted to portray Jesus as a model for the martyrs and Christians who professed their faith in him as the Messiah (1 Tim. 6:12f.). To form an accurate picture of Jesus' trial we must start with Mark and remember that he does not speak of two trials (a night sitting and a morning sitting); he speaks of only one trial which is interrupted by the account of Peter's denial. This literary device was intended to bring out the fact that Jesus' witness and Peter's denial took place at the same time and to underline the contrast between them. St. Luke was at pains to give a consecutive account of events and he disposed his material differently

⁶⁶*When it was day, the council of the elders of the people met together with the chief priests and scribes, and they brought him before their gathering.*

The Sanhedrin is portrayed for Greek readers as a " council of the elders of the people." Like the council of the elders in the Greek cities, the Sanhedrin was divided into a senate and a college of judges (chief priests and scribes). The soldiers of the guard brought Jesus into the council at daybreak. What happened there would be a source of encouragement for the infant church and those who preached the faith, when they appeared before the council of the elders in the Greek cities, to be interrogated about their preaching and their profession (Acts 16:20; 17:6).

⁶⁷*And they said: " If you are the Christ, tell us." But he said to them: " If I tell you, you will not believe me. ⁶⁸If I question you, you will not answer me. ⁶⁹From now on, the Son of man will sit at the right of God's power."*

The question the council put to Jesus was the crucial question which affected the whole people, the people of God: Is Jesus of Nazareth the Christ, the Messiah sent by God, to whom salvation history looked forward, and on whom Israel's salvation and the salvation of the nations depended? He had " gone about doing good and healing all those who were in the devil's power " (Acts 10:38). He had spoken as a prophet who enjoyed power. How was this to be explained? The people declared that he was the Son of David; they had hailed him as the eschatological saviour. Who was he? What did he say about himself? The question the council of the elders put was one which neither Israel, nor the world, nor any single individual could overlook once they had come to knowledge of the message concerning Jesus and the meaning of salvation history. No one who is convinced that God has not left the human race to its own devices can afford to overlook this question.

Jesus answered neither yes nor no to the Sanhedrin's question. He was unwilling to answer it, because those who put it to him did not want to believe. " If I tell you, you will not believe me." The council asked the question, not out of a desire for salvation, but because they wanted to find some ground of accusation for a political trial before Pilate. The title " Christ " or " Messiah " had national and political overtones. It was hoped that the Messiah would drive the Roman forces of occupation out of the country and win political independence. Why should Jesus admit in their presence that he was the Christ when they would not believe? They only wanted to use this admission to hand him over to the Roman authorities. Faith in him is necessary before a person can believe that Jesus of Nazareth is the Christ, the saviour sent by God. But only the man who raises the question of Christ's identity out of a sincere desire for salvation will attain faith in him. No one will find the way to faith in Christ unless he is willing to listen to his word and follow his way. The way to true faith in Christ is closed to anyone who raises this question merely to betray Christ or to accuse him. Even those who raise this question only because they want to know, and not because they want to follow him or be guided by him, will not find the way to faith.

Jesus had tried to lead the members of the Sanhedrin to see the answer to the question which they now put to him. He had raised the question concerning the authority John the Baptist enjoyed with the intention of leading them to an understanding of his own mission (20:1-8). He raised the question concerning the meaning of the mysterious words of the Psalm: " The Lord said to my Lord " (20:41-44). He tried to initiate them into the meaning of the expression " Son of David," and into his own relationship with God. But they made no answer, not because they were unable to give an answer, but because they were unwilling to acknowledge what the answer to his question involved. The question of Christ's identity affects the whole man; it affects a person's will as well as his intellect. It involves a change in a man's whole life; it is an " existential question." The man who wants to answer this question the way Christ wants him to must be prepared for " conversion " and for repentance; he must be prepared " to deny himself " and follow Jesus.

Who was Jesus, the prisoner who appeared before the supreme council? He answered the question put to him with a formula of revelation : " From now on, the Son of man will sit at the right of God's power." Jesus was speaking of the Son of man whom Daniel saw : " While I was still having this vision in the night, one came suddenly who looked like a Son of man, on the clouds of heaven . . . Sovereignty, honor, and a kingdom were now given to him " (Dan. 7:13). This Son of man would sit at the right of God's power, at God's right hand; God is here described as a power by circumlocution (Mk. 14:62). Psalm 110 (109):1 is connected with Daniel's saying about the Son of man : " The Lord said to my Lord : ' Sit at my right hand '." From now on, the Son of man will share in God's glory. What is the meaning of this veiled and mysterious reference to the Son of man? Why did Jesus speak about the Son of man at the very moment when the Jews asked him if he was the Messiah? This was a way of stating openly that he was the Son of man. Whenever he mentioned his future passion and death, he had always spoken of the Son of man. Now he stood before the court and was being condemned to death; from now on he would enter God's glory. Jesus claimed to be the Messiah, and God himself would vindicate this claim by exalting him as the Son of man. This revelation would do away with the scandal caused by Christ's humiliation which would make it impossible for the Jews to acknowledge him as the Messiah, especially the scandal arising from his passion and death on the cross. Jesus was the Messiah; but he was not the kind of Messiah the Sanhedrin imagined. He was the Messiah who would receive divine power and glory after he had walked the way of condemnation and death.

St. Mark reproduces Jesus' avowal in the words: " You will see the Son of man sitting at the right of the power and coming with the clouds of heaven " (Mk. 14:62). St. Luke suppresses the words: " You will see "; the members of the Sanhedrin would not see him. The glorified Christ would not appear to everyone; his coming in glory was not so close that the members of the Sanhedrin would witness it. St. Luke also omits: [You will see him] " coming with the clouds of heaven." In the persecuted and martyred church, it was important not merely to know that Christ would come, but to remember above all that he now reigns with God as the glorified Lord who shares God's power. This was the Christ to whom Stephen looked up and from whom he received the strength to endure a martyr's death: " See, I see heaven opened and the Son of man standing at God's right hand " (Acts 7:56).

[70]But they all said: " You are, then, the Son of God?" But he said to them: " You say it yourselves. I am." [71]Then they said: " Why do we need witnesses now? We ourselves have heard it from his own lips."

The Jews realized that Jesus was talking about himself. He called himself the Son of man and claimed a share in God's power and glory. His enemies drew the logical conclusion from this and asked: You are, then, God's Son? The Jews used the title " Son of God " in the sense of an appointment to an office and a sharing in God's sovereignty. In the words " God's Son," the members of the Sanhedrin summed up what Jesus had expressed in Daniel's words and the words of the Psalm: " Sovereignty, honor, and a kingdom were given to him," and: " Sit at my right hand."

Before answering their question, Jesus reminds the Jews that their knowledge was based on his word of revelation. They now said clearly what they had previously refused to say in their dispute with him about his authority and his interpretation of Psalm 110 (109). The question concerning his divine sonship transferred Jesus' identity as the Messiah from the political to the religious sphere. In its Greek translation " king," the title " Christ " (" Messiah ") could be abused for political purposes. The title " Son of God " was something which belonged to the purely religious sphere even in the pagan world. Therefore, Jesus admitted without reservation: "I am." The expression he used was also the formula of revelation used by God at the burning bush (Ex. 3:13). It was important to free the title "Christ" from all its national and political associations when the gospel was preached to Jews and pagans.

According to Mark, the question the high priest asked was: "Are you the Christ, the Son of the Most Blessed One?" (Mk. 14:61). Luke divided the question into two without, however, making an essential distinction between the two titles, such as for example: "Christ" = "Messiah," "Son of God" = "metaphysical Son of God" (by his essence). For the high priest as for Luke, the titles "Christ" and "Son of God" were synonymous. In the synagogue at Damascus, St. Paul said with reference to Jesus: "This man is the Son of God" (Acts 9:20), while the Acts of the Apostles tell us: He asserted "this man was the Christ" (9:22). The title "Son of God" throws light on the "Christ-Messiah" title.

When the council members asked Jesus whether he was the Son of God, they had no idea of the profound mystery involved in this title. They believed that God would appoint the Messiah to reign with him and give him a share in his sovereignty and power. That was why they referred to him as the Son of God (an adoptive son). When very early Christian texts called Jesus the "Son of God," they gave him this title primarily because he had been given a share in God's glory. "God raised up Jesus, as it is written in the second Psalm: 'You are my Son. I have begotten you today'" (Acts 13:33). God made Jesus his Son after he had raised him from the dead. In a profession of faith in Christ which St. Paul places at the beginning of the Epistle to the Romans we read: God "appointed Jesus as the Son of God with power . . . on the basis of his resurrection from the dead" (Rom. 1:4). But that was not all. The early church also realized that Jesus was God's Son even during his earthly life. The words attributed to God at his baptism and transfiguration prove this (3:22; 9:35). From the first moment of his existence, from his conception by the Holy Spirit in his mother's womb, Jesus was God's Son: " For this reason, the child which will be born will be called holy and God's Son " (1 : 35). God initiated the Church gradually into the profound mystery of Jesus' divine sonship. This tentative and gradual penetration into the mystery of Jesus' person gives us a better idea of the wonder of his person and his mission than the formal declaration: " I believe in Jesus Christ, his only begotten Son." The expression: " God's only begotten Son " conceals a profound depth of meaning.

Christ, therefore, acknowledged his right to three titles: " Christ" (" Messiah "), " Son of Man," and "Son of God." He did not attribute the title " Christ " or " Son of God " to himself directly. He described himself only as the " Son of man," and this in a hidden way, as if he were speaking of someone else. With the title " Son of man," he always connected the way he had to follow which passed through suffering to glory. This was the most basic and the most characteristic element of his self-revelation, that he would ascend through death to the glory of the Son of man who is enthroned with God.

The witness Christ bore before the Sanhedrin, as St. Luke relates it, was a " compendium of Christology " which had its source in all that Jesus professed to be. Jesus now proclaimed openly before the official representatives of the people all that he had told the apostles on the way to Jerusalem and all that he had taught the people in the temple. He had told his disciples, with reference to the people: " All that you have said in darkness will be heard in the light. What you have whispered in people's ears in darkened rooms will be shouted from the housetops " (12:3). This was verified in his own case, too, as he bore his witness before the council. Jesus bore his witness before the court of the Sanhedrin. He will always be the great model for martyrs in the church. " When they lay their hands on you and persecute you, giving you up to the synagogues and to prison . . . it will be an opportunity for you to bear witness " (21 : 12f.).

The council members confirmed that for them Jesus' word had

the value of direct testimony. " Why do we need more witnesses?" They regarded Jesus' avowal that he was the Son of God as proving that he was the Christ. They interpreted this messianic profession in a political sense. Their purpose was achieved; they were justified in handing him over to the Roman authorities and they were sure this move would be successful. The testimony a Christian bears concerning Christ is a two-edged sword: " We are Christ's incense in God's presence, both among those who are saved and among those who are lost. To some we are an odor of death which brings death, to others an odor of life which brings life " (2 Cor. 2:15).

Given up to the Gentiles (23:1–25)

The Romans allowed the various people subject to them to retain their own legislation and administer justice themselves. The Jews enjoyed special privileges. Under the Roman procurators (after 6 A.D.), the Sanhedrin at Jerusalem had the power to try those charged with capital crimes and pass sentence of death. The execution of this sentence, however, was reserved to the Roman governor, as seems to have been the case in all the Roman provinces (according to Jn. 18:31, the Jews told Pilate: " We are not allowed to put anyone to death."). When the Sanhedrin wanted the sentence of death they had passed on Jesus to be put into effect, they were forced to have recourse to the Roman procurator.

As the supreme judge, the procurator could simply confirm the sentence passed by the Sanhedrin and have it carried out, or he could hold a further trial himself. This was what happened in Jesus' case. The Sanhedrin was a college of judges, whereas the Roman governor judged alone. The assessors who normally accompanied him had no juridical authority; they merely acted as his legal advisers. In principle, the proceedings were public. The case began when the charge was laid. The method of proof was free; there were no formalities. The depositions of the accused and the various witnesses served as evidence The judge pronounced sentence from the tribunal, after consultation with his assessors, and this was executed immediately.

The gospels recount only some portions of Jesus' trial. Above all, they make no explicit mention of a formal sentence of death pronounced by Pilate. It has been inferred by this that his decision was not a sentence in the strict juridical sense; it was either a simple mandate of execution which confirmed the Sanhedrin's sentence, or an informal surrender of the accused to the Jews. To demand a juridical and technical account of the trial from the gospels is to misunderstand them; it would be asking for more than they ever intended to give us. They were interested principally in underlining the significance of Jesus' trial in salvation history.

Jesus' judge was Pontius Pilate, the governor (procurator) of Judea and Samaria (26–36 A.D.). Contemporary Jewish sources (Philo and Josephus Flavius) paint a very unflattering picture of him. He is portrayed as an unyielding and ruthless character who brought shame on his term of office by his corruption and his violent deeds. According to these writers, he was given to robbery, abuse of power, intimidation, frequent executions without trial, and intolerable cruelty. The gospels give us a completely different picture. There Pilate appears as a man who is anxious to act legally; he tried to see that Jesus received justice in the face of the Jews' hatred. On the basis of these conflicting testimonies, some writers claim that the gospel picture of Pilate is completely "unhistorical" (Klausner). This conclusion is wrong. There can be no doubt that the portrait painted by the Jewish writers is one-sided and hostile; it is based on facts which show the procurator in an unfavorable light. Under pressure of historical circumstances, Pilate went through a certain development. When he came to Palestine first, it was because he was anti-Semitic and had been made governor of the country by Sejanus, the all-powerful prefect of the guard under Tiberius. Sejanus was overthrown in the year 31 and after that Tiberius showed greater consideration for the Jews. Then Pilate was forced to adopt different tactics. He needed friends at Jerusalem, Tiberias (at the court of Herod Antipas) and Rome. There is no doubt that the gospels touched up Pilate's image; they were anxious to show that even the Roman governor had come to the conclusion that Jesus was not a political danger. It was the members of the Sanhedrin who plotted his death. This apologetic bias is most marked in St. Luke; he was writing for the part of the world in which the Roman empire wielded power. He wrote his gospel at a time when the church had already had considerable experience in the world. Furthermore, his outlook was influenced by a view of history which took full account of the fact that the church needed to find its place in this world and its circumstances, not least of which was the Roman state. Jesus' trial before Pilate benefited the church in two ways: it showed the martyrs how they should bear their witness before the Roman authorities, and it acted as an apology for Christianity in its relations with the Roman state.

Before Pilate (23:1-5)

[1]*The whole crowd of them stood up, and they brought him to Pilate.* [2]*Then they began to accuse him, saying: " We have found that this man is inciting our people to revolt and forbids the payment of taxes to Caesar. He says he is Christ the king."*

According to the Palestinian and Jewish custom, a large-scale deputation of dignitaries always appeared before the Roman authorities on official occasions. They put pressure on Pilate. St. Paul had the same experience in Corinth : " When Gallio was governor of Achaia, the Jews made a determined attack on Paul. They brought him before the judgment seat, saying : ' This fellow is trying to persuade the people to worship God in a way that is contrary to the law ' " (Acts 18 : 12). Christ's passion is a source of encouragement for Christians. There is nothing strange in it if they are persecuted as Jesus was.

For the great feasts, the governor left Caesarea on the coast, where he normally resided, and came to Jerusalem, where he stayed in Herod's palace in the northeastern sector of the city. This is where Jesus seems to have been taken. Roman tribunals were not interested in religious questions. Therefore, the charge against Jesus had to be political; the religious claims he made had to be distorted in a political sense. His missionary journeys were explained as an attempt to incite the people to revolt; his claim to be the Christ (Messiah) was interpreted as an act of high treason against the Roman emperor. In the east, the title given the emperor was " king." By imputing nationalist agitation such as this to Jesus, they branded him as a member of the Zealot movement. Therefore, he would have been bound on religious grounds to forbid the payment of the head tax to the emperor, even though what he actually said about this question might have been different. Jesus was charged with something he had always been careful to avoid; no account was taken of the care he took to keep from political activity. The charge was based on distortion and lies. The governor was roused against Jesus by the " whole crowd " of the councillors. In the same way, the authorities would later be induced to take legal action against Christians by allegations of the Jews. " But the Jews roused the leading women who worshipped God and the magistrates of the town. They started a persecution against Paul and Barnabas and drove them out of the district " (Acts 13 : 50). The church shares Christ's destiny and draws strength from the fate he endured.

³*But Pilate questioned him, saying: " Are you the king of the Jews?" He answered, saying: " You say I am."*

The governor instituted a hearing of his own (23 : 14). Of the three accusations, he took up the basic one, the accusation that Jesus pretended to be Christ, the king. He gave the question a secular and political twist as might be expected of a Roman procurator and as Jesus' accusers had insinuated it. He avoided the word " Christ " (Messiah). The question was: Was Jesus the king of the Jews? Was he a king in a political sense? A king in the Zealots' sense? They wanted to shake off Rome's domination over the Jews by force. If Jesus really claimed to be the king of the Jews in a political sense, sooner or later both he and his followers would rebel against Rome and refuse to pay tribute. All those who arose after Jesus' time and claimed to be the Messiah went this way, either of their own accord or when forced to do so by their followers. But was the claim to be the Messiah in itself a purely political claim? Jesus avoided giving a clear answer to Pilate's question : " You say I am," not I. His words are intended to make Pilate reflect. The governor was thinking in purely political terms; he interpreted the title " Christ " in a purely political sense. Jesus was not the king of the Jews in this sense. The reply he gave : " You say I am," was apparently phrased so as to avoid refusing the title " king " completely. Jesus is the

Christ; he is the Messiah and a king, but in a different sense. He entered Jerusalem as the messianic king—riding on a donkey! He came to Jerusalem, but he took possession only of the temple, not of the city. He exercised his sovereign authority, but only by teaching! What Jesus says in his own defense in St. John's gospel is implied in St. Luke's: " My kingdom does not belong to this world. If my kingdom was of this world, my servants would have fought to prevent my being handed over to the Jews. But my kingdom does not come from here . . . It is you who say that I am a king. It was for this that I was born; this is why I came into the world, to bear witness to the truth " (Jn. 18:36f.).

⁴But Pilate said to the chief priests and to the crowd: " I find nothing with which this man can be charged." ⁵But they redoubled their appeals: " He rouses the people to revolt, teaching throughout the whole of Judea, beginning from Galilee."

Jesus' principal accusers were the chief priests who were the leading members of the Sanhedrin. Behind them stood the crowd, a mob which had gathered for the trial. Pilate pronounced Jesus not guilty of the offense with which he had been charged. He had his suspicions about the Jews' loyalty to the emperor and, having heard Jesus, he knew that he had no political ambitions. He must have perceived the religious aspect of the matter, in which the accusation had its roots (see Jn. 18:38). He had no desire to become involved in religious disputes of any kind (see Acts 18:14f.).

Greater pressure was brought to bear on Pilate by the presence of the crowd and by the obstinate repetition of the charges. Pilate had already been worn down by similar tactics and forced to comply with their wishes. Now the emphasis was laid on Jesus' incitement of the people to revolt. Judea was part of the governor's responsibility; the interests of the Roman state were directly affected. Furthermore, Jesus' activity had started in Galilee, the home of political upheaval. It was there that Judas the Galilean had stirred up his revolt (6 A.D.), an incident in which the population census which was intended to facilitate taxation had played a great part (see Acts

5:37). Jesus was far from being harmless. He came from the land of rebels. Throughout Palestine, and even within the area of Pilate's jurisdiction, he brought people under his spell. Every possible means was employed to brand Jesus' success in the religious field as a political affair, so that he might be put out of the way.

Before Herod (23:6–12)

⁶But when Pilate heard [about Galilee], he asked if the man was a Galilean. ⁷When he learned that he came from Herod's territory, he sent him up to Herod who was also in Jerusalem at that time.

Herod Antipas, the prince of Galilee, was a Roman puppet prince who enjoyed judicial power. Jesus was from Galilee and had committed the " crime " with which he was charged there, at least in part. The procurator of Judea was free, therefore, to remit his case to the judgment of his own territorial overlord. At that time, Herod Antipas was in Jerusalem for the paschal feast. He normally resided in the Hasmonean palace west of the temple. This was the place to which the accused was sent up. It was hoped that this official act would produce at least a second judicial opinion, or perhaps even a definitive sentence (Acts 25:13ff.). Pilate was anxious to be rid of the unwelcome case. By this gesture of recognition, he probably hoped also to atone for the many occasions on which he had provoked the " Lilliputian Jewish prince " by his brusqueness; Herod enjoyed the emperor's favor. The gospel mentions the fact that Pilate remitted Jesus' case to Herod because of its significance in salvation history; Luke is not interested in the political or psychological reasons for the move. During the time of persecution, the early church in Jerusalem prayed to God: " You made heaven and earth and the sea and all that is in it. You said by the Holy Spirit through the mouth of your servant David: ' Why do the gentiles rage and the peoples plot in vain? Why do the kings of the earth rise up and the rulers come together against the Lord and his Anointed [Christ]? ' It is true, Herod and Pontius Pilate, with the gentiles and the people of Israel, came together in this city against your holy servant Jesus whom you anointed, to accomplish what your hand and your design had decreed should take place. Look, now, at their threats and enable your servants to preach the word courageously, by stretching out your hand to heal and causing signs and miracles to be done in the name of Jesus your servant " (Acts 4:24-30).

Both Jews and gentiles, Herod and Pilate, were at fault in their dealings with Jesus, the Lord of the world. Yet they were unable to destroy Christ; unwittingly, they helped him to win his universal kingship from God. The church which is threatened and persecuted draws strength from Jesus' passion. In the eschatological discourse, Jesus had foretold that his disciples would be brought before kings and governors for his name's sake (21:12); he himself experienced this first. The persecuted church shares the persecution Jesus endured. The martyrdom the church suffers is the result of the divine decree in the light of which alone Jesus' martyrdom, too, is intelligible. Christians are God's servants; they are united with his holy servant Jesus whom he anointed—in persecution and in glory.

*But when Herod saw Jesus, he was overjoyed. He had wanted to see him for a long time because he had heard of him and he hoped to see some sign from him, performed by him. *He interrogated him with many words but he answered him nothing.*

The Galilean prince was a witty and affable person; he was a man of the world and quite indifferent in religious matters; he loved luxurious buildings and kept a sumptuous table. He was a man who was fond of his peace and quiet; he was an able diplomat and he loved anything sensational. He was like the people of Athens of whom we are told: " There is nothing for which they have more time than recounting or listening to something new " (Acts 17:21). Herod was delighted when he saw Jesus. He hoped to see some miracle from the wonder worker. Conjurers used to pass the time for courtiers with their tricks. Perhaps Jesus could amuse them by some nerve-tingling act! St. Paul would later encounter a similar reaction from the Epicurean and Stoic philosophers on the Areopagus: "These are strange things you are telling us! We would just like to know what they mean" (Acts 17:19f.). God's holiest designs were reduced to the level of sensation-mongers. This, too, is a form of persecution.

Jesus was silent both in word and action. His miracles were signs of the dawning of God's kingdom; his word was a prophetic message which summoned those who heard it to faith, confronting them with a choice between salvation and condemnation, between life and death. Neither the word Jesus preached nor his power to work miracles was given to him for his own benefit. At the very outset of his ministry, Jesus had rejected a similar offer from the tempter (4:1-13). He did not accept it now either, although the choice was between freedom and condemnation. The curiosity which demands a sign is always disappointed (9:9; 8:19ff.). The only sign given to those who demand it is the preaching of repentance (11:29ff.).

Jesus' silence was the sign of the suffering servant: "Like a lamb being led to the slaughter, he does not open his mouth" (Is. 53:7). For the Greeks, silence was a symbol of the divinity. Behind Jesus' silence there stood, not that powerlessness which waits for the day of vengeance, but mute obedience to God's designs.

¹⁰*The chief priests and the scribes stood there and accused him vehemently. ¹¹But Herod and his soldiers gave him up to mockery and insulted him. He had a white garment thrown over him and sent him back to Pilate.*

The Jerusalem authorities could have had reason to be afraid that the Galilean prince would support Jesus who was also a Galilean, and so frustrate their plans to destroy him. He had already listened willingly to John the Baptist (Mk. 6:20) and had shown an interest in Jesus (9:9). Their accusations were vehement. What they lacked in power to convince they made up for in persistence. However, the trial before Herod also resulted in an acquittal. Jesus was ludicrous rather than dangerous, an impractical dreamer rather than a rebel. He might be a candidate for a throne, but he was not a king; he might be a visionary but not a revolutionary. Herod had a white garment draped around Jesus, the " *stola candida* " as it was called. Now he wore the dress of a candidate for office. He was scorned and made to look ridiculous as a candidate for the throne. Jesus' claim to be a king was not asserted with the power or the glory proper to a king (see Jn. 18:36) as people expected. But his claim was not taken seriously; it was laughed to scorn. A poor fool! An impractical enthusiast. To the Jews a stumbling block; to the gentiles mere foolishness (1 Cor. 1:23)!

12But Herod and Pilate became friends with one another that day. Up to this, they had lived in mutual hostility.

Pilate had erected a number of votive images in his palace at Jerusalem. The Jews regarded this as a desecration of the Holy City by pagan images and a provocative action. A delegation of Jews brought a complaint against Pilate before the emperor Tiberius in Rome. Herod Antipas had been a member of this delegation. This may have been the reason for their mutual hostility. By handing Jesus over to his tribunal, Pilate publicly acknowledged Herod's sovereignty and prepared the way for a resumption of normal relations. The gospel regarded their reconciliation as a significant event in salvation history. Herod and Pilate, the Jews and the gentiles, found themselves united in their opposition to God's holy servant, the Messiah whom he had anointed. Both Jews and gentiles declared him innocent, but both incurred guilt in their dealings with him. The great work of reconciliation which was to be fully accomplished when Jesus was exalted in glory (see Is. 49:7–13) was already beginning. Jesus " is our peace " (Eph. 2:14).

Jesus is Condemned (23:13–25)

13But Pilate called the chief priests and the leaders and the people together 14and said to them: " You brought this man to me as one

*who incited the people to revolt. See, I have heard him in your
presence and found nothing in any of the charges you bring against
him.* ¹⁵*Herod, too, found nothing; he sent him back to us. And see,
he has done nothing which deserves death.* ¹⁶*I will let him go free
after I have had him punished."*

The crowd in whose presence Pilate conducted the hearing had
grown bigger; it included the chief priests, the leaders, and the
people. First, only the whole crowd of council members (and the
guard, 23:1) were present; then the chief priests and the crowds
appeared on the scene (23:4). Now the chief priests and leaders
(the elders or the other members of the Sanhedrin besides the chief
priests) and the people—the people of God, who had previously
supported Jesus—were all there. The whole Jewish people had to
come to terms with Jesus; they were now faced with the most
crucial choice in their history. Herod and Pilate joined forces with
the gentiles and the people of Israel, to do what God's hand and
his all-powerful decree had appointed should be done.

Pilate announced the outcome of the hearing. The charge was
summed up in one item: inciting the people against the Roman
state. The investigation had proved that the charge was unfounded.
The trial had been held publicly before all the people; they could
see for themselves that Pilate had not acted illegally. Moreover,
Pilate's decision was confirmed by that of Herod. The outcome of
the hearing was summed up in the words: Jesus is guilty of no
crime that deserves death. Jesus' innocence of any political crime
showed that his interests did not conflict with those of the state.
This finding was of capital importance to the church which was
spreading throughout the Roman empire. The Roman state formally
acknowledged that Jesus' ministry and the message he preached did
not constitute a political danger. The judge sensed the mood of the
chief priests and the people who supported them; he knew what
they wanted. He declared himself ready to make a concession;
before setting Jesus free, he would have him scourged (Mk. 15:15).
This was a barbaric practice. The victim was stripped and tied to a

pillar or a stake, or else thrown on the ground; then he was beaten by a number of torturers until they were tired, or until the flesh hung from his body in shreds. As a rule, scourging accompanied crucifixion (Mk. 15:15). Pilate wanted to employ it as a separate punishment (Jn. 19:1–5). St. Luke avoids the word " scourge." Neither does he say whether this torture was actually inflicted on Jesus. He wanted to spare the Romans. Pilate yielded to the crowd's insistence; he set out on a road which proved to be fatal. He became the agent of the Sanhedrin who were determined to do away with Jesus. Their sin was greater than Pilate's (19:11).

¹⁷On the day of the feast, he was bound to set one [prisoner] free for them. ¹⁸But the whole crowd shouted, crying out: " Do away with this man, and set Barabbas free for us." ¹⁹He had been thrown into prison because of a revolt which took place in the city and for murder.

At the paschal feast, the governor was obliged to grant the Jews the freedom of one prisoner. This was obviously the result of a legal privilege granted to the Jews by the Romans. The crowd tossed Barabbas's name into the proceedings. He was a freedom fighter and a political agitator; in the course of a revolt, he had been guilty of murder. He was guilty of the crime with which the Sanhedrin charged Jesus. The crowd requested the liberty of an agitator and a murderer, and demanded that Jesus should be done away with by violence. After the resurrection, Peter said to the Jews: " The God of Abraham and the God of Isaac and the God of Jacob, the God of our fathers, has glorified his servant Jesus whom you betrayed and rejected in Pilate's presence, when he had passed sentence acquitting him. You disowned the holy and the just man, and demanded that a murderer should be given to you. You killed the author of life " (Acts 3:13f.). The stark contrast is not without an overtone of frightful tragedy. The people decided in favor of an unscrupulous anarchist against the " holy and just man," in favor of a man who destroyed life against the source and leader of life.

²⁰*But Pilate addressed them once more, because he wanted to let Jesus go free.* ²¹*They shouted back, saying: " Crucify him! Crucify him!"* ²²*But he said a third time: " What wrong has he done—this fellow here? I have found nothing in him for which he deserves death. I will set him free, after I have had him punished."*

From the moment Jesus was charged with high treason, the death penalty was always there in the background. Then the time came when it was demanded openly (23:18) and finally it was specified as death by crucifixion (23:21). In Roman law, treason was a capital crime. It was punished either by death on the cross, or by wild beasts in the arena, or by deportation to an island, according to the civil status of the person concerned. The leading members of the Sanhedrin plotted Jesus' death by crucifixion. They were determined to destroy him completely. Anyone who was crucified lost his life and his honor, as well as his existence in God's eyes. Scripture says: " Cursed is the man who hangs on the cross " (Deut. 21:23; see Gal. 3:13).

A third time, Pilate declared Jesus innocent (23:4.13–16.22). His declarations became progressively more emphatic. The first was the outcome of his own investigation of the case; the second was confirmed by Herod, and the third involved a comparison with a rebel and murderer. That was the kind of man who could be guilty of the crimes with which Jesus was charged. What wrong had he done—this fellow here, Jesus? " *Ecce homo* " (Jn. 19:5).

Each time Pilate declared Jesus innocent, the attitude of the crowd hardened. The chief priests and the crowd became more obstinate in their resistance (23:5); the whole crowd cried out uninterruptedly: " Do away with him " (23:18). They shouted back uninterruptedly in reply to Pilate's words: " Crucify him! Crucify him!" Three times Pilate tried to get them to accept his decision. He remitted the case to Herod (23:7); he expressed his willingness to have him tortured (23:16); he repeated the offer of this cruel compromise (23:22). It was not the Roman judge who was responsible for Jesus' crucifixion; it was the Jewish crowd who accused Jesus before his tribunal. St. Luke emphasizes the ever-

227

increasing obduracy of Christ's enemies, not Pilate's weakness in compromising with them or his criminal failure to act. The Jews' resistance to God had now reached its limit. After looking back over the history of God's dealings with his people, Stephen, in his speech before the Sanhedrin, expresses his conviction in the words: "Stiff-necked and uncircumcised in hearts and ears! You are always resisting the Holy Spirit, just like your fathers. Was there any prophet your fathers did not persecute? They killed those who foretold the coming of the Just One, whom you have now betrayed and murdered " (Acts 7:51f.).

23But they pressed him with loud cries, demanding that he should be crucified, and their cries prevailed.

Pilate submitted to the fanatical screams of the crowd. Jesus' accusers " pressed on him with their cries "; he was " submerged " by their fanatical demands. Their shouts gained the upper hand. Their howling rage appears almost as an impersonal force. The power of darkness was at work in this massed cry. Behind the crowd and their leaders, the powers of darkness were fighting against the Lord of glory (22:53; see 1 Cor. 2:6ff.).

24And Pilate decided that their demands would have to be satisfied. 25He let the man they asked for, who had been imprisoned for revolt and murder, go free, while he handed Jesus up to their will.

The text does not contain an explicit sentence of death on the part of Pilate. There are, however, indications that such a sentence was in fact handed down. Pilate ascended the judgment seat to pronounce sentence (Jn. 19:13); the proclamation of Jesus' guilt which was attached to the cross shows that Jesus was condemned for treason (23:38). The sentence was executed by Roman soldiers (23:47). Why, then, does the evangelist express himself in such veiled terms: " Pilate gave him up to their will "? It was the will of the Jews who were gathered before Pilate's tribunal that Jesus should be crucified. In his first sermon on the feast of Pentecost, St. Peter explains: " Men of Israel, listen to these words. By God's fixed decree and foreknowledge, Jesus the Nazarene . . . was given up, and you killed him, nailing him to the cross by the hands of lawless men " (Acts 2:22f.). The greatest responsibility for Jesus' death on the cross was borne by the leaders of the Jews and the people of Jerusalem who, by their clamoring, allowed themselves to be used as agents of their hatred. There is no suggestion of a collective guilt affecting all the Jews. Jesus unmasked the guilt the scribes and the chief priests incurred in his death in the parable of the wicked vinedressers (20:16, 19). The inhabitants of Jerusalem were warned that their city would be destroyed, because they had not recognized or welcomed God's gracious visitation when he came to them in Jesus (19:43ff.). It was by the will of the Jews who stood before Pilate that Jesus was crucified.

The Roman governor handed Jesus over to the Jews. He had done everything possible to prove Jesus innocent of any political offense. The Jewish crowd, under the guidance of the Sanhedrin, had forced him to yield. Pilate, therefore, was exonerated to a great degree. St. Luke was not interested in investigating and apportioning the blame for Jesus' death. For the mission confided to the church, it was much more important to bring out clearly the Roman governor's testimony that Jesus and his mission were above suspicion politically and did not constitute a threat to the state. The Roman state had no reason to persecute the church. Starting with its founder, the church had no political aspirations; it had no desire for power. Therefore, the Roman authorities should not allow themselves to be led astray by the calumnies of the Jews which Christ's apostles encountered in all the cities of the Roman empire.

For the church, Jesus' trial remains an obligatory norm governing its relations with the state. However, it is also a source from which the state can learn a correct understanding of the church. Jesus' experience before Pilate's judgment seat is a source of encouragement for the church when it receives the same treatment from judges and those in authority as Jesus received from Pilate. Jesus was sacrificed so that Pilate might not be involved in political difficulties, just as the Roman procurators, Felix and Festus, later sacrificed Paul and handed him over to his fanatical enemies (Acts 24:25ff.; 25:9). In principle, the time of the church is a time of persecution. The distress and trials which characterize this period will end only when the Son of man comes. The memory of the Lord consoles the church; he endured this destiny of suffering first. He was condemned as a traitor and an instigator of revolt, while the real traitor and murderer went free.

The Sanhedrin, therefore, were able to carry out their decision to put Jesus to death. The account of how they accomplished this began with Judas's promise to give him up to them. It ends with the words: "He [Pilate] gave Jesus up to their will." The words "give up," "surrender," characterize the whole passion, and not merely the beginning and the end of Jesus' trial. Various Jewish records of trials and martyrdoms tell us that the martyrs were given up into the hands of those who tortured and killed them. Therefore St. Luke portrays Jesus as a martyr. The expression " he was given up " conveys at once the historical event and its explanation. When Jesus was given up and surrendered, it was not the work of a human agent; ultimately it was God's doing. It was the Lord who gave him up because of our sins (Is. 53:12). Jesus was given up to the will of the Jews and so God's own will was accomplished which was revealed in scripture (24:26f.). His martyrdom was not merely the result of unbridled human power; it was a divine drama of salvation.

Jesus' Death (23:26–56)

Jesus' last journey and his death are portrayed in such a way that Jesus stands before the church as a martyr. His life and his mission reached their full achievement in his martyrdom. The success of his martyrdom became visible even before he breathed his last. In Jesus the persecuted church saw the " power in powerlessness " of a martyr's death.

The Way of the Cross (23:26–32)

²⁶And as they led him away, they seized Simon, a man from Cyrene who was coming in from the country, and laid the cross on him, so that he could carry it after Jesus.

The sentence was usually carried out immediately after it was pronounced. The execution was the duty of the procurator's guard, as Pilate had inflicted a military penalty. The phrase: "They led him away" really means for St. Luke: He was led away. So far, he has said nothing about Roman soldiers; he does not even mention that they insulted Jesus (Mk. 15:16f.). It was not the Romans who bore the responsibility for Jesus' torture and execution—at least the chief responsibility (Jn. 19:11). The distance from Herod's palace to the place of execution outside the walls of the city (Mt. 28:11; Jn. 19:20) was about three hundred yards. It passed through busy streets; the penalty of crucifixion was intended as a deterrent. As was the custom, Jesus carried the cross-beam of the cross; the upright was already in position, awaiting him at the place of execution. The evangelist says nothing about all that lay concealed in the simple expression: "They led him away." He stresses only the elements in which Christian martyrs could find strength and courage.

On the way, they took Simon of Cyrene and forced him to carry the cross for Jesus. He was seized. St. Luke chooses a "civilian" expression to replace the military term St. Mark used (15:21): "They arrested him"; they "requisitioned him." The Roman forces of occupation had the right to commandeer anyone they wished for public service. St. Luke, therefore, spares the Romans; Jesus' execution is not represented as having been carried out by the Roman forces. Simon was coming from the country, from a piece of ground which he may have bought for his burial. He was a Jew of the diaspora who had probably come from Cyrene to prepare for the next life in the proximity of the temple; it was commonly hoped that the resurrection of the dead would begin on Mount Sion. Simon carried the cross behind Jesus; in so doing, he accomplished all that Jesus demanded of his disciples: "If anyone wants to come

231

after me [to be my disciple], he must renounce himself and take up his cross daily " (9:23). " The man who does not take up his cross and follow after me cannot be my disciple " (14:27). Simon represents Christ's true disciple, the Christian martyr. The significance of Christian martyrdom consists in carrying one's own cross after Christ who carried his cross. The daily cross which the Christian life imposes in the demands made by each day shares in Jesus' way of the cross; the church is a persecuted church.

27A great crowd of the people and of the women followed him, who mourned and wept over him. 28But Jesus turned to them and said: " Daughters of Jerusalem, do not weep for me. Rather, weep for yourselves and your children. 29For see, the days will come when people will say: ' It is well for the barren, for the wombs which never bore children and the breasts that have never suckled!' 30Then they will begin to say to the mountains: ' Fall on us,' and to the hills: ' Cover us.' 31If this is what they do to the green wood, what will happen to the wood which is dry?"

The " people," the people of God, appears on the scene once more together with the women. They performed the lament for the dead which was customary at Jewish burials (8:52). When a lament was raised for leading personages, the group of mourners was widened to include the whole people. The Jews forbade a public lamentation for anyone who was executed (Deut. 21:22f.). Yet Jesus was lamented; the women beat their breasts and wept on the way to the place of execution. He was lamented as a teacher and a prophet, and as his people's king. The women who mourned over him bore courageous witness that Jesus was no criminal. In the same way, God-fearing men mourned for Stephen the martyr (Acts 8:2).

Jesus spoke to the women who mourned over him as a prophet of sublime majesty. His words were clothed in the language of the prophets of doom: " Daughters of Jerusalem " (Is. 3:16); " the days will come " (Amos 4:2); " they will say to the mountains: ' Fall on us ' " (Hos. 10:8). It was as a prophet that he had exercised his ministry, and it was as a prophet that he brought it to completion. Now he suffered the fatal destiny of all prophets at the hands of the city which murders prophets (13 : 34). He was faithful to the last. Endurance was his greatness, as it is the greatness of Christians; the time of the church is a time of persecution (21 : 19).

When Jesus went to his death, it was more than a mere lamentable personal calamity. " Do not weep for me!" His execution would bring down God's sentence on Jerusalem. " Weep for yourselves and for your children." This city had constantly resisted the prophets and put them to death. It had reached the limit of its blindness in what was now happening; soon it would meet its sentence of punishment. Its fate would be intolerable. What was otherwise regarded as the greatest happiness would then be a source of unhappiness. Childless women would be proclaimed blessed. Life would be so unbearable that people would prefer to die. The judgment inflicted on Jerusalem brought to an end a thousand-year history of infidelity and revolt against God. At the same time, it was a figure and a symbol of the general judgment which will be inflicted on all that is evil, on every rejection of God's offer of grace, and on all the powers which are opposed to God.

Jesus thought more about the fate which awaited Jerusalem and its inhabitants than he did about his own suffering. " Weep for yourselves and your children." His prophetic words were an exhortation to conversion and repentance. The sight of the city (19 : 41) and the encounter with its inhabitants who were well disposed towards him forced him to reveal his love for it and what he knew about its end. The way of the cross which he followed accomplished all God's plans. It was with a lament for Jerusalem that he had entered the city of his death where he would meet with refusal and rejection. It was in the sight of these women who mourned over him, while they should have wept for the city, that he left it to meet the death it had prepared for him. Jerusalem had failed to recognize what could promote its peace.

The gravity of the hour was clear in Jesus' death. Judgment was beginning with him, the just one. He was the suffering servant who suffered on behalf of the many; but this did not mean that the judgment threatened for those for whom he suffered was annulled. What happened to Jesus was a warning and an appeal for repentance. If God's sentence of punishment was so severe in his case, although he was innocent, what would it be like for those who were guilty? Jesus here appeals to a proverb: " If fire burns even what is green, what will become of the branches which are dry?" As a martyr who atoned for others, Jesus wanted to rouse his hearers. St. Peter says of the church of the martyrs: " The time has come for judgment to begin with God's house. But if it begins with us, how will it end for those who refuse to obey the gospel? If a just man scarcely attains salvation, what will become of those who are godless and sinners?" (1 Pet. 4 : 17).

³²*Two others who were criminals were led out with him, to be executed.*

The Romans were accustomed to carry out a number of executions simultaneously, which would not have been permitted under Jewish law. According to Mark, the two criminals seem to have been freedom fighters; according to Luke, they were not political offenders, but evildoers, sinners. Jesus was numbered among criminals and sinners. What he himself had told his disciples before they set out for the Mount of Olives was now a reality; this was the fate appointed for him by God, as the scriptures had foretold (22 : 37; Is. 53 : 12). He took his place among the wrongdoers and suffered their punishment, to atone for them. The criminals were " with him," his disciples!

On the Cross (23 :33–43)

JESUS IS CRUCIFIED (23 :33–34)

³³*When they came to the place which is called The Skull, they crucified him there, together with the criminals, one on his right and the other on his left.* ³⁴*But Jesus said: " Father, forgive them, because they do not know what they are doing." They cast lots to divide up his clothes.*

The place of execution was called " The Skull." This is a translation
of the Hebrew name " Golgotha " (Jn. 19:17). Like the name
" head " (Arabic: " *ras* ") which is so common in the east, it implied that it was a gently rising hill. Jesus ended his mission and
brought it to its full accomplishment on the gallows hill. " He was
despised and rejected by men " (Is. 53:3).

There they crucified him. Standing on the hill were a number of
uprights, each of them fitted with a wooden support in the form of
a seat in the middle and a groove for the cross-beam at the top. Jesus'
hands were nailed to the cross-beam (24:39; Jn. 20:25). This was
then hauled up, together with its burden, onto the upright; the
cross-beam and his feet were then secured in position. In antiquity,
crucifixion was regarded as the " cruelest and most fearful of all
means of execution " (Cicero), the " most pitiful of all ways of
dying " (Josephus Flavius), and the " penalty of slaves " (Tacitus).
The cross reduced Jesus to the level of the most dishonorable criminals. He entered Jerusalem as the Prince of Peace; he met his end
as a disturber of peace and order, on the gallows hill outside the city
of peace. He was crucified between two law breakers, like a common
criminal. But it was precisely for this reason, because he was numbered among the malefactors as a martyr and God's suffering servant, that a ray of hope shone forth: " Therefore, I will give him
a share among those who are great; he will divide the spoils with
those who are strong. It is for this that he empties his life in death
and lets himself be numbered among the malefactors " (Is. 53:12).
The picture of Christ gave Christians courage when they were put
to death as criminals, for the sake of Jesus' name.

Jesus prayed for his enemies and those who tortured him. Torment and injustice could not stop him from loving others. Even in
defeat he remained the victor. He practiced what he had preached.
He had preached love for one's enemies; now he prayed for his
enemies, as he himself had demanded his disciples should do (6:35).
Even in the hours of darkness, he remained true to himself in his
words. He would bring Judas to his senses, even as he was betraying
him. He healed the ear of the servant who was wounded as he came

to help in arresting him. He prayed for his enemies as they nailed him to the cross. Jesus crucified is an " illustration " of his own preaching, the model of all Christian living, prayer, and suffering. " It is to this that you are called; Christ suffered for you and left you an example, that you might follow his footsteps " (1 Pet. 2:21).

In the prayer he offered, Jesus acted as an advocate and high priest (Heb. 7:25; 1 Jn. 2:1) on behalf of those who " betrayed and murdered him " (Acts 7:52). He invoked all the intimacy which bound him to God and God to him which was expressed in the word " Father " (" *Abba* ") to gain the object of his prayers. Moreover, he made excuses for what his executioners, and his enemies among the Jews who were behind them, were doing. " They do not know what they are doing." In saying this, he did not deny their guilt. If they had not been guilty, Jesus' intercession would have been meaningless. His trial showed that his enemies were given to lying, hatred, and perversity; they had not scrupled to put pressure on the judge to attain their ends.

But were they fully conscious of what Jesus' execution involved? They were crucifying Christ, the Son of God and the Son of man (22:66ff.). We have seen what Peter said; he reproached the Jews of Jerusalem: " You killed the author of life," but he added immediately: " I know well, my brothers, that you acted in ignorance, as did your leaders " (Acts 3:15, 17). St. Paul agreed with this in the sermon he preached to the Jews at Antioch in Pisidia: " The people of Jerusalem and their rulers did not recognize him [Christ]. By their sentence they fulfilled the words of the prophet which are read out every sabbath " (Acts 13:27). Peter and Paul did not exonerate the Jews from all blame either; ignorance and failure to recognize Christ were not confined exclusively to the intellectual sphere; they also involved a free decision of the will. " Failure to recognize Christ did not mean simply that they were not properly orientated, which as such would be excusable; it also involved a neglect of duty which deserved God's anger and needed to be forgiven." However, it was only after Jesus' resurrection that refusal to believe in him as the Messiah became inexcusable. Until then,

God overlooked " the times of ignorance "; he did not inflict the punishment people deserved. But now that the resurrection had taken place, things were different (Acts 17:30). Prayer expressing love for one's enemies and imploring forgiveness for them appeared like a ray of light in the time of persecution. As he was struck by the stones and fell to his knees, St. Stephen the first martyr cried out with a loud voice : " Lord, do not count this sin against them " (Acts 7:60). He raised his eyes to the glorified Christ to whom God has given the power of judging and prayed in his spirit. Jesus is the model and the strength of the martyrs.

Jesus far surpassed the Jewish martyrs. They were great men and deserve all honor. It is impossible to read the account of the martyrdom of the Maccabee brothers and their heroic mother without being moved (2 Mac. 7). But how did they behave towards their enemies? They threatened the king who had them tortured with the words : " Do not think that you will go unpunished, you who dared to fight against God " (2 Mac. 7:19). They reviled their enemies and scorned them; they roused them to fury, execrating them, and announcing dire penalties for them. Jesus forgave his enemies; he made excuses for them and prayed that they might be forgiven.

The Jews expected a man who was being executed to make an admission of his guilt. The good thief did this (23:41). Jesus was the holy and just one; he bore the guilt of the many and prayed for them, especially for those who had sinned against him. Before he died, he fulfilled all justice, the justice he himself demanded from his disciples. He was merciful as his Father in heaven is merciful (see 6:36).

Those who were executed were crucified naked; their clothes and few personal belongings fell to the executioners. They cast lots to decide what should fall to each. The casting of lots for Jesus' clothes is described in words taken from the passion Psalm (Ps. 22[21] :19). It was part of God's design, of his plan of salvation, that Jesus should die in the most abject poverty and infamy. On his journey to his " being taken up," Jesus had often spoken with insistence of poverty and the need to become poor. Everything he possessed was taken from him, and he surrendered it all because it was God's will. When he entered this world, Mary wrapped him in swaddling clothes; before he departed this life, his clothes were shared among his executioners.

Everything Jesus had was taken from him; his freedom by the crucifixion, his honor by his being classed with criminals, and his clothes to which the executioners laid claim. He gave up everything to do good to those who hated him. Only one thing was left him —the Father—*Abba*. He would make those who were poor rich, as had been promised in the passion Psalm just quoted: " To him will I give my praise in the great assembly. I will fulfill my vows in the presence of those who worship you. Then the poor will eat and have enough. Then those who seek the Lord will praise him. Their heart will live forever. Remembering this, all the ends of the earth will turn to the Lord. Every age and people will cast themselves down in your presence to worship. Before him only will they fall down. All the princes of the earth will bow before him, all those who go down to the dust . . . Posterity will serve him who gave up his life. They will tell the future generation about the Lord of all, proclaiming his goodness to a people still to be born: ' It is he who has accomplished all this!' " (Ps. 22[21]: 26–31).

JESUS IS MOCKED (23:35-38)

[35]*And the people stood there, watching. But the leaders, too, mocked him, saying: " He saved others; if he is God's Anointed, the Chosen, let him save himself."*

A distinction is made between the people (the people of God) and its leaders. The people took up a position and stood there. They watched. These were the people who had listened to him in the temple, but played no active part in his trial. Now they appeared on the scene once more. Like the leaders, the people, too, mocked him. They were incapable of mastering what they saw and experienced as they stood beneath the cross. Jesus' death on the cross is the great challenge to faith, a challenge which must be overcome in temptations which will be constantly renewed. Can this man who hangs on the cross be the redeemer, the Messiah, if he cannot save himself? The people said nothing and took no active part in mocking Jesus. Interiorly, however, they were unable to cope with the scandal of the Messiah's death on the cross. Surely God was bound to intervene, when his Anointed, his Chosen, was being killed—or when a martyr dies a miserable death?

The leaders of the people " wrinkled their noses," curling their lips; they considered themselves justified in despising Jesus. The words they used summed up all that was contained in Jesus' different titles, " saviour," " God's Anointed," " Messiah " (9:35), " chosen," " suffering servant " (9:35; Is. 42:1), and " Son of God." If Jesus were all that these titles claimed, and enjoyed the power they expressed, he must demonstrate this power here and now and save himself. His mission began with a similar temptation (4:3), and he met it again in his home town of Nazareth (4:23). Finally, it marked the end of his earthly journey; it was a choice he had to make before he was glorified. It was incomprehensible that Jesus' power should be demonstrated in his powerlessness. A paradox such as this could be understood only in the light of scripture of which there is an echo in the words: " They turned up their noses." " But I am a worm, not a man, the scorn and derision of the people. Those who see me mock at me; they curl their lips [turn up their noses] and shake their heads " (Ps. 22[21]:8).

36The soldiers, too, mocked him. They came up to him and offered him vinegar, 37saying: " If you are the king of the Jews save yourself." 38An inscription was placed above him: " This is the king of the Jews."

The Roman soldiers, too, mocked Jesus. This is the first time the evangelist mentions them. They offered him vinegar in his thirst— a distant echo of the words of the Psalm: " In my thirst they gave me vinegar to drink " (Ps. 69[68] :22). They tortured Jesus in his distress. Everything revolved around the title " King of the Jews "; this was Jesus' " guilt." What kind of a king was this, hanging on the cross, helpless, and on the point of death? He was a true king of the Jews, a nation whom the Romans had subjugated, who were of no consequence. The king of the Jews was unable to save himself, much less his people. The crucified Messiah-king was a scandal to the Jews; to the gentiles, it was utter foolishness (1 Cor. 1:23).

As criminals were on their way to the place of execution, a white placard was hung around their necks or carried in front of them. This contained a description of their offense in black or red lettering. It was eventually fixed to the cross. Even the inscription which was fixed to the cross was intended to deride Jesus' kingship. This fellow hanging on the cross—the king of the Jews! Pilate and the soldiers made fun of Jesus, just like the Sanhedrin and the Jews. Jews and gentiles combined in scorning Jesus' kingship. The insults offered to Jesus also affected his church, his people, and his witnesses who are his martyrs.

The Good Thief (23:39–43)

³⁹*Even one of the criminals who was being executed blasphemed him: "Are you not the Christ? Save yourself and us!" ⁴⁰The other, however, answered him with a rebuke, saying: " Do you not fear God, you who are under the same sentence? ⁴¹We are being punished justly. We are getting what we deserve for our crimes. But this man has done nothing wrong." ⁴²And he said: " Jesus, remember me when you come into your kingdom." ⁴³And he said to him: " I tell you truly: today you will be with me in paradise."*

" In that night [when the Lord comes], there will be two men in the same bed, and one will be taken, the other left " (17:34). The separation of good and bad characteristic of that final hour was visible also as Jesus hung on the cross. The two criminals were crucified with Jesus; they hung on the cross, just like him—

together with Jesus. Yet the outcome of their lives was so different! Both were " with him," one of them only exteriorly, the other interiorly in a spirit of faith. Even being " with him " is no use without a personal decision for him (13:26f.).

One of the criminals joined in mocking Jesus. If Jesus was the Christ, God's Anointed, the Messiah, he must save himself and the two who shared his fate. He demanded that Jesus should prove he was the Messiah by saving him. His words were blasphemous; he condemned God's plan of salvation which was being accomplished in Jesus. The other criminal walked the path of faith which begins by fearing God and showing reverence for him. He fell in with God's design and his wisdom in which he believed. He acknowledged Jesus crucified as the Christ.

The man who is truly repentant acknowledges his fault and the justice of the penalty God inflicts on him. The good thief looked upon his crucifixion as a sentence he had earned for his crimes. The sight of Jesus moved him to recognize his guilt; he was convinced that Jesus was innocent as he hung upon the cross. His sins were forgiven because he gave God the glory and made no effort to achieve justification by himself. As he was dying, he acknowledged the justice of God's judgment; he accepted his death in obedience to God's will and as Jesus' companion.

Contrition which is effective and repentance must be accompanied by the conviction that God is ready to forgive. The good thief put his hope in Jesus. In him, he saw the saviour. He believed that the Father gave Jesus his kingdom, because he followed the way of the cross (22:29f.). Jesus gives the kingdom to those who adopt his way as their own (22:29). The thief placed his future in Jesus' hands. In the Old Testament, those who were tempted and in great distress appealed to God to remember the covenant and all his activity which he had accomplished for the patriarchs to whom he gave his promises. The good thief begged Jesus to remember him.

Everything that he accomplished for man's salvation God has placed in Jesus' hands. Prayer to Jesus had its origin in the agony of the cross; his glorification was beginning already. Such prayer would never cease. St. Stephen prayed: " Lord Jesus, receive my spirit " (Acts 7:59). Christians are described as people who invoke Jesus' name (Acts 2:21).

Jesus answered the good thief's prayer. The today which brings salvation had dawned. After his death, Jesus would enter paradise where his Father would give him the kingdom; he would give him supreme sovereignty and the eschatological " meal " (22:30). There the good thief would be with him. God gives Jesus paradise and Jesus gives it to his followers. The fact that the penitent and believing thief was " with him " formed the basis for his share in Jesus' paradise. Being " with him " is in itself paradise. Stephen prayed: " Lord Jesus, receive my spirit " (Acts 7:59), while St. Paul said: " I long to be released and to be with Christ " (Phil. 1:23; see 1 Thess. 4:17).

Jesus continued to be the redeemer and saviour of sinners until he died. His defense of the sinful woman in the Pharisee's house, his teaching in the parables concerning the things which were lost (15), and the gracious welcome he gave Zacchaeus the chief tax collector, were all crowned by his treatment of the good thief who was assured of salvation at the last moment. The root source of God's mercy is revealed in the cross of Christ who died on behalf of the many. In late Jewish literature concerning the martyrs, we frequently find that some gentile standing by was converted and shared the martyr's fate, so that he also shared their reward, like the good thief. Jesus, therefore, is God's suffering servant and a martyr.

Jesus' Death (23:44–49)

A God-given Interpretation (23:44–45)

[44] *It was already about the sixth hour and darkness came over the whole earth until the ninth hour, because the sun stopped shining.* [45] *The temple curtain was torn apart in the center.*

As an historian who is anxious to give exact figures (3 : 23), St. Luke decides that the traditional hours given for the passion are not exact. The sixth hour was noon, and the ninth hour was 3 p.m. During these three hours, darkness covered the whole earth. St. Luke attempts to give the reason for this: the sun stopped shining. God intervened in the world's course. Jesus' death was an event which affected the whole world; it affected men and the universe of the heavenly bodies. The coming of the Son of man as an eschatological event will be introduced by cosmic upheavals. The cosmos shared in Jesus' death in the same way; the sun refused its light, its lifegiving and creative power. When God darkened the sun, it was intended to be a sign of the judgment to come. Jesus, too, had reminded the women who lamented over him of the judgment to come (23 : 27f.). By Jesus' death, God wishes to lead the world to repentance.

The holy of holies in the temple was separated from the sanctuary by a curtain which shut it off completely. Only the high priest could pass through this on the Day of Atonement once a year, when he went to perform the rite of expiation. At Jesus' death, this curtain was torn apart by divine intervention; the carefully guarded entrance to the holy of holies was ripped open; the place of God's revelation in the Old Testament was profaned. God abandoned the place of his revelation; the old temple and its institutions were at an end. With Jesus' death, the old world and the old economy of salvation perished; a new order of salvation and a new world came into being.

JESUS DIES (23:46)

[46] *And Jesus cried out with a loud voice, saying: " Father, into your hands I commend my spirit." When he had said this, he breathed out his spirit.*

It may not be completely unusual for people to cry aloud immediately before they die. A person who was crucified, however, would die of slow exhaustion and lapse into unconsciousness. Jesus' loud cry from the cross prompts us to reflect. Was it a sign that he had superhuman powers at his disposal to the very end, so that he gave up his life voluntarily (Jn. 10 : 17f.)?

Jesus ended his life with a prayer. Every time his death and glorification were mentioned together during his life, he prayed; at his baptism (3 : 21), at his transfiguration (9 : 28), and now, as he was about to enter his glory through death. He took the words of his prayer from the Psalms, the great book of prayer God had given his people (Ps. 30 [31] : 6). But as always he introduced the words of the Psalm with the invocation " Father " (" *Abba* "). Innocent and persecuted, he committed his life to God's power, to the Father's love. Jesus yielded up his spirit completely to the Father, the spirit which was the vehicle of life. This passed over into the sphere of the Father's power; it became his property. God is faithful; he is a trustworthy God, a Father. In his hands, in his fatherly goodness, Jesus' soul would be safe. He would not destroy it; he would save it and keep it safe. Jesus' life ended on a note of self-surrender, obedience, and trust. By giving his life to God, he praised God as the One who had given it to him and from whom he would receive it anew.

The Jews used these words as an evening prayer. The temple trumpets announced the hour for the evening prayer about 3 p.m. On the cross of Calvary, Jesus pronounced this prayer in union with his people. He pronounced it in a loud voice as pious custom demanded. Jesus had probably used this evening prayer from the days of his childhood. Now, his childhood prayer became his dying prayer. The first word he spoke in which he revealed himself as God's Son was a word about the Father: " Did you not know that I must be in the place which belongs to my Father?" (2 : 49). The last word he spoke once more recalled the Father into whose hands he committed his spirit, because he had to be with him.

St. Stephen the first martyr departed this life with the words: " Lord Jesus, receive my spirit " (Acts 7 : 59). What was a prayer to God the Father on Jesus' lips became a prayer to Jesus on

244

Stephen's lips. The Father has given Jesus all power; in him is the fullness of salvation. Stephen died a martyr in imitation of the teacher and Lord of martyrs. St. Peter wrote to the early Christians : " None of you should be punished as a murderer or a thief, as a malefactor or a person who interferes in other people's affairs. But if a man is punished as a Christian, he must not be ashamed. He must glorify God in this name . . . Therefore, those who suffer because it is God's will should commend their souls to the Creator who is so faithful by doing good " (1 Pet. 4 : 15–19).

When he had prayed, Jesus breathed out his spirit; he died. At death, life leaves the body, but the real I, the soul, survives death. God will keep the souls of the just in paradise for the day of the resurrection (23 : 43).

RAYS OF GLORY (23 :47–49)

⁴⁷*But when the centurion saw what happened, he gave glory to God, saying: " Truly, this man was a just man."*

The centurion in command of the escort guarding Jesus witnessed the great drama which took place on Golgotha. The screams of rage and agony of the unfortunate victims, together with their curses and despairing outbursts, made the task of carrying out a sentence of crucifixion a frightful one. But Jesus did not curse his executioners; instead, he prayed that they would be forgiven. Instead of giving way to despair, he committed himself trustingly to a Father-God. He was silent and invoked no curses on those who mocked him. This was something which exceeded the limits of human strength. The centurion was convinced that God had a hand in it. God was active in Jesus. And so he gave glory to God. At Jesus' birth, the shepherds glorified God (2:20). When Jesus gave proof of his power in word or action, the people gave glory to God (13:13; 17:15; 18:43). At the end of his life, the pagan centurion added his voice to this chorus of divine praise. The message proclaimed by angels and men when Jesus entered the world, and later when he entered the city of Jerusalem, was now fulfilled: " Glory to God in the highest " (2:14; 19:38). God glorified himself in Jesus. In his life, his mission, and his death, he revealed himself as the " God of glory " (Acts 6:2); he revealed his majesty and his all-embracing sovereignty, his holiness, and his wisdom.

For the centurion, the drama on Golgotha was proof of Jesus' innocence. He was a just man. This was how Pilate's wife had described him (Mt. 27:19). Pilate, too, was convinced of this, when he said: " I am innocent of the blood of this just man " (Mt. 27:24). The early church regarded the centurion's words about Jesus as more than a proof of his innocence. For Christians, " the just one " was a messianic title. St. Paul was given the command: " The God of our fathers has chosen you to know his will, to see the just one, and hear his voice from his lips. You must be his witness for all men concerning all that you have seen and heard " (Acts 22:15). The prophets foretold the coming of the just one (Acts 7:51f.). Jeremiah says: " See, the days are coming when I will raise up a just shoot for David. He will reign as king and govern wisely; he will make right and justice prevail in the land " (Jer. 23:5). Justice was the characteristic of the messianic era. The Messiah was the one who would accomplish God's will to the full. He was the holy and just one (Acts 3:13). The sight of Jesus on the cross, therefore, should lead a person to confess him as the Messiah, not to deny it.

The pagan centurion's confession was a reproach to the Jews who did not believe in Jesus. St. Stephen rebuked them with the words: " Stiff necked and uncircumcised in hearts and ears! You are always resisting the Holy Spirit, just like your fathers. Was there any prophet your fathers did not persecute? They killed those who foretold the coming of the just one, whom you have now betrayed and murdered " (Acts 7:51f.).

A martyr's death saves the man who is condemned with him, and even his executioners. The Acts of the Apostles associate Saul's name very closely with Stephen's death as a martyr: " He gave his voice for his execution " (Acts 8:1). Before the Sanhedrin, the same lying witnesses made the same accusations against Stephen (Acts 6:14) as they had against the Lord (Mk. 14:56f.). The same reference to the glory of the Son of man who has been exalted at God's right hand occurs both in the synoptic account of the passion (Mk. 14:62f.) and in the story of Stephen's martyrdom (Acts 7:55f.). Stephen was dragged outside the city (Acts 7:58), like the Lord and the rest of the faithful. His last words resemble those of Jesus (Acts 7:59f.). The power of Jesus' martyrdom, the glory of God, lives on in the martyrs.

[48]*And all the crowds who were present at the spectacle saw what had happened. They beat their breasts and went back to their homes.* [49]*But all his acquaintances stood at a distance, with the women who had followed him from Galilee, watching this.*

Jesus' martyrdom was a spectacle. St. Luke's description is influenced by the descriptions of the Old Testament martyrs: " The crowd from the city gathered to watch the sad spectacle " (3 Mac. 5:24). The people beat their breasts as a sign of sorrow and regret (18:13). St. Luke's words are reminiscent of a passage of Zechariah: " I will pour out a spirit of compassion and entreaty over David's house and the citizens of Jerusalem. They will look on the man who has been pierced, and they will mourn for him like a man mourning an only son. They will weep bitterly for him, like a man weeping for a first-born son " (Zech. 12:10). The remarkable person referred to here, who has been described as " God's martyr," is a figure of the Good Shepherd (Zech. 11:4-14). He was put to the sword by God's own design (Zech. 13:7-9). But then an extraordinary thing happened: the people raised a bitter lament over the man whom they themselves had pierced and laid low (Zech. 12:10). Why did they mourn him? It was really an expression of grief at their own guilt in the martyr's death, and of sorrow for the misfortune which this death brought upon the people of God (Zech. 13:7-9). However, this lament took place against a background of hope; it was prompted by the gift of a divine spirit which they received and it marked the beginning of a new life:

" Then a fountain will be open for David's house and for the citizens of Jerusalem to counteract sin and uncleanness " (Zech. 13:1). By God's design, Jesus was put to death by his own people. He was the Son of David, the Good Shepherd, and Israel's king; at the same time, he was the first-born Son and the only beloved in a unique sense. Now the people of Jerusalem mourned him; they were guilty of putting Christ to death. When the women lamented over him as he walked the way of the cross, Jesus warned them of the judgment which was to come on Jerusalem (23:28ff.). But the lament raised by the crowds from Jerusalem foreshadowed the coming outpouring of the Spirit. Many of them would be converted by the proclamation of Jesus' death and resurrection after the descent of the Holy Spirit (Acts 2:37f.).

All Jesus' acquaintances had abandoned him, when he was arrested and condemned—and God failed to intervene on his behalf. The words of the prophet were fulfilled. As usual, St. Luke merely hints at this: " You estranged my acquaintances from me. You made me an object of aversion to them " (Ps. 88 [87] :9). " My friends and neighbors flee at the sight of my wounds; those who were closest to me keep their distance " (Ps. 38 [37] :12). Jesus' friends still stood at a distance, but they had come and they remained there. They rediscovered themselves in the presence of the crucified and through him. The martyr gave them courage and gathered them together.

The women who had followed him from Galilee and were his disciples (8:2) also came there to see the end. They arrived there and remained at the spot. His acquaintances and the women were witnesses of his death as they had been witnesses of his life. The church was beginning to congregate, as we are told in the hymn of the suffering servant: " From out of this wearisome life he sees the light. He filled many indeed with his knowledge. My servant relieved many of their guilt " (Is. 53:11). The eleven apostles and the women who had followed him from Galilee, together with Jesus' mother Mary and his brothers (his " acquaintances "), formed the basis of the church (Acts 1:13f.).

⁵⁰*And see, there was a man named Joseph who was a member of the council and a good and just man.* ⁵¹*He did not approve of their decision or their actions. He came from Arimathea, a Jewish town, and he waited for God's kingdom.* ⁵²*He approached Pilate and asked him for Jesus' body.* ⁵³*And he took him down and wrapped him in a linen cloth and laid him in a rock tomb in which no one had ever been buried.*

According to Roman law, a person who was executed lost all right to the honors normally paid to the dead. His body had to be left unburied until the birds and the animals had left nothing but the bones. Anyone who removed the body of an executed person on his own authority exposed himself to punishment. Jewish law, on the other hand, would not allow the body of a person who had been hanged to remain on the tree over night: "If a man has been executed for a capital crime, and he is afterwards hung in a tree, his body must not be left hanging in the tree over night. He must be buried on the same day. A man who has been hanged is cursed by God. You must not defile the country the Lord your God has given you as your inheritance" (Deut. 21:23). The Jews forbade a lament for a man who had been executed, but they allowed the body to be buried. However, this was done in a place apart and without ceremony. Sinners could not be buried beside good people, for fear these might be tainted with disgrace. The Jewish authorities took care that Jesus was not left hanging on the cross (Jn. 19:32). But was he to be buried like a criminal, without ceremony and without honor in a criminal's burial ground?

Now a surprising thing happened. A councillor, a member of the Sanhedrin who probably belonged to the elders (the lay nobility), took charge of Jesus' body. The gospels pay a glorious tribute to this man's memory. His name was Joseph. The town where he lived or from which he came was Arimathea, a Jewish town on the coastal plain (Ramathain near Lydda). He was a good and upright man, a noble character in whom God's word bore fruit (see 8:15). He looked forward to the coming of God's kingdom, and his hope and longing meant that he was disposed to listen to Jesus' preaching. He was not convinced of Jesus' guilt in the matter with which the Sanhedrin charged him. Consequently, he had not approved of its decision or its actions. God brought a disciple to Jesus from among the criminals who were crucified with him, who is with him in paradise; from among the pagan soldiers, he raised up one who bore him witness and praised his justice as God's work; from the Sanhedrin which condemned him, he brought to him a man who acknowledged him as the one who inaugurated God's kingdom and paid him his tribute of faith and recognition, as he passed through the door from death to glory. When God calls a man, he does not ask where he comes from. If a man is open for God " with a beautiful and good heart ", and is not self-righteous, so that he trusts only in the coming of God's kingdom, God will take him into the community of Jesus' disciples which is a community of salvation, no matter where he finds him.

Joseph had to get permission for Jesus' burial from the Roman authorities, from Pilate. Roman law prescribed that those who had been executed by the Romans could be buried only with the permission of the proper Roman authorities. If Joseph wanted to get this permission, he would have to overcome two difficulties; he was not a relative of Jesus, and Jesus had been condemned for high treason. Pilate surrendered the body. He was convinced of Jesus' innocence, all the more so as a member of the Sanhedrin interceded for him. The gospels think in terms of salvation history. Despite the obstacles, Jesus received an honorable burial; his glorification began immediately after his death. In this way, the words of the prophet were fulfilled: " His grave was appointed for him among the evildoers, but after his death a place was given him with a rich man " (Is. 53:9). The martyr was acknowledged and glorified. In the same way, Stephen was buried by Godfearing men (probably Jews who admired him) who raised a great lament for him (Acts 8:2).

Everything was done that an honorable burial demanded. The body was taken down from the cross (and washed; see Acts 9:37). Then it was wrapped in linen and laid in a rock tomb. There Jesus lay in a sepulchral chamber on a ledge of rock or in a cleft cut into the rock. No one had ever been buried in Jesus' tomb. In the same way, he had entered Jerusalem riding on an animal on which no one had ever ridden (19:30). He was the holy one; such reverence was fitting in his presence. He was taken out of the sphere of all that was profane and set apart from sinners (Heb. 7:26). In his death and burial, he was acknowledged as the " holy and just one," something the Jews had denied him when they chose Barabbas in his place (Acts 3:14).

The phrase " Jesus was buried " is found in the oldest professions of faith. " I handed on to you what I myself had heard; Christ died for your sins according to the scriptures; he was buried, and he was raised up, according to the scriptures " (1 Cor. 15:3f.). " The inhabitants of Jerusalem and their rulers did not recognize him. By condemning him, they fulfilled the words of the prophet which are read out every sabbath. They found no guilt in him which deserved death, yet they demanded his death from Pilate. When they had done everything which was written of him, they took him down from the cross and laid him in the tomb " (Acts 13:27ff.). The fact that he was buried proved that he was dead. It also proved that he rose from the dead. The tomb was at once an end and a beginning, a memorial to his death and to his resurrection, to his humiliation and his exaltation.

⁵⁴It was the day of preparation and the sabbath was beginning. ⁵⁵The women who had followed him from Galilee accompanied them and saw the grave and how his body was laid in it. ⁵⁶Then they went back and prepared spices and anointing oil, and on the sabbath they rested as the law commanded.

Friday was a day of preparation for the sabbath. As Jesus' body was laid in the tomb, the preparation day was coming to an end. The sabbath was already beginning. The evening star was shining and in the houses the lamps were burning which proclaimed the day of rest as a day for giving glory to God. Light was already beginning to shine through the darkness of Good Friday. Jesus' burial was not shrouded in a night of hopelessness; it already radiated life, light, and glory. Good Friday, the sabbath of repose in the tomb and Easter Sunday are all united in the Christian paschal celebration.

The women who had followed him from Galilee (8:2) and had been witnesses of his death by the cross also witnessed his burial. They saw the tomb and they saw that the body was laid in it. They would also be the first witnesses of the empty tomb after Jesus' resurrection. Although their testimony was belittled by many people, and discounted by those who described it as " idle gossip " (24-11; see Jn. 4:42), it deserves to be noticed. The ground was being prepared for the missionary activity of women.

The sabbath rest made it impossible for the moment to perform the usual offices of respect for Jesus by anointing his body. However, the women prepared everything they needed, so that what was impossible before could be done at first light on Sunday. The sabbath between Jesus' death and his resurrection was the great day of rest. The women rested and Jerusalem rested from its work. Jesus' body rested in the tomb, while his soul rested in the hands of his Father. " On the seventh day, God rested from all the work he did " (Gen. 2:2). A great turning-point in salvation history had been reached. The whole of creation held its breath before the new dawn for which everything was already prepared, the women with the anointing oil—the witnesses of the first news of the resurrection —and the first light—full of hope—of the sabbath without end (Heb. 4:1f.).

Jesus' Glorification (24:1–53)

St. Luke's account of the first Easter is distinguished from the others by three peculiarities. The risen Christ appears only in and around Jerusalem; not one of his appearances brings us back to Galilee. In St.

Matthew's Gospel, Jesus appears only in Galilee, while St. John mentions apparitions in both Jerusalem and Galilee. Even in his account of the resurrection, therefore, St. Luke remains true to the whole plan of his historical work. By God's will, the way Jesus followed led to Jerusalem, where his "departure" took place, and where everything else that was written about him had to be accomplished (see the account of the journey, 9:51ff.). It was at Jerusalem that his chosen apostles were endowed with strength when the Holy Spirit came upon them, and it was from there that they set out to be his witnesses to the ends of the earth (Acts 1:8). All the events St. Luke mentions take place on the same day, Easter Sunday. If we had only his gospel and not the Acts of the Apostles, there could scarcely be any doubt about this. St. Luke seems to have been moved to present the facts in this way by religious and liturgical considerations. The very early church celebrated the liturgy (1 Cor. 16:2; Acts 20:7) on the "first day" of the week, the "Lord's Day" (Rev. 1:10). This day recalled the Easter event. "Therefore we celebrate the eighth day with joy. It was on this day that Jesus rose from the dead and ascended to heaven, after he had appeared to his disciples" (*Ep. of Barnabas* 15:9). The Christian celebration of Sunday has its origin in the events of Jesus' life.

Three Easter events were experienced by three groups of witnesses, the women from Galilee (vv. 1–12), two of those who were close to the apostles (vv. 13–35; see 24:9), and the eleven (vv. 36–53). The whole church (Acts 1:13f.), therefore, proclaims the Easter message; it lives and acts by virtue of the Easter event; it is a paschal church.

The Easter Message (24:1–12)

The early Christians were convinced that God raised Jesus from the dead. They professed this belief in various formulas of faith (1 Cor. 15:3–4); they expressed it in their preaching (the sermons in the Acts of the Apostles), and they celebrated it in hymns (Phil. 2:6–11). St. Luke proves the "reliable character" of the evidence on which this faith rests by means of the "story of the empty tomb" with which all the gospels open their account of the first Easter, so that the objections raised are silenced. Secure in the possession of this Easter faith, therefore, St. Luke sets out with evident joy to tell us how the disciples came to believe in the risen Christ despite all their human reservations.

253

¹On the first day of the week, at very early dawn, they came to the tomb, carrying what they had prepared. ²But they found the stone moved away from the tomb. ³When they went in, they did not find the Lord Jesus' body.

The women who had witnessed Jesus' burial became witnesses of the empty tomb. Between the burial and the discovery that the grave was empty lay the day of rest. In their anxiety to perform the charitable task of anointing Jesus' body, the women went to the tomb very early in the morning. Who could have reached it before them?

They made a remarkable discovery: the huge stone which was used to seal the tomb had been moved away. The tomb was empty. Both of the facts which the women noticed called for an explanation. But what explanation was there? The women at first could think of no explanation. For them, there was no solution to the mystery; they were at a loss. They never thought of the resurrection, or that the body could have been stolen, as the Jews claimed in their efforts to disprove the apostles' preaching concerning the Easter event (Mt. 27:62–66; 28:11–15).

The explanation for the two facts they had discovered was given to them in a startling way.

⁴And it happened, while they were still at a loss about this, see, two men came to them in shining garments. ⁵As they were afraid and turned their faces towards the ground they said to them: " Why do you seek one who is alive among the dead? ⁶He is not here; he has been raised from the dead. Remember how he spoke to you while he was still in Galilee, saying: ⁷" The Son of man must be given up into the hands of sinners and be crucified, and rise again on the third day '." ⁸And they recalled his words. ⁹And they returned from the tomb and made known all this to the eleven and to all the others.

Their dazzling white robes indicated that the two figures were messengers from God. They were bathed in the light of God's glory (2:9). The news they brought was a message from God. Their sudden appearance also indicated that they were messengers from heaven (2:9; Acts 12:7). They appeared out of the blue before the women (2:9; Acts 12:7). Because there were two men, their testimony was conclusive (Deut. 19:15). The message they proclaimed was the church's Easter message: God raised up Jesus who had been laid to rest in the tomb after his death. He was alive. A live man does not live among the dead. He could not be sought in the tomb; he was not there. This was a truism and it was expressed in the form of a proverb. The message of Jesus' resurrection is a message from God. It was not inferred from the empty tomb; it was a revelation from God. The empty tomb bore out the divine message.

What the heavenly messengers said was confirmed by Jesus' prophetic word. He had foretold his death on the cross and his resurrection on the third day, while he was still in Galilee (9:22, 24). His betrayal into the hands of sinners, his crucifixion, and his resurrection were all rooted in the " must " of the divine plan of salvation. This saving plan was heralded by Jesus, the greatest and most powerful of all the prophets, and it was accomplished when he was raised from the dead. Ultimately, the most fundamental guarantee of the trustworthiness of our Easter faith is not the empty tomb, or the appearance of messengers from heaven; it is the prophetic word, God's word, which was spoken in the last instance by his Son (Heb. 1:2) and brought to its final state of perfection. Heaven itself refers us to this word; the women were told to remember the prophecy Jesus made during his earthly life.

When they recalled Jesus' prophecy, the women realized that it confirmed the Easter message they had received from heaven, and they themselves became instruments of the Easter preaching. According to Mark (16:7f.), they were told to make the news known to the disciples and to Peter, but did not do so. According to Luke, they announced the news without having to be told. Anyone who has listened to the good news becomes its apostle

(2 : 18; 2 : 38). Far from being overcome by fear and trembling at the extraordinary news they had heard, and saying nothing (Mk. 16 : 8), the women were forced by the joy contained in the Easter message to make it known. The time of the missionary church was beginning.

¹⁰It was Mary of Magdala, Joanna, and Mary the mother of James, and the others who were with them, who told this to the apostles. ¹¹Their words seemed to them as so much idle gossip, and they remained without faith.

Three of the women are mentioned by name. Mary of Magdala and Joanna " the wife of Chuza, Herod's steward " (8 : 3) remind us of the Galilean ministry : "And the twelve were with him and some women " (8 : 1f.). The apostles had really no reason to refuse to believe the women's story, yet they did not believe them. To the apostles their story seemed like a hallucination, a complete delusion. Faith in the Easter event encountered only opposition on the part of the apostles. It did not spring from credulity.

¹²But Peter rose up and ran to the tomb; when he bent down, he saw only the linen winding cloths. Then he went away, wondering about what had happened.

The leader of the apostles assured himself that the tomb was empty. He examined the burial chamber carefully and saw nothing there except the linen winding cloths in which the body had been wrapped. He could think of no explanation for what had happened. It seemed to him that he was faced with some divine intervention, but he left the tomb without giving a thought to the Easter message. A man who wonders and is amazed may be on the threshold of faith, but he does not yet believe; he has not yet cast off all doubts. There was no way from the empty tomb and the discarded cloths to faith in the resurrection. Yet the evangelist was convinced that after the resurrection Jesus' body was no longer in the tomb; it was not to be found there. Jesus had risen with his body.

The Risen Christ is Recognized (24:13–35)

After the resurrection, Jesus assured his church: " See, I am with you all days until the end of the world " (Mt. 28:20). In this way, he brought God's dwelling among the people of the covenant to its final perfection: " Where two or three are gathered in my name, I am there in their midst " (Mt. 18:20). In the resurrection, God brought the Christ-event to its climax; he set the final seal on Christ's preaching, and he confirmed the faith Christians professed in him. When the early Christians celebrated the eucharistic meal, they realized that the risen Christ was present among them. The phrase " Maranatha " (1 Cor. 16:22), " Come, Lord," was first used in the liturgical service of the very early church in Palestine. From there, it passed as a stereotyped formula into the liturgical usages of Greek-speaking Christians without even being translated. This phrase is a profession of faith in the risen Lord who is to come again. The risen, glorified Christ is present at the celebration of the Lord's Supper. It is in him that the church has its being; he confirms its preaching; he is the content of its worship. All these motifs find an echo in the " most beautiful and the most impressive " of all the Easter stories. This is the story of the two disciples who met the risen Christ on the road to Emmaus. In this passage, St. Luke is not writing merely as an historian; he is not merely defending the Easter faith as an apologist, or even proclaiming the Easter message as an evangelist—he writes as a religious narrator with the intention of bringing out the joy of Easter and making the hearts of his readers burn with longing for the risen Christ. The story has a counterpart in St. John, in the account of the risen Christ's encounter with Mary Magdalene. There as here, the risen Christ was present without being recognized; on that occasion, the word he spoke, " Mary," opened her eyes; here, the disciples' eyes were opened when he broke bread.

¹³*And see, two of them were journeying on the same day to a village called Emmaus, sixty stadia from Jerusalem.* ¹⁴*And they talked among themselves about all that had happened.* ¹⁵*And it happened that, as they talked and discussed together, Jesus himself drew near and began to journey with them.* ¹⁶*But their eyes were held, so that they did not recognize him.*

The two men were journeying on Easter Sunday from Jerusalem to the village of Emmaus about eight miles away (*el-qubebe,* northwest of Jerusalem). They belonged to the circle of those who were closest to the eleven. All their thoughts, their conversation, and their discussions centered around Jesus, showing that they were disciples of his. Jesus caught up with them after he had followed them unobtrusively. He journeyed with them. It was as one on a journey that the whole gospel of St. Luke had portrayed him. The church is a church which is on a journey, and Jesus journeys with it.

The two disciples did not recognize Jesus, just as Mary Magdalene had not recognized him, when he appeared (Jn. 20:14). The power which held the disciples' eyes fast was the incomprehensible character of the Easter message: a corpse does not suddenly return to life and rise from the grave. It was through God's intervention, through his power, that Jesus rose from the dead. When the risen Christ appears to a man and becomes visible, it is by God's gift: " God raised him up on the third day and revealed him, not to the people in general, but to us, the witnesses God had appointed beforehand, who ate and drank with him " (Acts 10:40f.). The life of the risen Christ was not merely a continuation of his earthly life. When he appeared to his disciples and was revealed to them, it was only by God's gift that they recognized him as the risen Jesus. It is God who is responsible for the events of salvation history—and it is he who gives them their explanation.

[17]But he said to them: " What kind of talk is this that you exchange among yourselves, as you go along?" And they stood still, with sad faces. [18]One of them who was called Cleopas answered, saying to him: " You must be the only one living in Jerusalem who does not know what happened there in these days!" [19]And he said to them: " What?" And they replied: " About Jesus of Nazareth who was a prophet, powerful in word and action before God and all the people, [20]how our chief priests and leaders gave him up to be sentenced to death and crucified him. [21]We hoped that he would bring de-

liverance to Israel. But, with all that, today is already the third day since this happened. ²²*Some women from among our number caused us some excitement; they were at the grave early in the morning,* ²³*but they did not find his body. They came and said that they had also had a vision of angels who said he was alive.* ²⁴*Some of those who were with us went and found everything as the women had said, but they did not see him."*

To the two disciples Jesus' fate was inexplicable. One suggestion merely led to another; discussion on a human level could never solve the mystery. Their sad faces betrayed their disillusionment, the hopelessness which weighed them down, and their paralyzing grief. This was the frame of mind which the events of Good Friday had inspired in the horrified disciples.

Cleopas spoke for the two of them and his words contain a picture of Jesus of Nazareth, as he had been in the days before his resurrection. He was powerful in word and action. He acted with power against the diabolical forces which are in the world. The words he spoke came from lips which were all-powerful; they overcame the power of the forces of the devil which was revealed in sickness, sin, and death. After he had cured a man who was possessed, the people exclaimed: " What kind of word is this, that he commands the unclean spirits with power and strength and they go out?" (4:36). " The Lord's power was there, so that he cured them " (5:17). God anointed him with the Holy Spirit and with power; that was why he went about the country doing good and healing all those who were in the devil's power (Acts 10:38). God lent credibility to his words by the acts of power, the miracles and signs, which he performed by God's means (Acts 2:22). Jesus was a prophet like Moses " who was powerful in his words and actions " (Acts 7:22). It was as such that God revealed him, as such that he was recognized by men (Lk. 7:16). Even after Good Friday, Cleopas still had no doubt that Jesus of Nazareth was a prophet.

In Jerusalem, something happened which threw the whole city into a state of excitement (see 24:18). The chief priests and the leaders of the people—Cleopas includes himself as one of the people —gave Jesus up to Pilate, to have him condemned to death; it was they who crucified Jesus. Jesus' death meant the end of the hope the two disciples had placed in him. To them, he seemed to be more than a prophet who was endowed with power; they had hoped that he would realize Israel's great hope and "deliver them from the hands of all those who hated them" (1:68, 71; 2:38). The prophecy made concerning the child Jesus seemed to them to be fulfilled in his life and ministry. The great mass of his disciples who had seen his powerful actions hailed Jesus as the Messiah-king (19:37) and expected that he would inaugurate God's rule in Jerusalem immediately (19:11). That the Messiah should end his life on the cross in misery and suffering, that he should be thrust out of the Holy City and die as a criminal, was contrary to all the messianic hopes of the Jews. How could he deliver Israel from the hands of their enemies, if he himself was subject to them?

The apostles' preaching concerning Jesus of Nazareth began with his ministry and mentioned his being given up to death. But then followed the triumphant sentences: " God raised up this man on the third day and enabled him to appear . . . He has been appointed by God as the judge of the living and the dead " (Acts 10:38–42). " The whole house of Israel must know with certainty that God has made this Jesus Lord and Christ [Messiah], the man whom you crucified " (Acts 2:34). The proclamation of the resurrection was the crowning point and the key stone of the church's preaching concerning Christ: " If Christ has not been raised from the dead, your faith is worthless; you are still in your sins " (1 Cor. 15:17).

The two disciples were familiar with the message of Jesus' resurrection; they knew about his prophecy that he would rise on the third day (9:22; 24:6). They had heard the message the women brought. They had seen the empty tomb. But they did not see him. The apparitions of the risen Christ confirmed the Easter message. But were the apparitions enough? Jesus was walking with his disciples here, yet they did not recognize him. How can a person arrive at faith in the fact that Jesus is alive, that he is with us?

²⁵And he said to them: " How senseless you are! How dull of heart to believe all that the prophets have said! ²⁶Was not the Christ bound to suffer this and enter so into his glory?" ²⁷Then, beginning with Moses and all the prophets, he explained for them what was said about him in all the scriptures.

Why were the disciples' hearts closed to the Easter message? Their understanding was blocked; their hearts, the source of all decisions in religious matters, were dull and unresponsive. God had inspired his prophets to proclaim the Easter message; anyone who listened to them in a spirit of faith would have suffered no disillusionment at Jesus' death on the cross; his hope in him would not have been disappointed. Faith, however, involves a certain understanding for God, and a heart which is open to his message. The disciples' eyes were held, so that they did not recognize the risen Lord who was walking with them; in the same way, their " hearts " were closed, so that they did not understand what the prophets had said. A man's heart must be broken open before he can receive the Easter faith.

By God's design, Jesus' way to the glory of the Messiah led through suffering and death. " God accomplished what he had foretold by the lips of all his prophets, namely, that his Messiah would suffer " (Acts 3 : 18). " By God's fixed design and foreknowledge, he was given up and nailed to the cross by the hands of lawless men " (Acts 2 : 23). The Messiah's way through suffering to glory was a divine " must "; it was part of God's plan which included both elements, the cross in this life, and glory in the next.

Christ passed through suffering to his glory. Glory is a divine power, God's own splendor, his own manner of being. After his passion, Jesus enjoys for ever the glory which was visible for a brief moment at the transfiguration (9 : 32). It is in this glory that he will be one day revealed : " They will see the Son of man coming with power and great glory " (21 : 27). The transfiguration was an anticipation of the final age. In the meantime, the glory of the Son of man is hidden, although Jesus already possesses it. After his death,

he entered into his glory, just as he entered into his kingdom
(23:42). His Father appointed this glory for him, because he had
walked the way of trial and suffering (22:29). " God made Jesus
whom the Jews crucified Lord and Messiah " (Acts 2:36).

The risen Christ interpreted scripture for the disciples. Scripture
contains an abundance of material concerning him, in the law and
in the prophetical books, in all the scriptures, in all the books of the
prophets. Christ, his passion and his glory, is the subject of the Old
Testament. The risen Lord gave the disciples, and the church
through them, the most important of all the " rules of interpretation " for the proper understanding of the scriptures. The risen
Christ is the key to the scriptures; it is of him that they speak (Jn.
5:39–47). The prophets " pondered when and what time Christ's
Spirit who was at work in them referred to, as he foretold the sufferings of Christ and the glory " (1 Pet. 1:10f.). The man who does
not know the scriptures does not know Christ; the man who does
not know Christ does not know the scriptures. Only the man who
has " turned to the Lord " can grasp the meaning of scripture. He
must first realize in a spirit of faith that Jesus of Nazareth is the
promised Messiah and the Son of God who rose from the dead and
was raised to glory. " To the present day," says St. Paul, " they
[the Jews] are covered by the same veil, when the Old Testament
is read to them. It has not been taken away, because it can only be
taken away in Christ. To the present day, a veil lies over their
hearts when Moses is read out." But this veil will be drawn back
one day, when Israel is converted to the Lord (2 Cor. 3:14–16).

*28And they drew near the village to which they were journeying and
he pretended that he wanted to journey further. 29And they pressed
him, saying: " Stay with us. It is towards evening and the day is
coming to a close." And he went in to stay with them. 30And it
happened when they reclined at table with him that he took the
bread and pronounced the blessing prayer, and broke it and gave it
to them. 31Then their eyes were opened and they recognized him,
and he disappeared from their sight. 32And they said to one an-*

other: " Did not our hearts burn within us, when he spoke to us on the road, at the way he opened the scriptures to us? "

They had reached their journey's end, the house of one of the disciples. Jesus wanted to be invited and implored before he stayed with them. Oriental custom demands that a person who accepts an invitation must allow himself to be pressed with friendly insistence (14 : 23). The traveler who interpreted the scriptures for the disciples, and revealed the mystery of the suffering and glorified Messiah to them, was welcomed as a guest with eager joy. In the apostles who explain the scriptures in the light of the risen Christ as they go on their journeys, it is the Lord himself who comes to their listeners (Mt. 10 : 40ff.).

Jesus took his place at table with the two disciples and assumed the role of the father of the house to which he was entitled as a guest by breaking the bread. The Jews began their meals by blessing and breaking the bread. On a historical level, what took place at Emmaus that evening may have been an " ordinary meal." However, St. Luke presents it on a higher level. He portrays it as a eucharistic meal. Our account of the meal at Emmaus on the first Easter Sunday comes, not from the lips of Cleopas, but in St. Luke's words. How did he interpret this meal? " Breaking bread " for him meant celebrating the Eucharist (Acts 2 : 42, 46; 20 : 7). The words used to describe the first Eucharist also occur in the account of the meal at Emmaus. " He took bread, pronounced the thanksgiving prayer, broke it, and gave it to them " (see 22 : 19).

It was in the evening, as the day was drawing to a close, that Jesus ate the Last Supper with his disciples and transformed the paschal meal into a eucharistic meal. It was in the evening, too, that Christians assembled for the eucharistic meal (Acts 20 : 8f.). The story of the disciples at Emmaus is not merely an edifying anecdote; it contains an important truth. Scripture bears witness to the risen Christ, but the Eucharist makes the risen Christ himself present in living form. The Eucharist is the great sign of the Lord's resurrection, the sign by which we can know that the Lord is alive and present. The Eucharist is not merely a memorial of the Lord's death; it is also a memorial of his resurrection. Death and resurrection are bound together inseparably. The celebration of the Eucharist makes the sacrifice of the cross present once more, but it does the same for the resurrection of him who lives forever. It is the sign by which we know that Jesus has truly risen. It is this which gives us the ability to recognize the Lord.

Is it purely by accident that the phrase " remain with them " occurs three times? The disciples implored Jesus : " Stay with us "; he went into the house " to stay with them "; he took his place at table with them. As the risen Lord, Jesus remains with his disciples until the end of the world (Mt. 28:20). It is in the Eucharist that the risen Christ remains with his church. John, with whom St. Luke has numerous affinities, describes remaining with Jesus as the most precious fruit of the Eucharist : " The man who eats my flesh and drinks my blood remains in me and I in him " (Jn. 6:56). When the risen Lord remains with his disciples, it is not merely to be present with them; his presence is an active presence which brings salvation. One element of his saving activity is the gift of being able to recognize the risen Lord. At Emmaus, the disciples' eyes were opened and they recognized Jesus.

As soon as the disciples recognized Jesus, he disappeared from them. The whole story led up to their recognition of the risen Lord. What the apparition of the risen Christ could not accomplish was accomplished by the celebration of the Eucharist. Neither the interpretation of scripture nor their grasp of it could achieve this; it could only lead up to it. As soon as Jesus' apparition had achieved its purpose, he disappeared. Jesus no longer dwells among men, as he did in the days after Easter. He has entered God's glory, and God " dwells in inaccessible light. No man has seen him, or can ever have sight of him " (1 Tim. 6:16). By God's gift, Jesus appeared visibly to those who had been appointed as witnesses of the resurrection (Acts 10:40), although he is otherwise invisible. Jesus returned to this state of invisibility after the disciples had recognized him.

Now the disciples also understood what had taken place within them when Jesus opened the scriptures to them on the road. Their hearts were burning. They probably recalled the words of the lamentation Psalm: "I was silent and dumb; I remained speechless, filled with distress. Then my grief was stirred up; my heart burned within me. In my sighing, a fire blazed up" (Ps. 39 [38] :3f.). With his heart burning, the supplicant struggles for hope and assistance in his empty and apparently meaningless life. When the risen Christ interpreted the scripture for them, the disciples' hopes were revived, the celebration of the Eucharist assured them that Jesus was alive and that the person who had journeyed with them was the risen Lord. They needed both the scriptures and the Eucharist. The scriptures set their dulled hearts on fire, while the Eucharist did away with their inability to understand (see 24:25). The faithful become conscious of the risen Lord's presence when the scriptures are interpreted in the light of the Easter event and the eucharistic meal is celebrated; their hearts are set on fire and they recognize him.

³³They rose up that very moment and returned to Jerusalem, where they found the eleven and those who were with them gathered together. ³⁴They said: "The Lord has really risen and appeared to Simon." ³⁵And they told them what had happened on the road and how they recognized him, when he broke bread.

After the great experience in which they had recognized God's saving activity in the risen Christ, the two disciples returned to Jerusalem where "the eleven and those who were with them" were gathered. They returned, like all those who experienced God's gracious visitation, the shepherds (2:20), Jesus himself (4:1-14), the apostles (9:10), the seventy (10:17), the leper who had been cured (17:15), and the people who witnessed Jesus' crucifixion (23:48). They all turned back "to give God praise and honor for all they had seen and heard," to relate and to proclaim what God had done, and to acknowledge something they had never acknowledged before. The two disciples set out that very moment; the need to praise God and proclaim him forces people to hurry (1 : 39; 2 : 16; 19 : 5). The news that Christ had risen had to be brought to Jerusalem, because it was from there that it went out all over the world (24 : 47; Acts 1 : 8).

The eleven and those who were with them were already convinced that Jesus was alive; the risen Christ had appeared to Simon Peter. The first apparition was granted to Peter (1 Cor. 15 : 4f.; see Jn. 20 : 2). He had been given the task of strengthening his brothers (22 : 23). The church was built up on faith in the risen Christ. The experience the two disciples underwent on the road to Emmaus and at the breaking of bread was in keeping with the Easter message preached by the very early church. The church's faith was based on the faith of the eleven and this was confirmed by the vision of the risen Christ which was granted Simon Peter.

St. Luke was interested in particular traditions which were marginal when compared with the strictly apostolic tradition. He mentions the mission of the seventy disciples (10 : 1ff.); he records the recollections of various women who met the Lord, and he was also familiar—perhaps through Cleopas—with the story of the two disciples to whom the risen Lord appeared on the road. St. Luke regards these " secondary witnesses " as trustworthy, but the church's faith is not based on their testimony. The church's faith is based on the foundation formed by the apostles who had Peter to confirm them. The experiences of these " secondary witnesses " confirmed the testimony of the eleven.

Scripture, the celebration of the Eucharist, and the church's profession of faith are the basic pillars on which the reliable character (1 : 4) of our faith in Jesus' resurrection is founded. It is significant that the story of the disciples who met the risen Christ on the road to Emmaus closes with the words: " They recognized him when he broke bread." In the celebration of the Eucharist, the community of the faithful meet to read the scriptures, to profess their faith, and to break bread. The Lord is present at the breaking of bread and through him God grants Christians the gift of being able to recognize the risen Christ. An understanding of the Easter mystery, therefore, is not merely an effect of faith; faith itself is a radiant expression of the mystery. Faith is an effect of God's divine intervention in raising Christ from the dead. It is a cause and an effect at once; it effects our encounter with the resurrection and it presupposes it.

The Risen Christ's Command and his Departure (24:36–53)

Jesus' Easter day closes with an appearance of the risen Lord before all the disciples. On this occasion, the reality of his glorified body is presented in such a way that all doubts are dispelled (vv. 36–43). Jesus gives his disciples a new insight into scripture and a command to preach the gospel to the world (vv. 44–49). His departure is then described (vv. 50–53).

THE REALITY OF CHRIST'S GLORIFIED BODY (24:36–43)

Luke's account betrays an apologetic tendency. Certain circles refused to believe that Jesus rose from the dead with his body. The bodily nature of the resurrection had to be demonstrated to counter them.

³⁶*As they were discussing all this, he himself stood in their midst and said to them: " Peace be with you." ³⁷They were thrown into a state of alarm and were afraid. They thought they were looking at a ghost. ³⁸And he said to them: " Why are you so agitated? Why do these [doubting] thoughts arise in your hearts? ³⁹See my hands and my feet, that it is myself. Touch me and see! A ghost has not flesh and bones as you see I have." ⁴⁰When he had said this, he showed them his hands and his feet.*

Jesus had disappeared from the disciples at Emmaus without warning; similarly, he appeared in the midst of the eleven and of those who were with them without warning. He was no longer bound by the laws of space and movement in space. The mode of existence of the risen Christ was no longer the mode of existence of the Jesus who had walked this earth, the Jesus of Good Friday. The unexpected and incomprehensible appearance of the risen Lord threw the disciples into a state of terror. Jesus' resurrection and his appearance in bodily form transcend the limits of human understanding; they go beyond all human hope. Even when they saw him and heard his peaceful greeting, the disciples were not convinced that it was he. Yet they already believed in the resurrection (24:34).

The disciples saw the apparition, but they took it to be a ghost without a body, a spirit or, according to an old manuscript reading, a product of their own phantasy, a diabolical illusion. The doubts and mistaken interpretations which occurred to the disciples anticipated the doubts and false explanations of those who later attacked the preaching of the resurrection. The debates sparked off by Christian missionary activity are reflected in the way the facts are presented. The appearances of the risen Christ were not phantasies; they were not merely interior " visions."

What the disciples saw was Jesus himself. The apparition was identical with him. " It is myself." His hands and feet were proof of this; they bore the marks of the nails (Jn. 20:25, 27). Jesus appeared to them in genuinely bodily form. The disciples could touch the Lord's body; the apparition had flesh and bones, the components of a real body. Even if their eyes were deceived, their sense of touch could not be deceived; this is the most " concrete " of all the senses. Jesus showed the disciples his hands and feet. Did they make the experiment? According to his own words, they needed nothing more.

⁴¹But, as they still remained unbelieving—for joy—and were overcome with amazement, he said to them: " Have you anything here to eat?" ⁴²So they gave him a piece of roast fish, ⁴³and he took it and ate it before their eyes.

Fear and terror were transformed into joy. Jesus' convincing offer and his words did not move them to believe immediately; they were only amazed. The evangelist excuses them with the words: " They were still unbelieving—for joy." The news of Jesus' resurrection was too good to be true. But perhaps his resurrection and his appearances were merely a product of human yearning, a figment of the disciples' imagination; they had been with the Lord and had placed all their hope in him; he was the greatest thing in their lives. A Christian's entire hope is concentrated on the truth of Jesus' resurrection. It had to be solidly established. The disciples' joy was well founded. They now received a fresh proof of the reality of the resurrection and the bodily character of the risen Lord. Jesus ate a piece of roast fish in the presence of his disciples. To obviate any attempt to reduce Christ's risen body to the level of a mere apparition, the early Christian preaching appealed to the meal the risen Lord had eaten with his disciples. " God raised him up on the third day and revealed him to us . . . who ate and drank with him after his resurrection from the dead " (Acts 10:40f.). After his rising from the dead, Jesus no longer needed nourishment; he had already entered eternal life (24:26). Paradoxically, he proved he was alive by using something which is a sign of our mortality. The mode of existence of the risen body can be described only in images which are inadequate (1 Cor. 15:35-49).

Jesus who was crucified and buried and rose again from the dead enjoyed a mode of existence which was peculiar to him. He appeared in bodily form with a body which could be seen and touched, and by means of which he could make himself heard. He was not a ghost, but a person of flesh and bone who was prepared to allow himself to be touched. To banish all doubt about his bodily reality, he ate food before the eyes of those who gave it to him. Yet Jesus was different from what he had been before his death. He was free from all the limitations of bodily existence, and he had absolute control over the changing forms in which he appeared (Mk. 16:12). No matter how much his bodily reality was emphasized, it still evoked doubts; it terrified those who saw it and prevented them from believing for sheer joy. The risen Lord appeared and disappeared without his coming or going being observed. A person's eyes had to be opened by God before he could be recognized. He had already been taken from suffering and an earthly existence into God's glory; yet he still had some affinity with what was earthly and was, in that sense, in an incomplete state. The mode of existence of the risen Christ cannot be described perfectly; it can scarcely even be outlined without falling into contradictions.

THE TESTAMENT OF THE DEPARTING LORD (24:44-49)

In the last words he addressed to the apostles, the risen Christ gives them a new insight into scripture (vv. 44f.), and teaches them about the universal character of salvation (vv. 46f.). He also promises them the Holy Spirit for their work of proclaiming salvation (vv. 48f.).

⁴⁴But he said to them: " These are the words I spoke to you, when I was still with you. Everything written in the law of Moses and in the prophets and in the Psalms about me had to be fulfilled." ⁴⁵Then he enlightened their minds, to understand the scriptures.

The Lord bequeathed to the apostles and to his church the word he had spoken during his life on earth, the tradition which enshrined all that he had done. His personal presence in the church is invisible; the church cannot hear him. However, in addition to this presence, it also has the tradition which enshrines his mission, the memory of Christ's life on earth. This time is described as the time in which Jesus was still with his apostles—visibly and palpably so. The time was near when he would leave them, when even the apparitions of the risen Christ would be no more, and the church would look forward to his coming (17:22). It was for this time that the words Jesus spoke on earth and the " sight " of his actions were bequeathed to us as a precious heirloom. Jesus' life is regarded as a historical fact to which the church looks back and which has an effect on our faith and life here and now.

Jesus' earthly ministry is framed between two references to the scriptures being fulfilled. At the beginning of his public life, he said: " Today this word of scripture is fulfilled in your hearing " (4:21). Before he was taken up into heaven, he reminded his disciples that he had said: " Everything that has been written must be accomplished." The whole scripture with all its parts, the law, the prophets, and the Psalms (*Ketubim*) speaks of Christ. It is he who brings the law to its full accomplishment (16:71f.); he is the fulfillment of the prophecies (4:21), and it is he who inaugurates the worship of praise which is offered to God for all that he has accomplished in Jesus. Jesus' time is the time when the promises are fulfilled.

Jesus had explained the scriptures to his disciples during his life on earth, but their minds were closed to a proper understanding of them. They had not learned to believe that Jesus was the Messiah; the true picture of the Messiah was still hidden from them. Scripture spoke about the Messiah, about one who rose from the dead. They could not grasp this (18:31–34). The risen Christ, whom God showed to be the Messiah by raising him from the dead, opened their minds to the meaning of scripture. Faith in Jesus is the work of the risen Lord, as is the new insight into scripture. It is only when the Old Testament scriptures are understood in the light of Easter that they lead a person to recognize Jesus as the saviour of Israel and the world. After the resurrection, ignorance of scripture is sinful (Acts 3:17f.). For the Jews who refuse to believe, scripture is a reproach; for the church which believes in the resurrection and interprets scripture correctly it brings salvation.

⁴⁶And he said to them: " So it was written, that the Christ would suffer and rise from the dead on the third day, ⁴⁷and that repentance and forgiveness of sin would be proclaimed in his name for all nations, beginning from Jerusalem."

Scripture proclaims salvation for all nations; that is its essence, its fundamental intention. Salvation is founded in Christ's passion, death, and resurrection. It will be proclaimed in Jesus' name, by his command, under his influence. Salvation is to be found only in this name (Acts 4:12). Jesus' name really means his active presence. When the apostles preached in Jesus' name, they could rejoice in the promise: " I am with you all days until the end of the world " (Mt. 28:20). Salvation is proclaimed for all nations. This, too, was in fulfillment of the scriptures. The universalistic prophecy of the

271

Deutero-Isaiah was fulfilled in the Baptist's preaching: "And all flesh will see God's salvation " (3:6; Is. 40:5), in Simeon's hymn of praise: "A light to enlighten the gentiles " (2:32; Is. 42:6), and in Jesus' preaching: "They will come from the rising and the setting of the sun " (13:28f.; Is. 49:12). The proclamation of salvation begins in Jerusalem. Salvation comes from the Jews (Jn. 4:22). In Abraham, all the generations of the earth are blessed (Acts 3:25; Jn. 12:3). The subject of the proclamation is repentance and the forgiveness of sins. Conversion (repentance) is a prerequisite for the forgiveness of sins, from which life results. The glorified Christ is the " author of life " (Acts 3:15), but he is also the author of conversion and forgiveness: "God has exalted him at his right hand as a prince and saviour, to bring Israel conversion and forgiveness of sins " (Acts 5:31). The prophetic promise Jesus fulfilled in his ministry is fulfilled for the nations by the apostles: "to proclaim deliverance for those in captivity, and sight for the blind " (4:18; Is. 61:1; 42:7). According to St. Matthew, the risen Lord commanded his apostles: Baptize all nations (28:19). Baptism presupposes repentance and conversion; it sets the final seal on them.

The Old Testament prophecy concerning the salvation of all nations and the proclamation of salvation was fulfilled. The Acts of the Apostles prove this. The apostles proclaimed Jesus of Nazareth as the Christ (Messiah); they proclaimed his saving death—" he died for our sins "—and his resurrection. They offered their hearers repentance and the forgiveness of sins. In one of St. Peter's first sermons, he says: "We are witnesses of all he [Jesus] did in the country of the Jews and in Jerusalem. They killed him by hanging him on the cross. But God raised him up on the third day and revealed him . . . He gave us a command to preach to the people and to testify that he has been appointed by God as judge of the living and the dead. All the prophets testify concerning him that anyone who believes in him receives the forgiveness of his sins through his name " (Acts 10:39–43). The proclamation of the good news began in Jerusalem, from where it passed on to Judea and Samaria and the ends of the earth (Acts 1:8).

Luke presents as a prophecy what Matthew describes as a solemn declaration and a command given by the risen Lord (28 : 18–20). The proclamation of the gospel to all nations is put on the same level with Christ's passion and resurrection, as fulfilling the scriptures. St. Luke thinks in terms of salvation history. The time of the promise was followed by the time of Jesus' life, " the midst of time "; after the ascension, the time of the church began which is a time of witness and of missionary activity.

[48]" *You are to be witnesses of this.* [49]*And see, I am sending my Father's promise upon you. You must stay in the city until you are clothed with power from on high.*"

Jesus here asserts a fact and gives a command. The apostles were witnesses of the events which fulfilled the prophecies, Jesus' death and resurrection. They were witnesses also of the commission he gave them as missionaries and of his world-embracing proclamation of salvation. They had been with Jesus from the moment of his baptism in the Jordan to the moment he ascended into heaven (Acts 1 : 21). They had everything that could be demanded of a witness. The apostles' message was not a matter of human speculation or human wisdom, in the form of a myth, for example; it was a series of historical facts and the explanation God gave of them on the basis of scripture.

For his part, Christ promised the apostles the gift of the Holy Spirit for their task of preaching the message of salvation. His words of promise are introduced by the pronoun " I ", the " I " of one who has authority and full power at his disposal. As St. Matthew puts it : " All power has been given to me in heaven and on earth " (Mt. 28 : 18). As soon as he had gone to the Father (Jn. 15 : 26) and been exalted, he would send the Father's promise, the Holy Spirit whom God had promised for the time of salvation (Joel 3 : 1–5; Acts 2:16–21). The Holy Spirit with whom Jesus himself had been anointed for his ministry (Acts 10 : 38) would also be given to his apostles. The time of the church is the time of the Holy

Spirit. " Exalted at God's right hand, Jesus has received the promised Holy Spirit from the Father and has poured him out, as you can see and hear " (Acts 2 : 33).

First, the apostles had to wait for the Holy Spirit; they must sit in the city of Jerusalem, and remain there. The word may imply that they were to remain there, reflecting and meditating (10 : 39). We are told that, after the ascension, the apostles persevered with one mind in prayer, together with the women and Jesus' mother Mary and his brothers (Acts 1 : 14). The city in question was Jerusalem. Jerusalem was the center of the history St. Luke wrote; it was the city of Jesus' death, the city of the risen Christ, the city of the descent of the Spirit, the city on which God's vengeance fell, because it had not recognized his gracious visitations.

It was at Jerusalem that the apostles were clothed with power from on high. The power from on high was the Holy Spirit; power and the Spirit are intimately bound up with one another. It was in the power of the Spirit that Jesus returned to Galilee after he had defeated the tempter, to begin his mission and proclaim the welcome year of salvation (4 : 14). The power of the Spirit was given to the disciples after Jesus had conquered the tempter by his passion and death and had been exalted in heaven. In the power of the Spirit, they continued Jesus' mission among all nations. " The apostles bore witness to the resurrection of the Lord Jesus Christ with great power " (Acts 4 : 33). It was not by their own power that they worked miracles (Acts 3 : 10); it was by the power and in the name of Jesus Christ (Acts 4:7, 10). Jesus' time began with a " dawning from on high " (1 : 78); the time of the church began with " power from on high." The apostles were clothed with this power, just as Jesus had been anointed with the Holy Spirit and with power (Acts 10 : 38). The apostles' " robes of office " consisted in power from on high which gave them a divine authority such as Jesus had. " They [the apostles] went out and preached everywhere, and the Lord worked with them, confirming the word by the signs which accompanied it " (Mk. 16 : 20).

The time of Christ's life was introduced with the message of grace: " The Holy Spirit will come upon you and the power of the Most High will overshadow you " (1:35). The time of the church was introduced by Christ's promise that he would send the apostles and those who were with them the Father's promise, the Holy Spirit, and that they would be endowed with power from on high. It was the Spirit who raised up the Holy One, God's Son, from Mary's womb (1:35), and it is the Holy Spirit who still raises up " saints," " sons of God," as Christians are called, through the church. Mary's fruitfulness, like that of the church, is the result of power from on high. Mary is the archetype of the church.

Jesus' Departure (24:50–53)

This section seems to contradict Acts 1:3-11. According to the Acts of the Apostles: " Jesus showed that he was alive after his passion by many proofs. Over a period of forty days he appeared to his apostles and spoke about the affairs of God's kingdom " (Acts 1:3). According to the gospel, on the other hand, it seems as if everything mentioned in Lk. 24 took place on Easter Sunday, and that the Lord's testament as he was about to leave the world (vv. 44–49), and his ascension into heaven (vv. 50–53), took place immediately after he had appeared to the apostles on the evening of Easter day. It seems the St. Luke's presentation of the events of the first Easter Sunday was influenced by liturgical considerations: every Sunday is an Easter Sunday for the local church. In the same way, he anticipated the account of the Baptist's death (3:18ff.), and ignored the historical sequence of events in favor of his literary and theological conception. He placed Jesus' sermon at Nazareth at the beginning of his ministry (4:14-30), as an outline of what was to come, although it is certain that it took place at a later date historically. Numerous points of contact between the gospel and the Acts show that St. Luke had already decided on the outline of the Acts when he wrote the gospel. Therefore, there is no reason to believe that in the Acts he intended to " improve " on the account of the ascension which he gives in the gospel. He was not influenced by historical or biographical factors.

[50]*Then he led them out near Bethany, where he lifted up his hands*

275

and blessed them. ⁵¹*And it happened that, as he blessed them, he departed from them and was taken up into heaven.*

" Near Bethany " means the region of the Mount of Olives near Jerusalem (19:28f.; Acts 1:12). It was from there that he set out to enter Jerusalem as the Messiah-king (19:28–38). His entry into glory, when he had accomplished his mission, could scarcely begin from any other place. Bethany was on the road which led from the desert to Jerusalem. The dawn of the time of salvation had been proclaimed with the words: " The voice of one crying in the wilderness: ' Prepare the Lord's way . . . All flesh will see God's salvation ' " (3:4ff.). It was on the way from the desert to Jerusalem that Jesus departed from his disciples and was taken up into heaven, from where he sent them the Spirit. The time of the church was beginning. At the end of the Acts of the Apostles, we are told with reference to the apostles' ministry: " You must know that God's salvation has been sent to the gentiles " (Acts 28:28).

Jesus had never before blessed his apostles, but now he gave them a solemn blessing. His upraised hands implied that he acted as a priest in blessing them. This scene is probably intended to recall the words of Sirach in which we are told about the high priest Simon: " Then he came down and raised his hands over the assembled communities of Israel. On his lips was the Lord's formula of blessing and he could glory in his name. Then they fell down once more, to receive a blessing from him " (Sir. 50:20f.). In the blessing he bestowed on his apostles as he was leaving them for heaven, Jesus revealed the blessing which he himself had brought: In him, all the generations of the earth are blessed (Acts 3:25). St. Luke's Gospel begins with a priest who could not pronounce a blessing after he had presented his offering, because he doubted (1:22). Zechariah's service was an incomplete liturgy. At the close of the gospel, we once more have a priest, but this time it is a priest who completes the offering he made with a blessing. The liturgy was brought to a fitting end. All the crucified and risen Lord's power to bless was concentrated in the blessing he gave his apostles.

As he was blessing them, Jesus departed from his disciples. His blessing remains with them, although he is now far from them. He departed from them. Did he depart from them in the same way as he had departed from the disciples at Emmaus? Did he simply become invisible? What is said here has a different implication. The full implication of his departure goes beyond the mere sense of the word. That was why, to remove all doubt, the words: " And he was taken up into heaven " (see Acts 1:9) were added to the text, even in important manuscripts. At the ascension, Jesus took leave of his disciples; the emphasis is on the leave-taking rather than on his ascension. The days during which the risen Christ appeared to his disciples were at an end. The days when Jesus went about doing good on earth were no more. He had reached the goal of all his journeying; he was taken up (9:51). The time of Christ, from his baptism to the ascension, was closed. There would never again be a time like this. The risen Lord now lives in " absolute distance," until he comes again.

⁵²*And they fell down before him, and then returned to Jerusalem with great joy, *⁵³*and they were always in the temple, praising God.*

The apostles fell on their knees before their Lord who was leaving them, just as the congregation falls down in prayer when the priest blesses them. The ascension took place to the accompaniment of a solemn liturgy, as the church congregated before the high priest who blessed them. It may be that the reference to the disciples falling on their knees to adore was inserted here under the influence of the book of Ecclesiasticus. Not all the manuscripts give it, and St. Luke may have given a more simple account. He describes what followed simply and with restraint, being content merely to mention what the apostolic church did after the Lord's departure. They returned to Jerusalem, thereby obeying the Lord's last command.

" With great joy." How could the apostles rejoice when Jesus was leaving them? Jesus' ascension brought his story on earth to an end, but it marked the final stage in his resurrection. It was a further step in the direction of the time when everything will receive new life, and God will send Christ Jesus to those whom he has chosen. " Heaven must take him up until the time for the restoration of all things comes, which God foretold from of old by the lips of his holy prophets " (Acts 3:20f.). The joy felt by those who had witnessed the ascension marked the beginning of the great joy which will accompany the final consummation. Once more, the end of the gospel reëchoes the beginning. When the Baptist's birth was announced, Zechariah the priest was told: " You will rejoice and be jubilant, and many will be glad at his birth " (1:14). Jesus' birth was announced with the words: " See, I bring you news of great joy which all the people will experience " (2:10). From beginning to end, the gospel was a message of joy.

On his entry into Jerusalem, Jesus had taken possession of the temple for himself and his people (19:45ff.). It was there that he laid the foundations of the church. And it was there, too, that those who had witnessed the ascension always met at the hours of prayer. The temple remained for a long time the meeting-place of those on whom the Holy Spirit descended at Pentecost. Here again the end of the gospel is connected with the beginning. The two occasions on which the child Jesus appeared in the temple marked the dual climax of the infancy gospel, and the temple was the home of those who " waited for the redemption of Israel " (2:38).

The praise offered to God by the church resounded in the temple. Through Christ, the high priest, God blessed the church formed by those who witnessed the ascension; the church in turn blesses God and expresses its grateful praise in its prayers and hymns. When the Baptist was born, Zechariah praised God with the words: " Praised be the Lord, Israel's God " (1:64, 68). Simeon took the child Jesus in his arms and praised God in his hymn: " My eyes have seen the salvation which you have prepared in the sight of the nations " (2:28, 30). Now the hope expressed in this praise was beginning to become a reality. Salvation has been prepared; it is offered to the gentiles in an atmosphere of praise. The liturgy of the eternal praise offered to God has begun.

278